More Praise for
The Secret Language of Leadership

"Out of the morass of strategies leaders are given to transform organizations, Denning plucks a powerful one—storytelling—and shows how and why it works."

>—Dorothy Leonard, William J. Abernathy Professor of Business, Emerita, Harvard Business School, and author, *Deep Smarts: How to Cultivate and Transfer Enduring Business Wisdom*

"*The Secret Language of Leadership* shows why narrative intelligence is central to transformational leadership and how to harness its power."

>—Carol Pearson, director, James MacGregor Burns Academy of Leadership, University of Maryland, and coauthor, *The Hero and the Outlaw*

"*The Secret Language of Leadership* is not only the best analysis I have seen of how and why leaders succeed or fail, it's highly readable, as well as downright practical. It should be mandatory reading for anyone interested in engaging a company with big ideas who understands that leaders live and die by the quality of what they say."

>—Richard Stone, story analytics master, i.d.e.a.s

"A primary role of leaders is to create and maintain meaning for their organizations. Denning clearly demonstrates that meaning-making comes from stories well told."

>—Thomas Davenport, President's Distinguished Professor of I.T. and Management, Babson College, and author, *The Attention Economy*

"Steve Denning is one of the leading thinkers on the power of narrative in business settings. His latest book is a smart, useful guide that can help leaders of every kind add value to their organizations and add meaning to their own journeys."

>—Daniel H. Pink, author, *A Whole New Mind*

JB JOSSEY-BASS

The SECRET LANGUAGE of LEADERSHIP

•

HOW LEADERS INSPIRE ACTION THROUGH NARRATIVE

STEPHEN DENNING

John Wiley & Sons, Inc.

Published by Jossey-Bass
A Wiley Imprint
989 Market Street, San Francisco, CA 94103-1741   www.josseybass.com

Wiley Bicentennial logo: Richard J. Pacifico

Jossey-Bass books and products are available through most bookstores. To contact Jossey-Bass directly call our Customer Care Department within the U.S. at 800-956-7739, outside the U.S. at 317-572-3986, or fax 317-572-4002.

Jossey-Bass also publishes its books in a variety of electronic formats. Some content that appears in print may not be available in electronic books.

Library of Congress Cataloging-in-Publication Data

Denning, Stephen.
  The secret language of leadership : how leaders inspire action through narrative / Stephen Denning.—1st ed.
       p. cm.
  "A Wiley Imprint."
  Includes bibliographical references and index.
  ISBN 978-0-7879-8789-3 (cloth)
 1. Leadership. 2. Communication in organizations. 3. Storytelling.
I. Title.
  HD57.7.D49 2007
  658.4'5—dc22

                                   2007028784

Printed in the United States of America
FIRST EDITION
HB Printing   10 9 8 7 6 5 4 3

Contents

Contents

The Secret Language of Leadership.

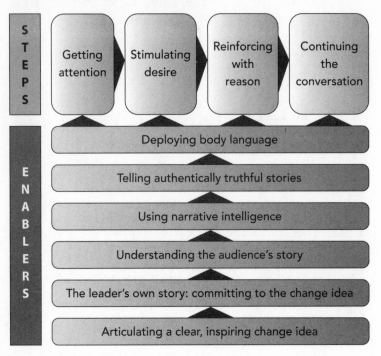

MY LEADERSHIP JOURNEY

My own leadership journey began abruptly late on Monday afternoon, February 5, 1996. That day, I'd asked for a meeting with one of the managing directors of the World Bank—one of the three people who reported to the president of the bank and were charged with running its operations. As the director of the Africa Region, I needed to see him because that curious thing known as "my career" had just then taken a turn for the worse.

The World Bank is an international lending organization located in Washington, D.C., and aimed at relieving global poverty. For several decades, I had held a number of positions and functions, including programming and budgeting, the West Africa riverblindness program, population, health and nutrition programs, and the quality control of operations. In the early 1990s, I had been director of the Southern Africa Department, where I had overseen the work of several hundred people working in ten countries. Now, as director of the Africa Region, I was responsible for the operations of more than a thousand staff working in forty-three countries. After that much experience as an executive, I believed that I understood *management,* although I was about to discover that I had much to learn about *leadership.*

Large organizations may look stable, but appearances are deceptive. In the past year, the president had unexpectedly died. Last month, my boss had decided to retire. Now someone else had just been named to my post.

The office of managing director is just two grade levels above director. To an outsider, those two grade levels might not seem like much, but from the inside, the difference was an abyss.

Like most organizations, the World Bank has a hierarchical management style. It's the same "look-up-and-yell-down" style as in the private sector.

At the beginning of the interview, I told the managing director that I'd heard the announcement that someone else was to fill my position. Did they have anything in mind for me?

"Not really," he replied with a smile.

I wasn't surprised. There had been inklings of trouble afoot. Just one month before, I'd been asked in the street if it was true that I was being pushed aside. My boss had confirmed that the scene was turbulent: his own decision to retire exposed me to the vagaries of the clan warfare that pervades large organizations.

The managing director quickly explained to me the diminishing range of my career options. The organization had no plans for me. There were no specific positions available. There weren't even any lists of possible positions on which I might figure.

He spoke to me dismissively, as though I had had no prior reputation, no credit for anything I had done over several decades, and no prospects. His world was a personnel chessboard and I was no longer a player. I had become a nobody.

When I pressed him, he said finally, "Why don't you look into information?"

Information? In February 1996, information in the World Bank had all the prestige of the garage or the cafeteria—a wasteland from which no traveler had ever returned. The message was unmistakable: I was being sent to Siberia.

Although the interview was bad news, the imperial style of delivery was something else. The managing director gazed on me as though he'd just swatted a fly.

At the time, I had no way of knowing that his own vast power was a facade. He had been chosen precisely because he was a loyal staff officer. I had no idea then that he, like all the new bank president's close associates, would be cast aside within a few years, when, in the inevitable custom of authoritarian contexts, the executioner becomes the victim.

The loss of my job hit me as a grave personal setback. Yet in retrospect, it's clear that there was nothing personal in it at all. The president, as it emerged in due course, planned to ditch everyone at my level, including the managing directors. He seemed to believe that if he appointed people himself, they would be more loyal and dedicated to his objectives. When this turned out not to be the case, he canned them with the same indifference that he dispatched the senior managers on hand at the time of his arrival.

For those slated for elimination, the president's technique was simple. He refrained from dismissing them outright. Instead he appointed them to posts with lesser responsibilities or status, or left them with no position at all. The idea was that they would resign to avoid the public humiliation of being treated so demeaningly.

In most cases, his judgment proved correct: they left without a protest, slipping quietly into the night. My case was different: I wasn't quite ready to leave.

I remained optimistic. Surely, I thought, there must have been a mistake. Surely my record counted for something. Surely, when lines of communication opened, my career would be back on track.

I set about looking into information, since I was interested in the topic, having been an early computer enthusiast. I saw that if I combined my knowledge of World Bank operations with my interest in computers, I could make a unique contribution.

The issues were immediately obvious—systems that weren't compatible with each other so that every question had multiple answers, a huge and growing duplication of effort, utter unresponsiveness to operations on the ground, antiquated, paper-bound relations with clients, and inexcusable delays in doing even the simplest thing.

I began putting together a plan for what I would do if I were to be offered a position in information. It became steadily more apparent that cleaning up information was a necessary but largely menial task. It would save the organization money but it wouldn't fix the fundamental strategic issue: a lending organization—even if it became more agile—could never solve the problem of global poverty. Global poverty would only be solved when people in poor countries themselves knew how to solve their own problems. Money could facilitate the relief of poverty, but it could never be the solution, unless combined with knowledge.

In 1996, the World Bank had a great deal of knowledge relevant to solving the problems of global poverty. We had world-class experts in a wide array of fields—agriculture, banking, finance, health, education, you name it—but access to this knowledge was problematic. If you were involved in a lending operation with the World Bank, you might discover some of this expertise, but otherwise you were out of luck. I began to think: suppose we were to generate quick and easy global access to our knowledge for everyone, wherever they were? Then we could become a pretty interesting organization, even an exciting organization.

Why not become a knowledge-sharing organization?

I thought this was not just a good idea: once you thought about it, it was breathtakingly obvious. There was just one problem. In the World Bank of early 1996, no one was willing to listen.

Eventually, in April 1996, after weeks of buttonholing anyone I could find, I managed to get a few people's attention. As a result, I was offered ten minutes in front of the Change Management Committee of the World Bank to explain my ideas on sharing knowledge. This committee comprised the managing directors as well as a few vice presidents and some senior advisers to the president. It had been set up to "orchestrate change" in the World Bank. It wasn't obvious to anyone that this was what it was up to, but clearly I needed its support. To be offered even a few minutes before it was a major breakthrough.

So now I had ten minutes in which to persuade a group of skeptical, change-resistant senior managers that we should embark on a new strategy to make sharing knowledge a central preoccupation of the organization.

My presentation, which is included in Appendix 1, was quite simple in structure. It talked about the problems the organization was facing in sharing its knowledge. It included a brief anecdote from Zambia, which suggested what the future might look like. And it gave a couple of simple road maps as to how we might get from here to there.

After I gave my presentation, I was taken aback by the overwhelmingly enthusiastic reaction. One of the vice presidents, Jean-François Rischard, raced up to me very excitedly. "Why don't we do it?" he asked. "What's the next step? Why isn't it being implemented? What's the blockage?"

At the time, my first thought was that this was a very strange conversation. Until ten minutes ago, vice presidents had hardly been willing to give me the time of day. And now it was as if I wasn't doing enough to implement Rischard's idea.

Then it dawned on me. How wonderful! The idea of sharing knowledge with the world was no longer just my idea. Now it was also *his* idea. And indeed it was Rischard who shortly afterward played a key role in communicating the idea of knowledge sharing to the bank president and sponsoring its implementation across the entire organization.

These were among the first inklings that there was something remarkable in that simple ten-minute presentation. And yet if I had been asked at the time why it was effective, I would have answered that the underlying idea was a good one and people recognized a good idea for its merits. At the time, I was only dimly aware that in most organizations good ideas go nowhere, because they aren't compellingly communicated. I had no notion then that I had, almost by accident, stumbled on a particular form of leadership communication that could galvanize action, even with difficult audiences. Even if I didn't yet understand what I was doing or why, I had begun to discover the secret language of leadership.

Later in the day, I learned that my presentation had been so well received that I was to be invited to give the same presentation to the entire senior management, except for the president.

The following week, when I made the presentation to this larger group, the effect was just as electric. A number of the vice presidents were highly energized. One of them told me: "This is the future!"

I was elated. I not only had a good idea: now I had support at high levels of the organization including vice presidents and some of the president's top advisers. I concluded: my career is back on track!

I was, alas, mistaken.

Several days later, I was summoned to the office of one of the managing directors. In walking toward his office for the meeting that evening, I was extremely upbeat. Given the reception of my presentation to the senior management group, I anticipated that the conversation would be about how to implement knowledge sharing.

Instead, I was told that the managing directors had considered my idea on making knowledge a key strategic thrust for the organization and had rejected it. I was to stop bothering the senior management any further, since it wasn't going to happen. There would be no position or role for me either in information or knowledge.

When I asked him what I was meant to do, he pointed to various lower-level jobs that were being advertised.

Needless to say, I left his office feeling crushed. I was back in no-man's land. What made the turn of events disturbing was not just the apparent collapse of my career, but even more so, the senselessness of it all. I knew I had a good idea. I knew the idea had strong support among a number of vice presidents. Yet somehow it was being scotched by an odd combination of corporate confusion and institutional politics.

I spent a dark night of the soul.

The next morning, despite little sleep, I was feeling better, even optimistic, and sensing that everything could be rectified. I went to tell the vice presidents what had happened. I was delighted to find that they were as shocked as I was: there was no way that the idea of knowledge sharing could be stopped in this cavalier fashion.

Immediately, things started to pick up: one vice president asked me to work with him, to make knowledge sharing a reality in his vice presidency. Then, other vice presidents joined in and invited me to help them as well.

As the scale of my informal assignment steadily grew, it was becoming apparent that the knowledge-sharing initiative was attaining organization-wide proportions. So the vice presidents decided to inform the managing directors what they were up to. I helped them prepare a joint memorandum, which they signed and sent to the managing directors. The memorandum didn't ask for permission or resources. It simply informed the managing directors of their plans.

A few days later, I was summoned by one of the managing directors and told to cease and desist. I should, he said, stop bothering people with my idea. Knowledge management wasn't going to happen.

I asked him why he was talking to me, since I wasn't even mentioned in the memorandum of which he was complaining. Why didn't he speak to the vice presidents, since they were the ones who had signed and sent it?

He replied that it was obvious that I was behind it and I should stop causing problems. I should apply for other operational positions, perhaps in a field office, preferably far away from headquarters.

During the ensuing summer, I attended a management program at the International Institute for Management Development in Lausanne, Switzerland. This gave me time to reflect on what had happened and what I would do next.

Here I had time to ask myself, What was my life about? What were my options?

Would it be possible to get my career back on track? Apparently, when the new president arrived, I had been in the wrong position at the wrong time with the wrong connections to the wrong managerial clan. With hard work, and knuckling under the new regime, would it be possible to reestablish myself?

I could see now that this wasn't realistic. I had been suffering from what is known in psychiatric circles as "the delusion of a reprieve." The condemned man, in the period after he is sentenced, suffers from the illusion he might somehow be reprieved. I imagined that there had been some mistake, that somehow the mistake would be corrected and all would be well.

Now, clearly, there was no mistake. There was no failure of communication. On several occasions, the managing directors had had opportunities to allow me to proceed, and they had actively blocked forward progress. Now it was clear: there would be no reprieve.

What to do? One option was to leave the World Bank and pursue my career elsewhere. That's what other senior managers who were being treated this way were doing. They resented being dealt with so demeaningly, and for the most part, they opted to depart. Why persevere in such an environment?

The question I pondered was, What was my life about? Was it about advancing up the managerial ladder in a large organization? I had to admit to myself that this had always been important to me—pride, ego, ambition were all part of the mix. Was my life really about a career?

Or was it about accomplishing something significant?

Based on my discussions in Lausanne, I knew I had a big, bold, promising idea for an organization whose mission was unquestionably noble—relieving global poverty.[1]

I knew the idea had generated enthusiasm among working-level staff on the front lines of the World Bank, who could see that both they and the organization would be more effective if it was implemented.

And a significant coalition of senior managers—perhaps one-third of the total—was now in place. They also believed that the future of the organization lay in sharing our knowledge to the world, to complement the provision of financial resources.

It was also well known that the president of the World Bank was open to big, bold ideas, was indeed searching for them. True, he had surrounded himself with managing directors who were acting as centurion guards to prevent any big, bold ideas ever reaching him. I calculated that if only I could get directly to the president, then the success of the idea would be inevitable. Even without that, surely it would be possible to launch a pilot scheme in one or more of the vice presidencies? Once that was implemented, then the idea could spread to the whole organization.

Now I had to choose.

Spend time resurrecting my career, either here or elsewhere? Or go flat out for change?

Coming back from Lausanne in September 1996, I made my decision. I opted to set aside any idea of career advancement and commit myself wholeheartedly to making change happen, accepting whatever indignities I might have to suffer. I would do whatever it took, even if the effort were to take a decade.

As it happened, an opportunity appeared within just a few days. And it was grander than anything I could have anticipated.[2]

Late on Wednesday afternoon, September 18, 1996, I was sitting in Jean-François Rischard's office. We'd been discussing how to move the knowledge-sharing initiative forward. We both thought that if we only could get to the president, given his stance and his personality, he was bound to support the idea. The timing was ideal, since the World Bank's annual meeting was just days away: the president's speech was a perfect opportunity to announce a bold new initiative. The problem was how to get to the president: he was surrounded by those pesky centurion guards.

After discussing the ways of getting the idea to the president, we finally decided that it was too risky. At the time, the centurion guards were on high alert, indeed expecting people to be submitting risky new ideas to the president. If we tried to get to him then, without their blessing, there would be terrible punishments and taxes.

So we decided the timing wasn't right. Instead we would wait until after the annual meeting. Then in the dark of night, when no one was watching, we would meet quietly with the president and sell the idea to him and we would be off to the races.

Just then, at the very moment we were concluding our conversation and deciding to lie low for the moment, Rischard got a phone call.

It was the president.

Apparently he was in a taxicab in a traffic jam in New York, reading a draft of the speech that he was to give in a matter of days to the annual meeting of the World Bank. He was calling on his cell phone to say that the draft speech was pablum, pure pablum—not a single new idea in it. Surely, he said, there was at least one good idea in the whole goddamn organization?

Rischard said that, as a matter of fact, there was, and began sketching the idea of knowledge management: how the Bank should pool its expertise on everything from civil service reform to electricity generation in central databases, massively expanding the reach of its ideas in the global struggle against poverty. He spoke for five minutes, then five more minutes, and presently he hit the fifteen-minute mark. The president was saying it was intriguing, actually quite good, and maybe he would think about it.[3]

That night, the president went to dinner and tried out the idea on his dinner guests. They said it was excellent.

The next day when he came in to the office, Rischard and I were asked to draft a speech that the president would give to the board of directors. Just over a week after that, on the morning of October 1, 1996, the president was giving the speech to the annual meeting of the governors of the World Bank, a huge public occasion—more than 170 finance ministers and all their entourages—explaining the new strategy of becoming a knowledge-sharing organization. We were going to become "the knowledge bank."

It's an understatement to say I was elated. In just a few days, the idea of knowledge sharing had gone from something undiscussable to something that was a central organizational strategy for the future. Visions of success and accomplishment danced before my eyes. The possibility of implementing the new strategy was now within my grasp.

What I didn't realize was that winning the support of the president wasn't the end of the war of innovation. It was simply the beginning.

It was not just that we were starting the long, hard slog of turning the vision of a knowledge organization into a reality.

The biggest shock was my discovery that the opposition from the managing directors didn't disappear with the president's endorsement. On the contrary, it intensified.

Obviously the support of the president was a hugely positive element. Jim Wolfensohn was mercurial, quick, able to see the promise in a bold new idea and decisive about endorsing it. His instant acceptance of knowledge sharing, his announcement of "the knowledge bank" at the annual meeting in 1996, his subsequent sponsorship of a formal strategy paper embracing external knowledge sharing in 1997, his adoption in 1999 of a formal mission statement for the World Bank that assigned knowledge sharing the same level of importance as providing financial resources—these were all crucial steps in launching and implementing knowledge management at the World Bank. Without them, we could never have achieved what was achieved.

The managing directors were a very different story. Up to that point, they'd permitted me to wander the corridors and buttonhole anyone who would listen to the idea of becoming a knowledge-sharing organization, because the possibility of that fantastic dream ever becoming a reality was nonexistent. They believed that I would tire of my quixotic mission and either find something more conventional to do or leave. They thought that their adversary was a person, albeit a determined one. They hadn't grasped that they were fighting an idea.

Now, with the president having unexpectedly endorsed the idea in the most public, formal forum available to him, it was obvious that they had underestimated the threat. Even if they couldn't see that the idea made sense or believe that it would ever become a reality, they now had to deal with the fact that the president had made a major commitment in the most public way to implement it. Now they couldn't oppose the idea outright, but as wily bureaucrats, they could and did find subtle ways to undermine or sideline it.[4]

Four years later, by 2000, despite the well-intended efforts of the managing directors to preserve the World Bank as a lending organization, substantial progress had been made. Knowledge sharing was in the mission statement of the organization, on a par with the provision of financial resources. It was in the organizational chart. It was in the personnel system. It was in the budget, albeit still underfunded in terms of real resources. And over a hundred knowledge communities were in place, most of them energetically sharing their knowledge. There were measurements of the effectiveness of the communities of practice. And there was external recognition: we were benchmarked several times as a world leader in knowledge management and as one of the world's most admired knowledge enterprises.[5]

Obviously, much remained to be done. Budgets needed to be sorted out. The less effective knowledge communities and vice presidencies needed to be dealt with. The blemishes in technology had to be rectified. But these challenges were largely those of *management*. It was a matter of strengthening, refining, and reinforcing what was already mainly in place.

By contrast, the work of *leadership* in knowledge management at the World Bank was by then largely complete. The DNA of the organization had been changed. Thereafter the specifics of the knowledge-sharing program might wax or wane, but the notion of external knowledge sharing had been ingrained in the World Bank's genetic code. Once people had seen the vision and realized that it could be implemented, it became an ideal the organization had no choice but to aspire to.[6]

Looking back on the experience, I can see that the World Bank in the period from 1996 to 2000 was an extraordinarily difficult environment, though probably not too different from what many change agents face in other large organizations today when they pursue transformational change.

In fact, the difficult environment at the World Bank was ideal for observing what it means to be a leader: the organization became a giant leadership laboratory.

One tremendous source of strength was the team of people that I had to help implement the vision. Roberto Chavez, Carole Evangelista, Adnan Hassan, Seth Kahan, Peter Midgley, and Lesley Shneier constituted one of the very few high-performance teams with which I have had the good fortune to be associated in my career. I benefited from their unflagging energy and support and learned much from them. Seth Kahan, for instance, taught me much of what I know about storytelling. Lesley Shneier showed everyone how to launch knowledge fairs. Adnan Hassan provided key strategic insights on the evolving role of knowledge.

I also benefited from a network of practitioners in the emerging field of knowledge management associated with the American Productivity and Quality Center in Houston and with Larry Prusak's Institute for Knowledge Management at IBM. These networks provided invaluable encouragement and guidance about how to turn the idea of knowledge management into a reality at times when the scene inside the World Bank looked extremely bleak.

And the challenges inside the organization were massive. The fact is, making knowledge management happen in a large, complex organization requires an extraordinary amount of collaboration from a huge number of people. In the absence of any hierarchical power to compel compliance, with no ability to direct or control or hire or fire or impose incentives or disincentives, and with only sporadic support from the president and continuing hostility from key senior managers, we were dependent on our ability to inspire people to buy into the idea and act collaboratively. We had no alternative but to invite people to espouse common objectives and modalities.

As a result, throughout the organization, people found themselves in a situation facing choices. Every day offered new opportunities for people to make decisions that determined whether they would contribute to the common goal of sharing knowledge or not. There were of course limits and constraints as to what they could do. But in the final analysis, what they did was the result of their own decisions as much as the context.

Different people acted differently.

For some, the lack of managerial clarity was a reason to hold back, doing nothing until the signals were less ambiguous. They would commit to sharing their knowledge only when they had clear directives, adequate resources, and clear unified support from those in charge.

For some, the scene was an invitation to set aside institutional goals and pursue individual interests. Some set out to build systems and approaches that they thought might nurture their own careers or promote their units but were barely compatible with the overall institutional goal.

And yet there were also many people who were inspired to overcome the mixed signals and the dysfunctional management scene. They saw the opportunity to forge ahead with the common objective of building robust institutional arrangements for sharing knowledge aimed at relieving global poverty. These people opted to unite toward implementing a goal that they saw as right. They ignored the difficulties and persisted in contributing to the collectivity.

Of all the staff involved in knowledge sharing at the World Bank, many rose to the occasion. They chose the difficult road of committing themselves to the common goal of making knowledge sharing a reality.

Yet as these leaders emerged, few of them were thinking of themselves as being in any way heroic, or even exercising leadership. They saw themselves as trying to resolve the crises of the day as best they could, doing what was necessary to get the job done. These people accepted the ambiguity and the chaos and the turmoil in which they found themselves and created their own meaning.

These people had a fundamentally different attitude from those who did not contribute or who resisted. They focused less on what the organization would do for them and more on what they could contribute to the mission. Their response consisted not merely in talk but in right action and right conduct. They took responsibility to find the answer to problems confronting them and set out to fulfill the tasks it set for them as individuals.

Rather than wait for leadership from above, they themselves became leaders. Lacking hierarchical authority, they created their own moral authority. Having been inspired to pursue a common goal of sharing knowledge with the world, they set out to inspire others to work together toward that goal.

The period from 1996 to 2000 in the World Bank was thus quite remarkable for the change that took place. In the space of four years, a strategic shift had been catalyzed in one of the world's most change-resistant organizations so that it had become a leader in a new field.

How could such a transformation have taken place? What were the elements of leadership that enabled such a change to take place? Why were so many people inspired to become champions when the obstacles to success were so huge? Could what was learned here be applied to leadership challenges that others might be facing both inside organizations and beyond?

By December 2000, I believed that I had some preliminary answers to these questions. So I left the World Bank as a full-time employee and began sharing my ideas with a wider audience. I went on the road and started passing on what I had learned about leadership with organizations all around the world.

I had come to see for instance that storytelling had played an extraordinary—and unexpected—role in the transformation at the World Bank. A certain kind of story had demonstrated an unexpected power to communicate a complex idea and spark action even in difficult, skeptical audiences. I called this kind of story a "springboard story" and wrote about it in *The Springboard* (2000).

Outside the World Bank, I found that people were keen to hear about my ideas and experiences, as many organizations were grappling with resistance to transformational change and struggling with how to inspire enthusiastic buy-in.

I was delighted to find that what I had learned about the specifics of leadership proved useful in countries as diverse as the United States, the United Kingdom, Denmark, the Netherlands, France, Germany, Austria, Australia, New Zealand, Japan, Singapore, and Venezuela. It worked in public sector and private sector organizations. It was effective in large organizations as well as small.

After several years, my work led to the articulation of other narrative patterns related to different challenges of leadership, including communicating who you are, enhancing the brand, transmitting values, sparking collaboration, sharing knowledge, taming the grapevine, and leading people into the future. I shared these findings in my books *Squirrel Inc* (2004) and *The Leader's Guide to Storytelling* (2005).

In those books, I explored the use of narrative tools, how they are deployed, how they differ from each other, and their strengths and limitations for the purposes of leadership. I focused principally on narrative, in part because it demonstrated remarkable power to connect with both the head and the heart and inspire leadership in others, and in part because storytelling was so underused in organizations.

At the same time, I saw that narrative wasn't the whole story. The secrets of leadership lay not only in the stories that were being told but also in the way the leadership goals themselves were formulated. Leaders could also deploy other tools like frames, questions, offers, challenges, metaphors, reasons, and so on. How did all these tools relate to each other? Which ones were best for which purpose? And how were all these communication tools combined into a seamless leadership message? How could leaders get people's attention? How could they combine storytelling with logic and reason? In effect, what was the full array of communication tools that constituted the language of leadership and how should they be used to greatest effect? More important: What was the role of leadership in the world?

These are the questions that this book addresses. It's about the nitty-gritty of transformational leadership. It describes what works and what doesn't work when it comes to changing the world and making it a better place. It's a book about the specifics of getting things done and inspiring other people to embrace new ideas and change.

It looks at leadership in finer granularity than is typical. It speaks of what leaders need to do and say when they want people not only to act differently but to *want* to act differently. The changes that leaders seek to effect in the world may be great or small. They may relate to changing an organization, or its brand, or a school, or a town, or a family, or a community, or a country, or even the planet. Whatever the scale or location of the change, the principles of leadership communication remain the same.

This book also shows that transformational leadership will require going down paths that are difficult, risky, and fraught with personal peril. It notes that making the world a better place is often at odds with personal advancement. The book is intended not for those who seek dominance or the ease of a wealthy, trouble-free existence but rather for those who aspire to a meaningful life. Rather than generating power *over* others, it shows how to create power *in* and *with* others.

This book shows what's involved in inspiring people to want to do something different and become leaders who themselves generate enduring enthusiasm. It translates general theories of transformational leadership into specific, identifiable, measurable, trainable behaviors that can be used to galvanize action. It's about the discipline of leadership communication: the secret language of leadership.

Washington, D.C.   Stephen Denning
July 2007

[PART 1]

WHAT IS TRANSFORMATIONAL LEADERSHIP?

[INTRODUCTION]

TEN MISTAKES TRANSFORMATIONAL LEADERS MAKE

> " The dogmas of the quiet past are inadequate to the stormy present. . . . As our case is new, so we must think anew, and act anew. We must disenthrall ourselves. "
>
> **—Abraham Lincoln[1]**

In the U.S. presidential campaign of 2000, Al Gore's robotic performances were the fodder of late-night comedy. The charisma-challenged candidate put everyone to sleep. His petulant sighs and stiffly aggressive manner made him look like the smart kid we all hated in eighth grade. No one wanted to listen to what he had to say. Despite a strong case on the merits, he lost the election.

Fast-forward to 2006, and what do we see? Millions of people have paid more than US$40 million to watch a movie of Al Gore's PowerPoint presentation.[2] And Gore's live talks enjoy the response of a rock star. Even deep in Republican territory like Boise, Iowa, Gore can pack a 10,000-seat arena—and tickets for his talk sell out faster than for Elton John.[3]

Why did Al Gore fail so badly in 2000, when in 2006 he was successful in communicating a difficult change message? It's sometimes said that the 2000 election was decided by the U.S. Supreme Court, or by the hanging chads of the voting slips in Florida, or even by the presence of the third-party candidate, Ralph Nader. But long before any of these factors touched the race, Gore had put himself in a position to lose the election by failing to understand the language of leadership. He had committed ten common leadership mistakes that aspiring leaders make.

Mistake #1: Unclear, Uninspiring Goal

On October 3, 2000, around 90 million viewers tuned in to see the first televised debate between Vice President Al Gore and George W. Bush. It was the most-watched single event of the U.S. presidential election campaign. It was the first opportunity for many Americans to assess the contenders for more than the flash of a television commercial or a glimpse on the evening news. Just thirty-five days before the U.S. presidential election, the race was still breathtakingly close: polls showed the two candidates to be in a statistical dead heat. The debate was a pivotal moment since most of the crucial swing voters would be viewing.

As the incumbent vice president, Gore had a great deal going for him. The country was at peace and enjoying unprecedented economic growth and prosperity. The national debt was being reduced. Welfare had been reformed. Crime rates were declining. Home ownership and job creation were at all-time highs. Major foreign policy successes had been accomplished with agreements in the Middle East, Ireland and the Balkans. Gore himself was one of the few vice presidents in history to have made a substantive contribution to an administration. He had played a role in the environment, technology, budget discipline, administrative reform, urban and foreign policy. And unlike most U.S. vice presidents, Gore had the strong, explicit backing of the then president, Bill Clinton, whose policies, despite a sex scandal, remained remarkably popular.

But for better or worse, Gore did not run as an incumbent. "This election," he told the Democratic convention, "is not an award for past performance. I'm not asking you to vote for me on the basis of the economy we have." Instead, the economic record, good as it was, was "not good enough." Crime had fallen, but "there's still too much danger and there's still too much fear." In the presidential debate, he hardly mentioned his record and did not associate himself with the president with whom he had worked for almost eight years.

Gore ran for election as a transformational leader. He was not running as vice president but as himself. His campaign was based not on what he had done in the past but rather on what he would do *in the future* as president. Instead of dwelling on the question, by analogy with Ronald Reagan in 1980, "Are you better off today than eight years ago?" he asked "Will we be better off four years from this day?" For most voters, the answer to the first question would have been a resoundingly positive "Yes!" The answer to the second question was much less certain. While Bush generally embraced the successful economic policies that Clinton had pursued for the past eight years, paradoxically Gore ran as someone who wanted to change policy. He presented himself as someone who wanted to fight.

But fight for what? By most accounts, the electorate hadn't been paying very much attention to the campaign. On the night of October 3, 2000, some 90 million people tuned in to find out what it was all about. What they learned from Gore was that he was going to fight for a large number of government programs. In the first ninety seconds of the debate, Gore managed to mention eleven such programs. These included balancing the budget, paying down the national debt, putting Medicare and Social Security in a lockbox, cutting taxes for middle-class families, ensuring safe schools, giving parents the tools to protect their children against cultural pollution, and investing in education, health care, the environment, and retirement security. That was just the beginning. As the debate wore on, he mentioned even more programs that he was fighting for.

Clinton had been warned by his advisers in 1992, "If you say three things, you've said nothing."[4] Clinton took the advice and concentrated on a single theme, "It's the economy, stupid." Here in 2000, at the outset of the debate, Gore was saying, not just three things, but eleven things in ninety seconds, and then some.

Absorbing the implications of eleven programs in ninety seconds would be tough for any audience, even an expert one paying rapt attention. For an electorate that wasn't paying much attention to the campaign, it was overload. Instantly, "Memory full!" signs were flashing in people's minds.

But was there an overall theme to what Gore was saying? The closest Gore came in the debate to answering that question was at the end of the debate when he said: "I would like to have your support for me because I want to fight for you as president and fight for all the people." In his two-minute closing statement, he used the words *fight* or *fought* seven times.

It was as though the goal itself was to fight. For an electorate that was tired of the partisanship of the Clinton presidency, the prospect of another four years of fighting was neither clear nor inspiring.

Mistake #2: Lack of Total Commitment for Change

"I'm not," said Gore toward the end of the first presidential debate, "a very exciting politician." When Gore said those words, it wasn't news: he was confirming what his critics had often said about him. But he was revealing something fatal in a transformational leader. He was conceding that even he wasn't fully convinced in himself as a leader. If Gore wasn't excited about his own candidacy and his change agenda, how could he expect the electorate to be?

The critics were correct that Gore's campaign hadn't been the most exciting. His public performances were stiff and uninspired. But to be a transformational leader, Gore needed to overcome this criticism. And the first step was to believe in himself and to have an unshakable faith that the changes he was pursuing were exciting in themselves and capable of inspiring excitement in others.

To those who knew Al Gore in private, his stiff public persona was a mystery. They knew him as a skilled storyteller, a practical joker with a quick, acerbic wit and a facility for coming up with the deadpan retort that eased the daily tension of the workplace. Yet he was reluctant to reveal his humor on the public stage, because of its sharp, cutting edge.[5]

Moreover, he was guarded because his advisers had told him not to discuss the very things he was passionate about. As a result, Gore tempered his views on issues. "He didn't talk about tobacco because he was worried about being called a tobacco farmer," said one of his campaign aides. "And he wouldn't talk too much about the environment because he was afraid his book would be used against him."[6] He didn't talk about his long-term partner and president, Bill Clinton, because his advisers felt voters would disapprove of Clinton's personal conduct.

In fact, Gore was still going through a personal struggle with his advisers as to what sort of a candidate and person he was. He had made wholesale changes to his team of advisers in the preceding year. The struggle was still visible in what he said at the debate itself. At the start of the debate, he came out as a rational bureaucrat, with programmatic solutions for every problem. By the end of the debate, he was presenting himself as the passionate advocate for change, determined to fight on behalf of the little guy. Who was the real Al Gore? Becoming comfortable with who he was and what he stood for was something that Al Gore had to do for himself. It was an internal decision to adopt a stance, an orientation toward the world.

With all the different personae warring within him, Gore opted to converse from behind a mask, hiding what was most precious to him while attempting to project a persona that he hoped might appeal to the electorate.

If Gore had been committed, mind, body, and soul, to a clearly articulated goal, come what may, whatever it took, then he would have seen the goal—and his own role—as exciting. But this was a bridge that Al Gore had not yet crossed. Because Gore was still vacillating in his own mind as to which persona to adopt, he himself wasn't excited—and so he was unable to inspire widespread excitement in the electorate.

Mistake #3: Incongruent Body Language

It was extraordinary that at the time of the first presidential debate in October 2000 Gore was still largely unknown to much of the electorate. His father had put the family name in the national political domain more than sixty years earlier. His own record of public service as congressman and senator from Tennessee and vice president of the United States covered twenty-four years. He was the coauthor of a best-selling book. He had given three prime-time addresses at successive Democratic conventions. He had participated in each of the past four presidential campaigns, including his run for the Democratic nomination in 1988. And yet his political persona was still a mystery beyond a few persistent stereotypes.[7]

The first presidential debate was a chance for Gore to reveal to the electorate in an unscripted environment what sort of a person he was. In a sense, the election was ultimately about Al Gore. The election was his to lose. In a time of peace and great economic prosperity, why should the electorate make a change? All he had to do was connect. But up till this point, he hadn't connected. He was still an unknown quantity.

On the substance of what was said during the debate that night, Gore was widely regarded as the winner. In the instant polls, CBS showed Gore winning 56 percent to 42 percent; ABC, 42–39; CNN, 48–41; and NBC, 46–36.[8] His arguments were clearer. He was more articulate than Bush, who stumbled for words and didn't seem as familiar with the issues. But this wasn't a high school debate: it wasn't enough to win on substance. The question on swing voters' minds was: What sort of a person is Gore?

On this issue, in terms of what Gore himself said that night, the viewers didn't get much help. Gore had a positive story tell, but he never got round to telling it. As a result, the viewers had to make their own judgment from Gore's body language as to what sort of a person he was. The picture wasn't pretty.

Gore spoke hurriedly, sounding brash and combative, rather than like the seasoned statesman he actually was. Several times, he jumped into the discussion, betraying his eagerness to argue. He knowingly violated the rules of the debate. He said, "I know we're not supposed to ask each other questions" and went ahead and asked Bush a question anyway.

He came across as aggressive and hard-hitting. He hammered his points relentlessly, mentioning "the wealthiest 1 percent" ten times and the "lockbox" into which he planned to place Social Security and Medicare a total of five times during the debate. Overall, his behavior suggested an element of inner insecurity.

Even more damaging was Gore's body language while Bush was speaking. He shook his head, pursed his lips, frowned, grimaced painfully, rolled his eyes, and sighed loudly at Bush's answers, as if to say, "Oh really now!" Gore looked supercilious, like a class showoff smirkily displaying his superiority.[9]

The result was that Gore came across as a rather unlikable fellow—knowledgeable and articulate, yes, but also relentless, overbearing, officious, petulant, hectoring, interrupting, bullying, not someone you would want as a next-door neighbor. To swing voters, the thought of having to watch and listen to another four years of this was not an alluring future.

While Gore's words said that he was ready to be president, his body language said something else. It was the body language that the audience listened to. So although immediate polls showed that Gore "won" the debate on substance, in the aftermath of the debate Bush moved forward in the polls and went on to win the election.

Mistake #4: Misreading the Audience

In October 2000, America was at the height of the dot-com boom. Economic growth, the stock market, employment, incomes, homeownership were all flourishing. As a result, most voters viewed themselves and the country as prosperous and were satisfied with the policies of the Clinton-Gore administration, even if there was significant disapproval of the Clinton's personal conduct.

Yet Gore spoke as though most people were suffering because of high drug prices, overcrowded classrooms, fear of crime, and the machinations of big business. He was offering to fight for them to deal with these problems. But most people didn't see them as major problems. They were satisfied with economic progress and the way the country was being run: in October 2000 few Americans were crying out for anyone to fight for them.[10]

Gore's proposal to fight for them was at odds with the overall mood of the country, particularly the swing voters who would decide the outcome of the election. Gore was offering to solve problems that weren't at the top of their agenda. Moreover, he was offering to solve them by resorting to government programs, which were not widely perceived as either efficient or effective.

For Gore to succeed as a transformational leader, he needed either to address issues that the electorate already recognized as serious problems or to convince voters that their problems were more serious than they realized. Since Gore did neither, he lost.

Mistake #5: Lack of Narrative Intelligence

For much of the debate, Al Gore spoke in abstractions about programs and policies, in large numbers and with considerable precision. He gave mind-numbing detail. He was asked complex questions and he gave long, complex answers. In substance, they were good answers. He demonstrated intellectual grasp of the issues. In the instant polls that were taken, Gore won.

Yet Gore knew that electoral campaigns were won or lost on the basis of stories. He knew that stories could connect with the audience. So he came prepared with stories. And he wove them into his answers. But they didn't work. Why?

Midway through the debate, Gore told the tale of a fifteen-year-old Florida girl in an overcrowded classroom.

> I would like to tell you a quick story. I got a letter today as I left Sarasota, Florida. I'm here with a group of thirteen people from around the country who helped me prepare. We had a great time. Two days ago we ate lunch at a restaurant. The guy that served us lunch gave me a letter today. His name is Randy Ellis. He has a fifteen-year-old daughter named Caley, who is in Sarasota High School. Her science class was supposed to be for twenty-four students. She's the thirty-sixth student in that classroom. They sent me a picture of her in the classroom. They can't squeeze another desk in for her, so she has to stand during class. I want the federal government, consistent with local control and new accountability, to make improvement of our schools the number one priority so Caley will have a desk and can sit down in a classroom where she can learn.

There were several problems with the story told in this way. First, Gore began by saying it was just "a story," as if to imply—prophetically, as it turned out—that it wasn't entirely true.

Second, the story had a lot of confusing detail at the start, including the lunch in the restaurant in Sarasota, the group that was there in Boston having a great time while helping him to prepare, and then about the guy who served him lunch in Sarasota and afterward gave him a letter. What did these details have to do with the story of Caley Ellis? Gore wasted precious seconds on irrelevant, confusing detail, not realizing that to use narrative effectively in this setting, it was critical to be succinct.

Finally, the heroine of the story, Caley Ellis, the Florida schoolgirl without a desk, was not typical of the education problems of the country, and hence the story wasn't one that most of the audience knew of or would connect with.

A second story, which Gore included in his closing remarks had even worse unintended consequences. It was a story about a woman called Winifred Skinner. The woman had been featured in the network news a few days earlier. Gore tried to weave in her story halfway through the debate, but managed to mention only her name, much to the mystification of the viewers. So in his closing remarks Gore opted to end by telling her story. The results were unfortunate.

What Gore Actually Said

> There is a woman named Winifred Skinner here tonight from Iowa. I mentioned her earlier. She's seventy-nine years old. She has Social Security. I'm not going to cut her benefits or support any proposal that would. She gets a small pension, but in order to pay for her prescription drug benefits, she has to go out seven days a week several hours a day picking up cans. She came all the way from Iowa in a Winnebago with her poodle in order attend here tonight. I want to tell her, I'll fight for a prescription drug benefit for all seniors and fight for the people of this country for a prosperity that benefits all.

How Gore's Speech Was Parodied

> My opponent wants to cut taxes for the richest 1 percent of Americans. I, on the other hand, want to put the richest 1 percent in an ironclad lockbox so they can't hurt old people like Roberta Frampinhamper, who is here tonight. Mrs. Frampinhamper has been selling her internal organs, one by one, to pay for gas so that she can travel to these debates and personify problems for me. Also, her poodle has arthritis.[11]

Gore's decision to close with this story caused multiple problems. A story at the end of a communication is weighed by the audience in terms of the evidentiary value it adds. Even a credible story about a single individual would in principle have added little. In this case, the suggestion that seventy-nine-year-old Winifred Skinner drove 1,300 miles from Des Moines to Boston to listen to the debate, suggested that this wasn't an authentic story, but rather a self-serving piece of public relations generated by the Gore campaign machinery. The strangely discordant details—being seventy-nine years old, driving 1,300 miles in a Winnebago, owning a poodle, and yet spending several hours a day having to pick up cans to earn money to pay for her medication—rendered the story so implausible that it became an easy target for opponents.

As a result, Gore's story was parodied on late-night comedy to the hilarity of the nation, thus cementing in place the perception of what was wrong with Gore's candidacy—someone who was trying to pull on the audience's heart strings with irrelevant, implausible stories.

Mistake #6: Not Telling the Truth

Throughout his career, Gore had acquired a reputation as someone with a tendency to exaggerate, to stretch the truth to suit the political moment and to embellish his own role in what had been accomplished. His own staff had drawn Gore's attention to his tendency to go out on a limb in the 1988 presidential campaign as a serious issue. The media—and his opponents—made fun of his supposed claims to have invented the Internet, to have discovered the toxic waste danger at Love Canal in New York, and to have been the model for the novel *Love Story*.[12] In reality, Gore was a serious public servant with a commitment to doing the right thing. But loose lips sink ships and Gore's verbal slips continued to dog him through his political career. His campaign had been ineffective at putting the credibility issue to rest. Most newspapers did stories at some point during the campaign as to whether Gore was a big liar or a little fibber.[13]

The issue had died down somewhat after the Democratic Convention in August 2000. But in the debate, it was obviously crucial for Gore to be scrupulously honest and to be ready to show that he was a straight shooter.

As is customary in political debates, both candidates tossed out numbers that night about different programs. Each disputed the other's statistics. As usual, the audience was in no position to figure out whose numbers were right. Bush, however, linked the dispute on numbers with the more general and memorable question of Gore's character and his apparently casual attitude toward veracity. Thus when Gore challenged some of his numbers, Bush replied:

> Look, this is a man who has great numbers. He talks about numbers. I'm beginning to think not only did he invent the Internet, but he invented the calculator. It's fuzzy math. It's scaring—he's trying to scare people in the voting booth.

If it had remained a question about whose statistics were more accurate, Bush's comment might have been no more than a cute, forgettable one-liner. On the spot, Gore had no response to the charge, even though he should have known it was coming. And it began to have real resonance when it transpired after the debate that three of the stories Gore had told contained some exaggerations.

It turned out that Caley Ellis's school did not make her stand in science class every day. That may have been true on that particular day when $100,000 worth of new science equipment was stacked up and waiting for installation. The school had a practically brand new campus. It was said to be one of the top schools in the nation. All students were in regular classes with nine hundred computers and six hundred Internet sites.[14]

Gore also overstated his role in the handling of some fires in Texas. The issue arose because the moderator, Jim Lehrer, had asked each candidate to point to a decision or action "that illustrates your ability to handle the unexpected, the crisis under fire." Bush responded by talking about the emergency responses to the disastrous fires that ravaged Texas in 1996 and complimented James Lee Witt of FEMA for the good work done in a crisis. Gore immediately attempted to claim some of the credit, saying: "I want to compliment the governor on his response to those fires and floods in Texas. I accompanied James Lee Witt down to Texas when those fires broke out. And FEMA has been a major flagship project of our reinventing government efforts. And I agree it works extremely well now." It turned out, however, that Gore had not accompanied Witt to Texas in

1996. Rather Gore had visited Texas with Witt in 1998 during a spate of smaller fires.

The story of Winifred Skinner was not shown to be factually incorrect, but the discordant details—a seventy-nine-year-old woman spending hours each day collecting cans, driving 1,300 miles in her Winnebago to hear the debate, and owning a poodle—made the story sound so implausible that it too added to the impression of untrustworthiness.

While the disputes over statistics were quickly forgotten as part of the normal give-and-take of political jibber-jabber, the actual or apparent exaggerations in Gore's stories were memorable and stuck in people's minds. They led to an indelible impression that Gore was a candidate who didn't tell the truth.

The reality was that Gore was a man of deep principle and distinguished public service, and was profoundly concerned about doing what was right. But that night, his language communicated something else. And afterward, his campaign was somehow unable to convey that his misstatements were trivial in the overall scheme of things, and that molehills were being turned into mountains. Gore even made the mistake of defending the Caley Ellis story as essentially accurate.[15]

In the final days of the campaign, Gore finally did take action to address the issue. He went on a special edition of *Saturday Night Live* and made fun of his tendency to moralize, saying: "I was one of the very first to be offended by the material on *Saturday Night Live*." And on David Letterman's late-night show, Gore parodied his own tendency to exaggerate, saying "Remember America, I gave you the Internet and I can take it away." As in all effective self-parody, Gore was now implying, "If I can make fun of these flaws, you shouldn't be worried about them either." But it was too little, too late. By then, most of the 90 million viewers of the October 3 debate had already made up their minds: Gore was not a truth teller.

Mistake #7: Attention Misdirected

For the most of the campaign, people weren't listening. The country was at peace. The economy was prosperous. There were no obvious pressing national issues. The candidates seemed to be saying similar things. When some 90 million viewers tuned in, the first presidential debate was a real chance to get the electorate's attention.

At the outset, Gore came on as the rational bureaucrat mentioning all the government programs he was going to implement. His objective was presumably to demonstrate competence. But in the mind-numbing recitation of programmatic arguments, it is probable that he lost the attention of many viewers then and there.

Yet Gore was aware of the power of narrative to get attention and he had come armed with stories aimed to do just that. In addition to the stories of the fifteen-year-old Caley Ellis who had to stand in her science class and the seventy-nine-year-old Winifred Skinner who had to collect cans to help pay for prescription drugs, he also told the story of the seventy-year-old Milwaukee hypertension patient, George McKinney. McKinney and his wife, Gore said, had to travel to Canada to buy affordable prescription drugs. This story showed that there was a problem, but it focused attention on another question that didn't help Gore: why hadn't the problem been solved in the seven years Gore spent as vice president? The stories drew attention to problems that had occurred during his administration, rather than to Gore's positive accomplishments or to his future programs.

Moreover, while Gore cited the Caley Ellis story to make the case for federal funding for education, the story actually showed the opposite, since this was an excellent school that didn't need federal funding. Thus the story reinforced his opponent's point that Gore was too eager to throw government money at problems, thus contributing to large-scale waste.

Thus Gore's stories got people's attention, but in a way that undermined his case. As one commentator put it, they made "despair look positively sunny." It was as though Gore was saying:

"1. I've been vice president for the past seven years.

"2. Here are some particularly wretched situations that Americans have found themselves in during that time.

"3. Therefore, you should vote for me for president."[16]

Mistake #8: Inability to Elicit Desire for Change

Rightly or wrongly, Al Gore presented himself as a candidate for change. Subsequent commentators have noted that Gore would have been more likely to have won the election if he had presented himself as an incumbent, dwelling on the many successes of the Clinton-Gore administration, adding the possibility of incremental change at the margin and urging, as George H. W. Bush had done in 1988, that this was no time for the on-the-job training of his less experienced opponent.[17] Instead, Gore opted to present himself as a challenger who would do things differently and fight for change on behalf of the little guy against the wealthy, the big insurance companies, the big oil firms and other special interests.

The difficulty for Gore, as indeed it is for most transformational leaders, was that there was no obvious demand for the fight he was planning to launch. The electorate was content with the current economic policies. They were prosperous. They were happy. The future looked bright. They were complacent. Why change?

What were the rhetorical options open to Gore to succeed as a change agent?

One was to describe the problems of people who weren't faring well in the economy. Gore did this, but merely stating the problems didn't generate desire for change. It was an appeal to the mind. To generate desire for change, he needed to appeal to the heart. Gore's abstract arguments didn't generate enthusiasm.

Another was to tell future stories about what he planned to do and how this would make things better. But future stories are always nebulous and difficult to make inspiring. Moreover, Gore didn't make clear how he would proceed except by using government programs or by fighting— not an enticing prospect for the electorate.

Gore did use a couple of striking stories set in the recent past—George McKinney and his wife, Caley Ellis, Winifred Skinner—that got people's attention. But they were negative stories of questionable credibility—the wrong kind of stories to stimulate a desire to change. Negative stories typically stimulate the listeners' reptilian brain with a fight-or-flight response; they don't generate enthusiasm for a future course of action.

What Gore needed, and what he failed to use, was the most powerful kind of motivational story—true, positive stories about the successful accomplishments of the past seven years. When well told, such stories could have generated positive stories about the future in the minds of the listeners and so stimulated enthusiasm for other changes. Instead of dwelling on those stories, Gore chose to tell stories about problems. A future full of problems and fights wasn't a future that the electorate wanted to contemplate.

Mistake #9: His Reasons Backfired

The more reasons Al Gore gave as to why he should be elected and what he would do if he was, the more boring he sounded and the less people listened. Why?

One clue comes from the work of Frank Luntz, the legendary Republican pollster, who in 1992 was running a focus group in Detroit to test television ads for Ross Perot, the presidential candidate. There were three ads: a biography, a Perot speech, and testimonials from other people. In these sessions, he set out to find the consensus and then see whether he could undermine it. What he found at first was that he couldn't undermine support for Perot. His support remained strong.

But at the session in Detroit, by mistake, Luntz ran the ads in reverse order: first, the testimonials, then the speech, and finally the biography. With this order, the people said that they didn't like Perot at all. His opinions seemed intemperate if they didn't rest on the foundation of his impressive rags-to-riches life story. Suddenly Luntz realized: the order in which you give people information influences how they think. If they're already positively oriented to the subject, their reaction to what you are saying is very different from what it would be without that connection. Luntz had discovered, accidentally, that it is vital to establish an emotional connection at the outset.[18]

Without the emotional connection to Gore and his change program, Gore's reasons lacked traction. The more reasons Gore offered, the more he started an argument with the audience, and the less likely he was to win their support.

Mistake #10: The Conversation Died

Leadership communications begin as monologue. If they are successful they turn into dialogue and then into conversation. The conversation emerges because of the enduring enthusiasm for change that has been inspired. The conversation mobilizes the energies of listeners who contribute to finding solutions of how to get there and inspire others to do likewise.

Gore's presentation during the presidential debate failed to do this, because it didn't inspire desire for change. Instead, Gore implied that he would use the power of the presidency to force change. He was going to put Social Security and Medicare "in a lockbox." He was going to "fight" to make change happen with the hierarchical power of the office of the presidency in adversarial struggles on behalf of the little guy against the wealthy, the big insurance companies, and big oil and special interests. Instead of trying to inspire people and organizations to want change, he was going to fight to require them to change.

In effect, he was asking for a four-year mandate to undertake adversarial warfare against the opponents of change, not to continue a conversation. As the electorate was tired of partisan fighting, it opted not to give him that mandate.

Learning the Language of Leadership

The object here is not to pick on Al Gore but rather to point out mistakes that are often made by aspiring transformational leaders. Gore wasn't passionately and unconditionally committed to a clear, inspiring change idea. Most of the time, he was trying to make his case through abstract arguments, discussing and analyzing problems and proposing solutions. This left the audience dazed rather than inspired. He failed to engage them at an emotional level through appropriate stories. The stories he did use directed attention to issues that undermined his cause rather than reinforcing it. His body language communicated an aggressive, unlikable person, rather than someone with whom the audience would want to interact. As a result, the conversation between Gore and the audience never got going—and so he lost the election.

Yet in 2006, Al Gore was able to sell out whole stadiums to people who wanted to hear his change message. What's the difference between the Al Gore of 2000 and the Al Gore of 2006?

In his movie, *An Inconvenient Truth*, Al Gore conveys passion for a subject he cares deeply about—the environment. Now he isn't merely repeating what his political managers or handlers have told him to say, as in his 2000 campaign. He talks frankly about his family's tobacco farm and the role that it may have played in his sister's death from lung cancer. It also helps that he has become less pompous in his public speeches and is able to poke gentle fun at himself.

Even more important, the Al Gore of 2006 has abandoned speaking in a tangle of complex abstractions and used appropriate narratives.

From the start of the movie, he gets our attention by telling a series of frightening stories about the scale and scope and causes of global warming and the reasons why no action is being taken, as well as engaging stories about himself, his life, his family, and what the environment means to him personally.

As the immensity of the problem we are facing becomes apparent, he asks the question: is it feasible to do anything about it? He answers this by pointing to the many cities, states, and corporations that have already decided to take action. And he gives some vignettes showing how the human race has managed to fix other huge global problems, including winning two world wars, curing smallpox, establishing civil rights, putting a man on the moon, and even fixing the hole in the ozone layer. These massive problems were solved by concerted action by governments and countries all around the globe. So we were able to solve huge global problems before. What if we were to do the same thing here?

Finally, he outlines the practical steps that would be needed to bring the problem under control, including more efficient use of electricity, more efficient buildings, improved vehicle efficiency, greater use of mass transit, greater use of renewable energy, and cleaner power plants and industrial activities. These actions are feasible. This is not a technical problem. This is not a political problem. It's a moral problem. When the whole future of the planet is at stake, it is time to rise up and secure the future.

Whatever one thinks about the scientific merit of Gore's arguments or his politics, his presentation has proved to be remarkably effective in getting people's attention and pushing them to act.[19] What we see in the Al Gore of 2006 is that he had a clear change idea that was capable of generating enduring enthusiasm and to which he was genuinely committed. He had learned how to connect emotionally with the audience through narrative. His body language had become calm and assertive, rather than aggressive, and he was able to reveal his droll sense of humor. He communicated by getting the audience's attention and stimulating desire for change. After he had stimulated an interest in change, he reinforced this with reasons. After the movie came out, he continued the conversation in talks, on television, and in person.

By 2006, Al Gore had learned the language of leadership.

1

THE SECRET LANGUAGE OF LEADERSHIP

> " Human communication has its own set of
> very unusual and counterintuitive rules. "
>
> **—Malcolm Gladwell**[1]

The head of a major drug company is in trouble because her firm's pipeline of new products has run dry. The managing editor of a major newspaper has difficulty inducing reporters in the newsroom to change their behavior to meet new types of competition.

A director in a global fast-food firm knows how to repair its swooning share price, but he can't get the CEO to listen. Young staff in a dysfunctional unit of an enormous engineering firm can't persuade its management that open source collaboration will help productivity, not harm it.

A health care provider can't get heart surgery patients to change their lifestyles: without healthy diet and exercise, they will be ill—or dead—within a year or two. A global conglomerate sees its share price tank; despite sterling earnings, profits, and growth, Wall Street doesn't understand its strategy.

A change-oriented presidential candidate can't connect with the electorate and loses an election he should have won. A nonprofit aimed at redressing global warming struggles to mobilize policymakers around the world in a more agile fashion.

A father puzzles what to do about a teenage boy who vanished into his room at the age of thirteen and hasn't been seen for several years. A mother ponders what to do about her teenage daughter who questions everything and won't submit to her authority.

What links these people—in this book as in life—troubled CEOs, stressed change agents, hard-pressed marketers, stymied idealists, mystery politicians, puzzled parents—is a wish to induce change. They have to transmit bold new ideas to people who don't want to hear them, and have the ideas implemented with sustained energy.

What Is Transformational Leadership?

In principle, we know *what* transformational leaders are meant to do. They change the world by generating enduring enthusiasm for a common cause. They present innovative solutions to solve significant problems. They catalyze shifts in people's values and ideologies. They demonstrate willingness to sacrifice personal interests when necessary. They help others get through critical moments of crisis. They inspire people to want to change, so that positive energy sustains the change over time. They don't just generate followers: their followers themselves become leaders.

But if the *what* of transformational leadership is reasonably clear, the *how* has remained almost totally obscure. How exactly do leaders communicate complex ideas and spark others into enduringly enthusiastic action? What words do they use to inspire others to become new leaders? Why are some leaders able to accomplish the feat while others fail miserably?

It's become fashionable to see leadership almost solely as an issue of inner conviction. Find the leader deep within yourself.[2] Become the person others will want to follow.[3] Discover your strengths.[4] Become emotionally intelligent.[5] Merely through increased self-awareness, self-regulation, and positive modeling, authentic leaders develop authenticity in followers.[6] When you visualize, then you materialize.[7] Be true to yourself and change happens.

Would it were so.

The reality is that sustained, enthusiastic change doesn't occur by osmosis or extrasensory perception. If leaders' inner commitment to change is to have any effect, they have to communicate it to the people they aspire to lead. True, the leaders' actions will eventually speak louder than words, but in the short run, it's what leaders say—or don't say—that has the impact. The right words can have a galvanizing effect, generating enthusiasm, energy, momentum, and more, while the wrong words can undermine the best intentions and kill initiative on the spot, stone dead.

The Pitfalls of the Traditional Approach to Communication

Think back for a moment to the last memo or essay or journal article you wrote, or the last time you gave a presentation. If you followed the traditional model of communication, you went through a familiar trinity of steps.

You stated the problem you were dealing with. Then you analyzed the options. And your conclusion followed from your analysis of the options.

Define problem >> Analyze problem >> Recommend solution

If this was your model, it wasn't unusual. You were doing what has always been done in organizations or universities. It's the "normal," the "commonsense," the "rational" way of communicating. It's an appeal to reason—a model that has been the hallowed Western intellectual tradition ever since the ancient Greeks. It reached its apogee in the twentieth century. And it works well enough when the aim is merely to pass on information to people who want to hear it.

But if you're trying to get human beings to change what they are doing and act in some fundamentally new way with sustained energy and enthusiasm, it has two serious problems. One, it doesn't work. And two, it often makes the situation worse.

Giving reasons for change to people who don't agree with you isn't just ineffective. A significant body of psychological research shows that it often entrenches them more deeply in opposition to what you are proposing.

In 1979, a psychologist named Charles Lord and his colleagues at Stanford University published their classic research on what happens when people are presented with arguments that are at odds with what they currently believe.[8] Lord's team selected twenty-four proponents and twenty-four opponents of capital punishment. They showed them studies that confirmed the penalty's deterrence as well as other studies that refuted it. What happened? The proponents of capital punishment interpreted the studies as supporting capital punishment, while the opponents of capital punishment concluded that the evidence refuted the approach. Both proponents and opponents found clever ways to reinterpret or set aside any contrary evidence so as to confirm their original positions.

For instance, whereas a participant in favor of capital punishment commented on a study confirming the deterrence effect that "the experiment was well thought out, the data collected was valid, and they were able to come up with responses to all criticisms," an opponent of capital punishment said of the same study, "I don't feel such a straightforward conclusion can be made from the data collected."

On another study showing the opposite, that is, disconfirming the deterrence effect, the roles were reversed. The opponent's meat became the proponent's poison and vice versa. The end result was that the proponents and the opponents of capital punishment became even more set in their positions. After they had reviewed the evidence, they were more polarized than before.

The phenomenon, which psychologists call the *confirmation bias*, was noted by Francis Bacon almost four hundred years ago: "The human understanding when it has once adopted an opinion . . . draws all things else to support and agree with it. And though there be a greater number and weight of instances to be found on the other side, yet these it either neglects and despises, or else by some distinction sets aside and rejects, in order that by this great and pernicious predetermination the authority of its former conclusions may remain inviolate."[9]

The confirmation bias isn't entirely illogical. Thus when I glance at a tabloid at the supermarket and read the headline, "Scientists Discover 4,000-Year-Old Television Set in Egyptian Pyramid," I smile and question the reliability of the tabloid, not my belief as to when television was invented. When we think we know something to be objective truth, our immediate reaction to news indicating the opposite is to jump to the conclusion that there must be something wrong with the source. And for many purposes, the confirmation bias serves us well.

But why aren't we more willing to reconsider our positions in the face of serious factual evidence that should at least give us pause? Aren't we thinking at all? Apparently not, according to a recent study by psychologist Drew Westen and his team at Emory University.[10] The team conducted functional magnetic resonance imaging (fMRI) brain scans on fifteen "strong Republicans" and fifteen "strong Democrats" in the course of the 2004 presidential campaign while they were reviewing blatantly self-contradictory statements by the two candidates, George W. Bush and John Kerry. As we would expect from earlier studies of the confirmation bias, the Democrats found ways to reconcile Kerry's inconsistencies and became even more strongly Democrat, while the Republicans had no difficulty explaining away George W. Bush's self-contradictions so as to become even more fervently Republican.

But the fMRI brain scans showed something new. While the participants were considering the inconsistent statements, the part of the brain associated with reasoning revealed no signs of activity at all. "We did not see," said Westen, "any increased activation of the parts of the brain normally engaged during reasoning. What we saw instead was a network of emotion circuits lighting up, including circuits hypothesized to be involved in regulating emotion and circuits known to be involved in resolving conflicts."[11]

But there was something even more startling. Once the participants had seen a way to interpret contradictory statements as supporting their original position, the part of the brain involved in reward and pleasure became active, and the conclusion was "massively reinforced . . . with the elimination of negative emotional states and the activation of positive ones."[12]

Remember that involuntary smile that sprang to my lips when I read the headline about the 4,000-year-old TV in the Egyptian pyramids? That smile wasn't as innocent as it looked. My brain was giving itself a psychic reward for having been able to stick to its original position. The emotional reaction, not my thinking mind, was causing me to be even more passionately attached to my original belief.

The confirmation bias helps explain why the traditional approach of trying to persuade people by giving them reasons to change isn't a good idea if the audience is at all skeptical, cynical, or hostile. If a leader offers reasons at the outset of a communication to such an audience, the maneuver will likely activate the confirmation bias and the reasons for change will be reinterpreted as reasons not to change. This occurs without the thinking part of the brain being activated: the audience becomes even more deeply dug into its current contrary position. Reasons don't work at the outset, because the audience is neither listening nor thinking.

Worse, we also know that skepticism and cynicism are contagious and can quickly turn into epidemics. They are instances of rebellious, antisocial behavior. In *The Tipping Point*, Malcolm Gladwell has described how such epidemics occur in many different settings.[13] We see it with hooligans. We see it with teenage smoking. When one person in a group is openly skeptical or cynical, it can create a license for others to be likewise: being a skeptic or a cynic can quickly become the cool thing. In the bar, after work, if the coolest person in the group says that the presentation that day was pure BS, how many others in the group are going to take the social risk of saying that they thought the presentation made a lot of sense? If they were thoroughly convinced, maybe. But if they themselves found the presentation confusing and hard to understand, the risk is that they'll go along with the cool guy, and agree that yes, it was all BS.

So although we might imagine that giving a presentation discussing and analyzing problems and reaching rational conclusions in favor of change can't do any harm, we need to think again. Giving a lecture full of abstract reasons arguing for change can quickly turn an audience into an army of strident cynics.

The Language of Leadership in Action

To find out what language is capable of generating enduring enthusiasm for change, I have spent the last decade studying how successful leaders communicate in scores of organizations, large and small, around the world.

What I've seen time again is that massive differences in the impact of leadership communication can be achieved by paying attention to the tiniest details of the words that are used, the patterns they form, the order in which the patterns are deployed.

Successful leaders communicate very differently from the traditional, abstract approach to communication. In all kinds of settings, they communicate by following a hidden pattern: first, they get attention. Then they stimulate desire, and only then do they reinforce with reasons:

Get attention >> Stimulate desire >> Reinforce with reasons

When the language of leadership is deployed in this sequence, it can inspire enduring enthusiasm for a cause and spark action to start implementing it. Moreover, successful leaders don't stop with a one-time communication. As implementation proceeds, it is inevitable that the cause they are pursuing will evolve. While that is happening, leaders and their followers stay in communication and co-create the future by continuing the conversation.

Of course, words alone won't work. The language of leadership is most effective when certain enabling conditions are in place, including a truthful commitment to a clear, inspiring change idea that is illuminated by narrative intelligence, appropriate body language, and an understanding of the audience's story. When all these enabling conditions are present and working in sync with the language of leadership deployed in the right sequence, transformational leadership takes off.

The Introduction illustrated the difference between the communications of Al Gore in 2000 and Al Gore in 2006. Here are two more examples of transformational leadership in action.

In the spring of 2002, Craig Dunn faced a perfect storm of bad news. AMP was famous in Australia as an icon of financial security, but the last few years had been a disaster for the company. Some major acquisitions in the U.K. had bombed and were now being undone. A major downsizing was under way. The stock price was plummeting. Rumors of an imminent hostile takeover were rampant. Many thought that AMP wouldn't survive.

Dunn, who had recently been appointed managing director of AMP's financial services business unit to help execute a turnaround, recalls going to a meeting of distributors in Melbourne at the height of the storm. "It was," he says, "just the worst meeting you ever went to. We had insults thrown at us. There was a lot of anger and disappointment. People had lost faith in the firm they partnered. And they had good reasons for feeling the way they did. We all had to face the fact that there had been a lot of poor management decisions in the recent past."

Little in Dunn's background had prepared him for this kind of challenge. Before joining AMP, he had worked as an analyst for KPMG in Europe and Indonesia, and then taken over as CEO of a Malaysia-based insurance company. In those roles, the environment was orderly. He gave people reasons and, by and large, they did what they were told. Now people were shouting and screaming abuse at him. They were furious. In such a crisis it was obvious that just giving people reasons wasn't going to work.

So he recalls going to a meeting in Melbourne and talking to the staff face-to-face. He began by acknowledging the problems AMP was facing, and said, "This is hard, this is difficult, but this is what the organization means to me."

Then he told them about a family in Adelaide that had bought one of AMP's insurance policies:

> The guy was still quite young, still in his early thirties, and he had a couple of kids. But he had contracted multiple sclerosis. He was just moving to the stage where he would be in a wheelchair. He had an income protection policy with us, and in that instance we went beyond what we were required to do legally. One of our claim managers had traveled over to Adelaide. He went through the house that we had just renovated for the family, and agreed to put in a new bathroom so that they could access it in a wheelchair, and to lower the kitchen benches.
>
> I told them what we had done for that family and what they had said to our claim manager. I was reminding people of what our firm was all about. And the value that we added to people's lives. It was true that the firm had lost its way in the past few years, but the sorts of

things that we'd done for that guy and his family in Adelaide were still happening. They were happening every day. I showed them that this was an organization worth fighting for.

And he went on to explain the actions that he planned to take to enable AMP to survive. Three years later, when AMP had not only survived the crisis but was back on the road to profitability, Dunn said: "What I came to see was that the communication is more emotional than logical: we had to draw upon people's emotional connection to the organization, to draw on that piggy bank of good will to the firm and use that as the way forward."[14]

Bill Gates is rightly given credit for issuing his "Tidal Wave memo" of May 26, 1995. In it, he communicated his decision to change course at Microsoft so that the nascent World Wide Web would become an integral part of the firm's computing software rather than a sideshow to the then-dominant desktop applications. The company's strong response crippled its competitor, Netscape, and won Microsoft more than 90 percent of the global browser market.

But as Gates points out in his book, *Business @ the Speed of Thought,* the issuance of the memo was more the end of the process than the beginning.[15] The memo had been preceded by a great deal of leadership activity needed to stimulate the desire for change.[16]

In the early 1990s, Microsoft wasn't thinking very much about the Internet, but it wasn't totally oblivious. In 1991 it had hired a twenty-two-year-old specialist, J. Allard, to help ensure that it would develop the right technologies for interoperability. By mid-1993, basic Web support had been built into Windows NT. Allard had seen the promise of the just-emerging technology and set about trying to convince others in the organization that they needed to make the Web central to all their software. He set up three machines on a folding table in the hallway of a Microsoft office block, and dragged everyone he could find, from product manager to group vice president, to show off the Web and get people enthusiastic about its potential. It wasn't just that the demonstration looked impressive; Allard could back it up with reason: the fact that in a ten-week period, customers downloaded twice as many copies of an MS-DOS upgrade from this Internet site as from CompuServe helped him prove that something big was already under way.

Then in early 1994, Gates's technical assistant, Steven Sinofsky, went to Cornell on a recruiting trip and got stuck there for several days as a result of a snowstorm. He used the time to check out how the university was using computers. He was amazed by the changes that had taken place since the year before. E-mail use by students was almost universal. Cornell's instructors were communicating with students online. A wide variety of information, including the library catalogue, schedules, grades, accounts, financial aid data, and a directory of who was who in the school community were available on the Web.

Allard and Sinofsky began writing memos and e-mail about how important the Internet was going to be. The e-mail began circulating among a large number of people in the firm.

In 1994, Gates was still thinking that the Internet was years away, because of the limited bandwidth available at the time to most Web users. The Microsoft strategy was to establish a network that would sit on top of the Web.

But the priority of the Internet in Microsoft was steadily rising from the bottom toward the top. The e-mail from Sinofsky and Allard circulated to a large number of people and sparked a firestorm of electronic conversation about what the Web would mean for Microsoft, how its programs would be affected, what capabilities they would need to have, and what new products should be developed. Sometimes ideas won quick agreement. Sometimes discussion was fierce. In the melee, many new ideas emerged.

"Hallways and e-mails," says Gates, "That's how it happened."[17] Gates himself became involved in e-mail exchanges with many different parts of the business. The Internet development plans were made available on the Microsoft network so that everyone could see them. In April 1994, as a result of the efforts of Allard and Sinofsky, Gates devoted Think Week to the Internet.

By early 1995 every team had defined its Internet charter and begun development. Internet add-ons, integration, and products were being actively produced.

So when Gates sent out his Internet Tidal Wave memo in May 1995, it was important, because it meant that Gates as the top manager was announcing a change of course. But the memo was nearer the end of the process than the beginning. It was the signal of a formal decision for a change that was already largely in place. Without the spirited conversation that had preceded the memo, it would have had little effect.

The Language of Leadership: Key Steps

What's going on in these examples? Let's look in a little more detail at each of the three key steps of the language of leadership, before turning to some enabling conditions—six elements that enable the language of leadership to achieve its maximum effectiveness.

Step #1: Getting the Audience's Attention

If leaders don't get people's attention, what's the point in even trying to communicate? If people aren't listening, speakers are simply wasting their breath. And in most settings today people are not listening in any attentive way. They are mentally doing e-mail, preparing for their next meeting, reminiscing about what happened at last night's party, planning lunch, or whatever. They may be aware in a vague, background way that someone is talking, and even conscious of the subject under discussion. The first step in communicating is to get their urgent attention.

How do you get people's attention? A couple of years ago, Tom Davenport and John Beck conducted an experiment with sixty executives to see what got their attention over a one-week period. Their conclusion: "Overall, the factors most highly associated with getting attention in rank order, were: the message was personalized, it evoked an emotional response, it came from a trustworthy source or respected sender and it was concise. The messages that both evoked emotion and were personalized were more than twice as likely to be attended to as the messages without these attributes."[18]

Social scientists have also shown that *negative* messages are more attention-getting than positive messages. Here are some of the more effective ways to get the audience's attention:

- Stories about the audience's problems (*"These problems are serious . . ."*)

- Stories about the likely trajectory of the audience's problems (*"These problems are getting worse . . ."*)

- A story of how the presenter dealt with adversity that is relevant to the issue under discussion—particularly if the presenter is new to the audience

- A surprising question or challenge in an area of interest to the audience

Al Gore's movie, *An Inconvenient Truth,* uses all these tools to get the attention of an audience that isn't particularly interested in making fundamental adjustments to their lifestyle as a result of global warming. Gore talks in conversations by a stream at his home of his family growing tobacco and his sister dying of lung cancer, thus helping to establish an emotional connection between him and his audience. Such an approach can be especially effective when, as in Al Gore's case, the audience may have a false impression of the kind of person he is.

J. Allard got people's attention by buttonholing everyone he could find and physically dragging them to come and look at the Web in action on the computers he had set up in the corridor. Sinofsky's e-mail about what was happening at Cornell helped alert others that something very different was under way. What if Microsoft were to miss the wave that was already rolling?

In Craig Dunn's case, he got the attention of the audience by acknowledging the problems that management itself had generated.

Step #2: Eliciting Desire for a Different Future

As Al Gore discovered in 2000, failing to distinguish between getting attention and stimulating desire can have disastrous results. That's because what gets people's attention typically doesn't stimulate a desire to act. Whereas getting attention is generally done more effectively by negative content, getting people to want to do something different needs to accentuate the positive. Negative stories, questions, or challenges wake us up. They activate the reptilian brain, suggesting fight or flight. They start us thinking, but they also generate worry, anxiety, and caution. They don't stimulate enthusiastic action.

Nor does the traditional practice of using a comprehensive set of analyses of the reasons for change generate enthusiastic action. For one thing, it's too slow. By the time the traditional presenter is approaching the conclusion, the audience has already made up its mind—largely on emotional grounds. For another, it's addressed to the wrong organ of the body. To gain enthusiastic buy-in, leaders need to appeal to the heart as well as the mind. The audience has to want to change. To be effective, a leader needs to establish an emotional connection and stimulate desire for a different future. Without the emotional connection, nothing happens. And stimulating desire is key, because decisions are made almost instantly, or as Malcolm Gladwell might say, in a blink.[19]

The task here isn't about imposing the leader's will on an audience, which, in any event, is impossible. It's not about moving the audience to a predetermined position that the leader has foreseen. It's about enabling the people in the audience to see possibilities that they have hitherto missed. It means creating the capability in the audience to see for themselves the world and their relations with others in a new and more truthful light. It involves pointing a way forward for people who find themselves—for whatever reason—cornered by the current story that they are living.

The idea that storytelling might be important is not particularly extraordinary: great leaders have always used stories to spark change. But the kinds of stories that are effective for leaders in stimulating desire for change are very different from what we might suspect. Some of the most effective stories are not big, flamboyant theatrical epics, well-told stories with the sights and sounds and smells of the context all faithfully evoked. Stories told with a bullhorn don't necessarily elicit desire for change.

In fact, some of the strongest stories are the smallest and the least pretentious. It's precisely because they are small and unpretentious that they work their magic. It's a question of understanding the right form of story to elicit desire: generally, it's a positive story about the past where the change, or an analogous change, has already happened, and it is told in a simple, minimalist manner.

Such stories look unassuming, but they can be astoundingly powerful. They operate by sparking a new story in the mind of the listener. It's this new story that the listeners generate for themselves that connects at an emotional level and leads to action. In the new story, listeners begin to imagine a new future. Thus:

- In *An Inconvenient Truth,* Al Gore used several stories to show that the human race had handled other massive global challenges before. These help spark a new story inside the minds of listeners: if we have solved problems like this before, then surely we can solve the problem of global warming!

- Craig Dunn told a story about the kind of role that his firm has played in the lives of real Australians, sparking a new story in the minds of the listeners: this is a firm worth preserving!

- Sinofsky's stories about what was happening on the Cornell campus pointed to the massive changes already under way on the Web. This led managers at Microsoft, including Bill Gates, to imagine a new story: if that's what the Internet could accomplish at Cornell, just imagine what it could do all around the world!

Quickly stimulating desire for a different state of affairs is the most important part of the communication: without it, the leadership communication goes nowhere. It's also the piece that is most consistently missing in the communications of aspiring leaders. And it's the trickiest facet of leadership, because it involves inducing people to want to do something different. The key insight is that if the listeners are to own the change idea, they have to discover it for themselves in the form of a new story.

And it's not "just" a story. What's generated becomes a new narrative to live by, a story that is both credible because it makes sense of their lives as they understand them, and capable of being put into practice. The newly emerging narrative is constructed both from the ongoing stories of the people and their organization, and from the new story put forward by the leader. It is born in the listeners' minds as a more compelling version of their ongoing life stories. The listeners themselves create the story. Since it's their own story, they tend to embrace it. What the leader says is mere scaffolding, a catalyst to a creative process going on inside the listeners.[20]

LEADING CLEVER PEOPLE

In a recent *Harvard Business Review* article titled "Leading Clever People," Rob Goffee and Gareth Jones do a disservice to the concept of leadership when they write, "If clever people have one defining characteristic, it is that they do not want to be led." Goffee and Jones argue that clever people need "benevolent guardians" rather than "traditional bosses." Because clever people are difficult, managers should use reverse psychology and suggest the opposite of what they really want.[21]

These are not helpful suggestions. The truth is that if leaders are unable to lead clever people, it means that they don't know how to be good leaders. What clever people object to is not being led, but being led badly. They object to being managed, commanded, controlled, or manipulated by people who aren't knowledgeable in the area where they are working or who are working in pursuit of goals that don't make sense. And they don't respect "benevolent guardians" any more than "traditional bosses." Reverse psychology works on clever people only when they have experienced a track record of bad decision making: in such settings, it's rational to give close attention to the opposite of what management says.

Although "benevolent guardianship" may do less poorly with clever people than traditional command-and-control management, it is a suboptimal solution. What clever people want, like all people, is *good* leaders, that is, people who can inspire enduring enthusiasm for a worthwhile cause.

Step #3: Reinforcing with Reasons

An emotional connection by itself isn't enough. Reasons are still relevant. The desire for change may wane unless it is supported and reinforced by compelling reasons why the change makes sense and should be sustained. But *where* the reasons are placed in a presentation is crucial.

When we encounter strange new ideas, we are subject to the confirmation bias and seek to preserve our existing viewpoint. By contrast, when we have made a decision to explore change, we actively look for elements that confirm the decision we've already made.

So if reasons are given *before* the emotional connection is established, they are likely to be heard as so much noise. Worse, if the audience is skeptical, cynical, or hostile, the reasons tend to flip and become ammunition for the opposite point of view. By contrast, if the reasons come *after* an emotional connection has been established with the change idea, then the reasons can reinforce it, because now listeners are actively searching for reasons to support a decision they have in principle already taken.

Giving people reasons at a time when they are ready to receive them is one of the keys to communication that leads to action. Reasons are put at a different position in the flow from the Western intellectual tradition. They come, not at the beginning or middle, but at the end.

Moreover, the most effective way to present reasons that will really resonate with your audience is to give people reasons in the form of stories. The most effective stories usually include:

- The story of *what* the change is, often seen through the eyes of some typical characters who will be affected by the change

- The story of *how* the change will be implemented, showing in simple steps how we will get from "here" to "there"

- The story of *why* the change will work, showing the underlying causal mechanisms that make the change virtually inevitable

Instead of relying on pure reason, on facts and figures and arguments, stories give reasons an emotional punch. They appeal to the heart as well as the mind, so as to cement the reasons in place and make the reasons memorable. These three steps—one, getting attention, two, stimulating desire for change, and three, reinforcing the desire for change with reasons, are the same whatever the leadership setting. Of the three steps, the middle step—stimulating desire for change—is the most important. Without desire for change, people will have no energy or enthusiasm. Indeed without desire for change, there is hardly any point in getting the audience's attention. And without desire for change, there is nothing for reason to reinforce. It's desire for change that drives the change process. So if transformational leaders do only one thing, they should make sure they stimulate desire for change.

The three steps form a flexible template. They offer a way of making sense of any leadership presentation. In some situations where resistance in the audience is particularly high, the speaker may need to spend a great deal more time getting attention than when the audience is already somewhat interested. By contrast, in an "elevator speech," there may only be time for the critical middle step—a story that kindles desire for change. Where generous time is available, the speaker may be able to give a large number of reasons in favor of change. The template can be tailored to meet the needs of the specific audience and the time available.

Leaders who talk in this way sound very different from typical authority figures of the past—managers, teachers, parents or politicians. True, some of those people were inspiring. But most of them communicated in the familiar top-down, paternalistic, authoritarian, domineering, I'm-in-charge-so-I-know-what's-right manner that people in positions of

The Secret Language of Leadership.

Effective presentation to get action

authority have been adopting for the last couple of thousand years. Too often they sounded hollow, flat, distant, uninviting, arrogant, almost inhuman.[22]

By contrast, the true language of leadership feels fresh and inviting, energizing and invigorating, challenging and yet enjoyable, lively, spirited, and fun, as when equals are talking to equals. It generates laughter and energy. It is not laughter at others, but laughter with others. It's the exhilaration of the discovery of possibility. Leaders show people that the end they thought they were coming to has unexpectedly opened: they laugh at what has surprisingly come to be possible.[23]

In short, it feels like being engaged in a great conversation that opens up new vistas and wider horizons.

And once started, the conversation must be continued. Leadership isn't about making a single presentation, after which the audience sees the light and rushes out to do what the leader says. It's about an ongoing openness to dialogue, combining a fierce resolve with a continuing willingness to listen.

The Language of Leadership: Key Enablers

The language of leadership will make the maximum impact if certain enabling conditions are in place. Without these enablers, the words that leaders use—the spoken language of leadership—risk sounding glib and superficial.

Enabler #1: Articulating a Clear and Inspiring Change Idea

When people are pursuing a clear and inspiring goal, they exude a quality that is real and recognizable but also difficult to describe or define. There's a look in the eye, the spring in the step, an eagerness in the voice, a willingness to interact with each other and with outsiders, an openness to innovation. They exhibit enduring enthusiasm in pursuit of the idea. There's excitement, anticipation, a feeling of movement, a sense of purpose and direction, an impression of going somewhere. When those qualities are absent, everything feels different: work becomes work, a chore rather than a joy.

Although a few exceptional people are able to pursue any activity with enduring enthusiasm, most people find it difficult to pursue an activity with sustained gusto unless they are pursuing it *for its own sake*, not merely to achieve some instrumental or external good such as money, status, prestige, power, or winning. The perceived inherent worth of the activity being undertaken is foundational.

Instrumental benefits may accompany activities being pursued for their own sake, but if they become the principal, or worse still, the sole, objective of undertaking the activity, then the activity itself becomes degraded: energy tends to fade and enthusiasm dies.

Thus the goal of Al Gore in 2006 was not just the instrumental goal of lowering levels of CO_2 emissions, but the moral goal of preserving the planet. The goal of Craig Dunn was not just the instrumental goal of improving the profitability of AMP; he was out to preserve a firm that does worthwhile things for the community. The goal of J. Allard and Steven Sinofsky at Microsoft was not just the instrumental goal of producing more profitable software, it was the inherently valuable purpose of integrating all software with the World Wide Web.

CAN WINNING BE THE GOAL OF TRANSFORMATIONAL LEADERSHIP?

Transformational leadership concerns activities that are pursued primarily for their own sake, not merely for the sake of instrumental benefits such as money, prestige, prizes, or the status of being considered a winner. If at any point, instrumental benefits become the principal goal of the activity, then the chances of its being the subject of sustained enthusiastic commitment are reduced, if not eliminated. An alternative view is articulated by Jack and Suzy Welch, in their book, *Winning:*

> I think winning is great. Not good—great. Winning in business is great because when companies win, people thrive and grow. There are more jobs and opportunities everywhere and for everyone. People feel upbeat about the future; they have the resources to send their kids to college, get better health care, buy vacation

homes, and secure a comfortable retirement. And winning affords them the opportunity to give back to society in hugely important ways beyond paying more taxes. . . . Winning lifts everyone it touches—it just makes the world a better place. When companies are losing, on the other hand, everyone takes a hit. People feel scared. They have less financial security and limited time or money to do anything for anyone else. All they do is worry and upset their families, and in the meantime, if they're out of work, they pay little, if any taxes.[24]

There are several reasons that a focus on the achievement of instrumental goals like money, prestige, prizes, or winning per se is unlikely to be the subject of sustained enthusiastic commitment.

One is pragmatic. It is an intractable fact of human nature that most people find it difficult to remain genuinely enthusiastic for a sustained period of time about primarily instrumental goals. When everything is done for the sake of something else and nothing is done for its own sake, then purpose is obliterated. When purpose is obliterated, life loses its meaning. When meaning dies, energy fades and enthusiasm dies.

Instrumental goals like winning are fundamentally about acquiring the title of "winner" as accorded by other people. When people spend their lives trying to elicit such decisions from other people rather than doing what they themselves believe is worthwhile, they end up as prisoners of other people's opinions. With no genuine views of their own, they have little to be enthusiastic about.

Moreover, it isn't true that winning lifts everyone it touches. Wherever there are winners, there are by definition also losers—usually many more than winners. As a result, winning is necessarily an aspect of win-lose activities. This is because external goals like money, status, prestige, and the title of "winner" are finite resources, and are governed by a win-lose dynamic. If A wins, B loses. If C becomes famous, everyone else is less so. If D is president, no one else can be president at that time. In the world of instrumental goals, truly win-win outcomes are rare, perhaps nonexistent. Even having money is not so much about the absolute fact of having money—it's about having more money than other people. In such zero-sum games, the inherent worth of the activity is often subordinated to the goal of getting ahead of others, and to doing whatever is necessary to achieve victory. When that happens, one has entered a rat race: the activity shifts from inspiring to deadening, from fun to dull, from energizing to burdensome: it becomes mere work. By contrast, when activities are pursued for their own sake, innovations that any one individual makes tend to be shared with others and so everyone benefits. An advance by one helps all. The dynamic is inherently win-win.

Finally, the suggestion that those who focus primarily on winning will eventually get around to doing something worthwhile in itself, such as "give back to society," has meager evidence to support it. Even if we set aside the inevitability of a large group of "losers" who by definition accompany the "winners" and who won't have anything to give back to society, the reality is that winning as a primary goal becomes a drug. Because winning doesn't satisfy in itself, people need more of it to keep going. Hence people who devote their life primarily to winning usually never get round to doing anything worthwhile in itself. Instead, they find themselves on their deathbeds, wondering where their lives went.[25]

Transformational leadership invites people to stop postponing their lives and start right now doing what is genuinely worthwhile—and inviting others to join in.

Enabler #2: Committing to the Story of Change

Managers are appointed by other people. Leaders appoint themselves. Deciding to be a leader is a choice we have to make on our own. No one else can do it for us. It's an internal decision to adopt a stance, an orientation toward the world, to pursue an activity for its own sake and to set out to induce others to do likewise. Are we genuinely ready for the challenge of leadership? Are we ready to commit mind, body, and soul to the goal?

This was a crucial difference between the Al Gore of 2000 and the Al Gore of 2006. In 2000, Gore hadn't yet crossed this bridge. By 2006, he was talking about a goal to which he was totally committed. As a result, he sounded very different. He was no longer wearing a mask, trying to project a persona that he hoped would appeal to the audience. Instead, he was telling the electorate what he, Al Gore the person, genuinely believed.

When leaders decide to commit themselves to change, they take a stand. They adopt a position. They cross a Rubicon. Conscious of the need for the change and what it will take, they commit to making it happen. They decide that it's worthwhile and that they're willing to pursue it, come what may, whatever it takes. Their inner commitment gives life to the words they use. It becomes a central part of their new life story.

Enabler #3: Mastering the Audience's Story

Story also has enormous implications for the way we understand our audience as well. We like to spend a lot of time thinking about the content of what we are going to say. No less important is figuring out the story that the audience is currently living. If we don't understand the story of the people we're talking to, how can we craft a new message that will resonate with them?

It's easy to underestimate the effort involved in getting inside the listener's mind. Abraham Lincoln once said, "When I'm getting ready to reason with a man, I spend one-third of my time thinking about myself and what I am going to say—and two-thirds thinking about him and what he is going to say."[26]

That's because as leaders we need to overcome what psychologists call *fundamental attribution error*. This is the tendency that we have as human beings to assign the cause for other people's actions to dispositions or personality-based explanations of behavior, whereas we tend to assign the causes of our own actions to the situation we are in. We tend to think: "I didn't get much done today because I got to bed late last night; you didn't get much done today because you're lazy." In effect, we have an unjustified tendency to see people's actions as reflecting "the sort of people they are" rather than on the social and environmental forces that influence their actions.[27]

We need to work hard to overcome fundamental attribution error and understand the world of our listeners in all its peculiarity, its strangeness, its stubborn differences. We have to stop thinking of people as obstacles, as enemies, as resisters, as opponents, as malcontents, as stupid or obstinate or irresponsible or ill-willed, and rather as people we deeply want to understand, people whose world in its own way makes sense, albeit in an incomplete fashion. And the best way to do that is to work on understanding the listeners' story.

We need to start from where the audience is, not where we are. We need to figure out why our followers don't see the change idea as positively as we do. Within what story do they find themselves cornered? What artificial walls have the listeners constructed around their current existence so that they don't see the same future we do? What imaginary constraints are hampering them from imagining something different? What mythical limitations are hobbling their vision? Which of their most heartfelt dreams are currently unfulfilled? If we can understand these aspects of the audience's story, then crafting a new story that will resonate with them is often relatively simple.

How do leaders make sense of the listeners' world even if they know the answers? Although agreement on a comprehensive framework for human personality is not complete, psychologists are tending to the view that the best way to make sense of this subjective world is through stories: stories are ideally suited to capture how a human actor, endowed with consciousness and motivated by intention, enacts desires and beliefs and strives for goals over time and in a social context.[28]

Formulating the listeners' stories can help leaders reach out imaginatively and get inside the subjective world of the people they are seeking to change, develop a sense of what it is like to be living in that world, and get a feel of its logic and power and order, even its compelling beauty.

Enabler #4: Cultivating Narrative Intelligence

Stories aren't the only rhetorical tool available to leaders. Later chapters introduce others: questions, metaphors, images, offers, challenges, conversations, arguments, data, and the like. But among the communication tools that are most effective in terms of inspiring action, stories tend to predominate.

In principle, we shouldn't be surprised at the primary role of storytelling in communications about change. We know that human beings think in stories. They dream in stories. Their hopes and fears reside in stories. Their imaginations consist of stories. They plan in stories. They gossip, love, and hate in stories. Their emotions have a narrative character.[29] Their decisions rest on narratives: as philosopher Alisdair MacIntyre has pointed out, "I can only answer the question, 'What am I to do?' if I can answer the prior question 'Of what story or stories do I find myself a part?'"[30] Storytelling is closely associated with the very conception of the self.[31]

Although we shouldn't be surprised by the idea that storytelling is important to leadership communications, the fact is that we are. In fact, at first glance, it often strikes business executives as profoundly counterintuitive. This is not what we were taught at school. It's not how we've been trained. It's not the norm in formal organizational meetings. Our mantra has been that analytic is good and anecdotal is bad: it isn't logical to generalize the idiosyncratic vagaries of a single story to an entire population. And so we go on making PowerPoint presentations full of abstractions and bullet points, like medieval doctors slicing patients' veins to remove excess blood, not realizing that everything we are doing and saying is making the situation worse.

The notion that a deep understanding of narrative is key to transformational leadership strikes many people as surprising and in some sense unacceptable idea. And yet it has an even more surprising dimension than that.

If it's true that we think in stories, and make decisions in the form of stories, then what this means is that *all* forms of communication directed toward action—not just stories themselves, but questions, metaphors, images, offers, challenges, conversations, whatever—are effective to the extent that they generate a new story in the mind of a listener. If yes, then the communication is effective. If not, then the communication fails. These varied communication tools are effective when they point to a story. Story provides a unifying concept to understand whether and to what extent any communication directed toward action will be effective.

And if that is so, then narrative intelligence—the ability to "think narratively" about the world—is central to leadership.[32] But what exactly does it mean to think narratively about the world? It means the capacity

44

to understand the world in narrative terms, to be familiar with the different components and dimensions of narratives, to know what different patterns of stories exist and which narrative patterns are most likely to have what effect in which situation. It also means knowing how to overcome the fundamental attribution error and understand the audience's story. It implies the ability to anticipate the dynamic factors that determine how the audience will react to a new story and whether a new story is likely to be generated in the mind of any particular audience by any particular communication tool.

The ability to think narratively—that is, narrative intelligence—reflects a recognition that the narrative aspects of the world matter because human goals matter, and narratives encapsulate human goals. The pattern of words that we use matters: are they abstract, cold, impartial, objective, inert, seemingly remote from human goals? Or do they have all the richness and texture and objectives of human existence, making them likely to engage an audience? And the sequence of patterns matters: one order generates excitement; the opposite generates hostility. And the stories that these patterns of words elicit in the listeners' minds matter. And the responses, witting or unwitting, in the form of a nod, a smile, or a frown from the listeners matter. And what the leader does about those responses matters, whether the responses are encouraging or discouraging. And the interaction among narratives matters, an interaction that is taking place in seconds: a single word, or phrase, or sequence, at the right time—or out of place—makes all the difference. The outcome—one way or the other—will be decided in a flash. An ability to act and react agilely in this quicksilver world of interacting narratives is the gist of narrative intelligence.

Overall, cultivating narrative intelligence will be a key enabler of using the language of leadership to full advantage.

Enabler #5: A Commitment to Telling Authentically True Stories

In some activities of the human species, such as espionage, lying is required: deception is the essence. In other activities lying is frowned on but widely practiced. Politicians and salespeople routinely shade the truth to win office or make a sale.

Transformational leaders are in a different situation. If they are to inspire enduring enthusiasm for change, they must tell the truth. Lying and leadership are like oil and water: they simply don't mix. The distrust that lying breeds is devastating to trust and credibility.

Honest mistakes are possible, of course, but it's vital that when a mistake is discovered, leaders level with people and explain the mistake and how it came about, rather than wait to be found out, as if deliberately hiding something.

And when leaders tell the truth, it's not just a matter of factual accuracy. It's not merely telling a story that's true as far as it goes. It's about telling the authentic truth, including everything that's relevant to understand the story. It needs to be a story that once people check it out—and if the story has an impact, they will check it out—and all the facts are known, people will still say, "Yes, that's pretty much what happened."

Here's a famous example of a story that is factually accurate as far as it goes, but isn't authentically true:

> Seven hundred happy passengers reached New York after the *Titanic*'s maiden voyage.[33]

No one could quarrel with these facts—but the story leaves out the little detail that the *Titanic* sank and fifteen hundred passengers drowned. And when those facts become known, if they aren't already known, then the negative backlash on the story and the storyteller is massive.

That was the problem with Al Gore's presidential debate story about Caley Ellis, the fifteen-year-old schoolgirl who had to stand in the classroom. What Gore said was factually accurate as far as it went. But when it emerged that she had to stand through class only on opening day—and that was because of extra equipment stacked in the classroom, not, as Gore had implied, on a permanent basis because of a lack of facilities, the backlash against Gore's candidacy was inevitable.

Although telling a story while omitting relevant facts is a very bad way to tell a story, ironically, many corporate communications follow exactly this pattern. They paint a rosy picture of some situation when—just around the corner, just below the surface—some omitted negative element lurks. The omission creates a massive backlash against the story and the storyteller once it becomes known, if it isn't already known—and instantaneously if it is known.

Enabler #6: Deploying the Body Language of Leadership

Cesar Millan doesn't train dogs: he rehabilitates them. It's the owners he has to train. And what he trains them in is leadership. He shows the dog owners how to embody in their behavior the calm assertiveness of leadership vis-à-vis the dogs they own.

The dogs he works with are difficult dogs—dogs of all breeds and sizes that have been terrorizing their host families, often for a considerable time. Typically they are dogs that combine warm, loving behavior with a dark side—barking, biting, chewing, jumping, pulling—all the things that vicious, uncontrollable dogs do. Often they are dogs that dog trainers have given up on in despair. Now these dogs are terrorizing their owners' households and turning their lives into nightmares. Often the families are desperate and on the verge of doing away with the dog. They call Cesar Millan as a last resort.

Some of the most striking examples involve contrasts in size—say, a tiny chihuahua owned by a burly policeman who is fearless in dealing with criminals on the mean streets of a big city, but is terrorized when the tiny, biting canine doesn't get what she wants. When you see what the dog gets away with, it's as though the chihuahua owns the policeman rather than the policeman owning the chihuahua.

Usually these dogs are even more difficult and aggressive with strangers than with their owners. But when Cesar Millan walks into the room, these dogs typically stop barking and snarling and pulling and jumping. Then they do a strange thing: they sit down. They gaze calmly and quietly at Millan and wait to see what he's going to do next. When these dogs see Millan, they immediately recognize that they are not dealing with one of the pliable human beings they have been terrorizing for so long. Dogs grasp in a flash that Millan is someone who can't be shoved around. They see at once that they are dealing with someone who means business. They sense in Millan someone who is 100 percent there for them. They understand the body language of leadership. They see immediately that they are in the presence of a leader.

There is nothing particularly extraordinary about Cesar Millan's physical appearance that would give him an edge in what he does. He is medium height and stocky in build, not physically dominant. Born in Mexico, he is mild in manner and pleasant in his demeanor. As you watch him go about his work with dogs and with people, it is evident that the calm assertiveness of his behavior comes not from any surface characteristic, but from within. It is evident in the way he holds himself, the way he moves, the way he looks at his surroundings, and the way he talks.

What's even more striking is how quickly and easily the calm assertiveness of leadership embodied in Cesar Millan is mastered by the dogs' regular owners. The body language of calm assertiveness is relatively simple to learn: square shoulders, open body stance, feet firmly planted on the ground, the right kind of eye contact. It adds up to "being there" for the audience.

Perhaps what's most extraordinary is that as soon as the regular dog owners embody these behaviors, they are at once treated as leaders by their dogs. They can immediately resume ownership of their own households. They discover that if they are there for the dog, the dog will be there for them.

The body language of leadership that Millan teaches to dog owners is the same body language that leaders need to master if they are to be effective in their communications with other human beings. Without the calm assertiveness of the body language of leadership, the verbal language of leadership will have little, if any, effect.

This is one of the differences between the Al Gore of the first presidential debate and the Al Gore of 2006: the aggressive brashness of the 2000 presidential debate has morphed into the calm assertiveness of *An Inconvenient Truth*. Whereas the Al Gore of 2000 was a tedious bore, the Al Gore of 2006 is rock-star popular. Small differences in body language can have a massive impact.

Mastering the Language of Leadership

For a very long time, we've been living with the idea that leadership and change are driven by the efforts of a few exceptional people. This book puts forward a different idea. It says that change and leadership don't require exceptional people at all. Leadership and change are driven by ordinary people who act and speak in a different way. Once people grasp what is involved in acting and speaking in that way and take the trouble to master it, then they find that *anyone* can drive change, if they want to.

For too long, we've been thinking that leadership was some kind of innate gift, a mysterious kind of genetically inherited charisma. But once we've deciphered the language of leadership and understood its essential enabling conditions, transformational leadership is no longer a mystery. Once the hidden patterns of the language of leadership are made explicit, leadership becomes accessible to anyone.

While the main elements of the language of leadership are relatively simple and quick to understand, putting them into practice is something else. The bare essentials can be grasped in minutes, but fully mastering them may take a lifetime.

For some, particularly those habituated to the practice of hierarchical command-and-control management, learning the language of leadership will entail deep change. It isn't some kind of party trick. It isn't just a set of superficial techniques—it's a different way of thinking, speaking, and acting. It requires that we understand our own values, thinking through what we are attempting, exhibiting more than a little humility, and being able to level with others and speak from a genuine point of view. It involves acquiring a new perspective on the world, a profound clarification of what it means to be leader.

The three steps of the central triad of the language of leadership—getting attention, stimulating desire, reinforcing with reason—offer a way of making sense of any leadership communication. They provide us with a flexible structure that can be populated with suitable leadership content. In Part Three, I discuss in detail how they operate: if you want to get right into the nitty-gritty of the leadership presentation itself, you may want to skip ahead and start there. Appendix 2 contains a set of exercises and templates that can facilitate preparation of the various communication tools discussed in the book.

But to get the maximum value from the language of leadership, it's a good idea to make sure that the enabling conditions are in place. Part Two addresses those issues. Is our goal clear? Is it potentially inspiring? Are we fully committed to it? Do we understand the people we are trying to convince? Have we developed appropriate narrative intelligence? Are we being authentically truthful in our communications? Is our leadership presence up to snuff? If any of these enabling conditions are not in place, the language of leadership will have some impact, but it won't be optimal. If the enablers are in place, they will ensure that the language of leadership inspires truly enduring change.

[PART 2]

THE LANGUAGE
OF LEADERSHIP:
KEY ENABLERS

2

ARTICULATING A CLEAR, INSPIRING GOAL

> " This is the true joy in life, the being used for a
> purpose recognized by yourself as a mighty one;
> the being thoroughly worn out before you are
> thrown on the scrap heap; the being a force of
> Nature instead of a feverish selfish little clod
> of ailments and grievances complaining that the
> world will not devote itself to making you happy. "
>
> **—George Bernard Shaw[1]**

In 1983, John Sculley became CEO of Apple Computer. He was brought in to help sort out the chaos created in part by the brilliance and inexperience of its chairman, Steve Jobs. Sculley had been a star manager at Pepsi and, once Jobs left Apple in 1985, Sculley was quickly able to rationalize its products and services and stabilize the corporation. In the early 1990s, however, new possibilities were opening up for Apple. Sculley saw that Apple could, like Dell, produce low-cost computers, or create portable, handheld devices like the PalmPilot, or like Microsoft capture the huge potential revenues to be gained from selling computer operating systems to businesses. If Apple exploited these possibilities, it could have a very much brighter financial future.[2]

Sculley tried multiple managerial methods to implement these strategic shifts. He moved to turn Apple into a more conventional corporation, hiring executives from old-line computer companies and dropping the firm's emphasis on consumer sales to enable a direct assault on business. He introduced structural changes, systems, and processes in order to stimulate buy-in for the changes he envisioned.[3]

To no avail. The Apple staff saw themselves as continuing to follow Steve Jobs's goal of creating cool, innovative electronic products—a purpose that they saw as worthwhile in itself. The staff really weren't interested in becoming just another computer company. They didn't embrace Sculley's instrumental goals, and he was forced out in 1993.

Sculley's talents as a manager didn't prepare him for the principal challenge of leadership, namely, how to inspire the staff to pursue new goals energetically and enthusiastically. The staff were still pursuing Apple's original purpose, which they saw as more compelling and seductive. The managerial tools of communication deployed by Sculley could not dislodge that purpose from their minds.

Sculley's successors at Apple met the same fate. Apple's board first appointed Michael Spindler, head of the company's successful European operations, as CEO. He was out after three years, after vainly trying to sell the company. The board then named Gil Amelio, who had led a successful turnaround at National Semiconductor. He raised revenue, improved quality, and slashed costs, but some staff saw him as a carpetbagger.[4] He was removed after only eighteen months, and the ousted Apple founder, Steve Jobs, came back as interim CEO. On his return, Jobs didn't try to change the company's purpose. Instead he resumed the focus on designing cool, innovative electronic products such as the iMac and iPod. The "interim" was removed from Jobs's title and Apple is once again flourishing in both the computer and music industries.

Articulating a Worthwhile Purpose

Transformational leadership entails engendering enduring enthusiasm for a cause. Why did Steve Jobs's goal of making cool, innovative electronic tools generate enduring enthusiasm while John Sculley's business objectives didn't? What is at the root of enduring enthusiasm?

The word *enthusiasm* comes from the Greek, *en theos*, a god within.[5] Thus the word's origins imply that transformational leadership involves "inspiring a god within one's followers." The "god within" is an energizing, ebullient, effervescent source of energy. It's restless, kinetic, and irrepressible. It is more than contentment: it leaps, bubbles, and overflows. It is contagious. It carries ideas forward and catalyzes action.[6]

While enthusiasm can be fragile and liable to fade, in some circumstances it endures over an extended period of time. Let's look at some examples.

Think of *two children learning to play the piano*. One child loves it. She thrills to the sound of music. She practices as often as she can because it's a joy. It fills her life with meaning. She inspires her friends with her playing. She has won a prize for her effort and accolades from her schoolteachers, but this recognition isn't nearly as important to her as the joy that she gets from the playing itself. Meanwhile another child studies the piano, playing the same pieces, because her parents have told her that she must. She dutifully practices the pieces she is assigned. Because she has a natural aptitude for music, she does quite well, but it gives her no more than mild pleasure. She finds her practices monotonous and forlorn.

These two young girls are engaged in the same activity, but they have a very different attitude toward it. One feels energized and enthusiastic about it and energizes others by her attitude. The other sees it as a drag and a bore.

Think about the practice of *sharing knowledge* in organizations, an approach known as knowledge management.[7] Since this movement began in organizations in the mid-1990s, some practitioners have approached the goal with sustained enthusiasm. They have committed their working lives to making the best knowledge available to those who need it when they need it. They practice the virtues of honesty and openness. They perceive their own personal growth in pursuing the practice and also contribute to the wider community of knowledge management practitioners across many organizations. Knowledge management may have commercial benefits for the organization in which they pursue their work, but for these people, the bottom-line benefits of knowledge management are less important than inherent value of sharing knowledge itself. If the organization in which they work should ever cease to support knowledge management, they would leave that organization and find another context where they could continue to pursue their goal.

Compare these people to others who are pursuing knowledge management solely because of its commercial return. For them, knowledge management is simply one of a number of management gadgets that can be used to enhance the firm's capacity to make money. So long as it is commercially profitable, they pursue knowledge management. If it ceases to have a handsome return for the firm, they set it aside for other more commercially viable practices. For this group, knowledge management has no inherent value: it is pursued for its instrumental benefits.

The description could continue with other types of activities: teaching, law, medicine, architecture, retail, restaurant or hotel management, engineering, farming, sports, or whatever else, illustrating the same distinction.

A principal difference between these two different ways of viewing an activity is that when the activity generates sustained enthusiasm, the activity is being *pursued for its own sake,* not merely to achieve some instrumental or external good such as money, status, prestige, power, or winning. The perceived inherent worth of the activity being undertaken is foundational.

In *Built to Last,* Jim Collins and Jerry Porras suggest that bold missions—what they called "Big Hairy Audacious Goals" or BHAGs—are at the heart of generating sustained enthusiasm, and I believe that they are partially right. Large, bold goals are more likely to generate excitement than difficult-to-understand, hard-to-remember mission statements. However some of the BHAGs they cite, such as Boeing's goal to build the 707, are finite in time and so sidestep the question of where to go after that. It's not enough to generate truly enduring enthusiasm that BHAGs be bold, hairy, and audacious. In addition, they must be worthwhile in themselves, so as to be self-motivating on an ongoing basis.

A wide range of activities can be pursued for their own sake, rather than for external, instrumental objectives. Mihaly Csikszentmihalyi's book *Flow* describes how even a few workers in boring routine jobs somehow manage—for a time—to view steadily improved performance as valuable in itself.[8]

Both Viktor Frankl and Alexander Solzhenitsyn have written persuasively how even prisoners in a concentration camp can find meaning in living in a certain way, as opposed to accepting the horrors of prison life as given. Objectively they were slaves, but subjectively they had sufficient psychic energy to create meaning for their lives.[9]

People who are able to find inherent value in whatever they are doing are sometimes called "autotelic personalities": they have the capacity to be intrinsically motivated by almost *any* activity. No matter how threatening or oppressive the external environment, they somehow manage to discover new opportunities for improvement. However, even autotelic personalities have difficulty sustaining their enthusiasm if the activity itself lacks a minimal degree of suitability for sustained enthusiastic commitment.[10]

Thus some activities are more likely than others to generate sustained enthusiasm. Ideally these activities have four main characteristics:

- The participants in the activity can see themselves making progress toward something that is *good for its own sake,* not primarily because it will lead to something else. The activity is, or can be seen as, inherently rewarding. Additional effort is a joy and not a burden: participants perceive that in the here-and-now the world is a better place because of this activity.

- The participants experience *their own personal growth and development* as part of the activity. If they do not perceive themselves as making progress, they risk becoming discouraged. Studies show that it's helpful if the participants get feedback in terms of the successes and failures they generate in the course of the activity, so that their behavior can be adjusted as needed. A balance between ability level and challenge—the activity is neither too easy nor too difficult—is also conducive to enthusiasm.[11]

- Through the activity, the participants see themselves as contributing to, raising the sights of, and *enhancing the efforts of other people* pursuing the same activity. If the participants are focused only on themselves, on enhancing their own practice, their enthusiasm is less likely to be sustained.

- Although the instrumental benefits of the activity are not the central driving force for undertaking the activity, the external effects are not irrelevant. Ideally, the activity should bring some positive instrumental benefits: income, status, prestige. But even without that, it should at least be *without negative instrumental effects.* If the medical or legal work or teaching or knowledge management bankrupts the community or causes physical harm, this will sooner or later become apparent and become a drag on exuberance and energy.[12]

If these four elements are in place, chances are good that the enthusiasm and energy level can be sustained. If one or more of them is missing, the activity risks tending toward entropy.[13]

The language of leadership can of course be used in an attempt to induce enthusiasm for activities with merely instrumental benefits, and that attempt may even be successful for a time. The enthusiasm is, however, unlikely to be sustained unless the goal can eventually be articulated as something perceived as worthwhile in itself.

As noted, the primacy of goals pursued for their own sake in transformational leadership does not mean that instrumental benefits are unimportant. In practice, instrumental benefits reinforce the pursuit of goals for their own sake. Thus it's easier to pursue an inherently worthwhile activity, be it art or law or medicine or journalism or knowledge management or teaching or whatever, when the instrumental benefits are there, too: one earns a living or acquires respect or prestige through the activity. In fact it is a very rare person who can pursue an activity for its own sake on a sustained basis if it never has any external benefits whatsoever.[14] However, if people focus principally on instrumental goals and ignore the inherent value of the activity, then the activity changes in nature. Enthusiasm is likely to die. Life becomes work—an irksome chore.

One central aspect of the language of transformational leadership is therefore to articulate goals and activities in terms that can be viewed by participants as worthwhile in themselves, not merely pursued because they lead to instrumental benefits:

- Unlike John Sculley's instrumental goals of making money from hardware and software, Steve Jobs's goal was one that the Apple staff saw as worthwhile for its own sake: producing cool, innovative electronic devices.

- The goal of Craig Dunn wasn't just the instrumental goal of improving the profitability of AMP, it was to preserve a firm that does worthwhile things for the community.

- The goal of J. Allard and Steven Sinofsky at Microsoft wasn't just the instrumental goal of producing more profitable software, it was the inherently valuable purpose of integrating all software with the World Wide Web.

The same logic applies to corporations: they are most inspiring when they pursue large goals that are worthwhile in themselves:

- The goal of Toyota is "to enrich society through the building of cars and trucks." The idea of enriching society means offering car customers reliability and mobility while investing profits in new plants, technologies, and employees. It reflects a company-wide obsession to keep on building better cars and to plan for the long term—financially, technically, imaginatively. "The company thinks in years and decades," Michael Robinet, a vice president at CSM Worldwide, a consulting firm that focuses on the global auto industry, recently told the *New York Times,* "They don't think in months or quarters."[15]

- In the mid-1940s, Johnson & Johnson adopted a credo by Robert Wood Johnson that defines the company's responsibilities as first, to the consumers and medical professionals using its products, second, to employees and managers, third to the communities where its people work and live, and fourth and last, to its stockholders.[16]

- Costco's goal is to provide its members quality goods at low markups. Under Jim Sinegal, who co-founded the company in 1983, Costco has obsessively pursued the goal. Its margins are among the slimmest in retailing. To the delight of its customers and to the annoyance of Wall Street, Costco declines to take advantage of windfall profits when it negotiates a lower price on an item: instead it passes the savings directly to customers.[17]

- Given that publicly held corporations are under continuing pressure to grow and do whatever is profitable, regardless of the intrinsic worth of the activity, it is often easier to pursue an inherently worthwhile purpose in a privately owned corporation. In *Small Giants,* Bo Burlingham has written about fourteen privately held corporations that explicitly decided to stay relatively small and close to their local communities in order to pursue worthwhile purposes.[18] The group includes Anchor Brewing, the original American microbrewery in San Francisco, and Zingerman's Community of Businesses, a group of small food-related firms in Ann Arbor, Michigan. Burlingham makes the case that these are firms that have chosen to be great, rather than big—a choice that closely held private ownership facilitates.

- In politics, Mahatma Gandhi sought not merely the instrumental goal of getting rid of the British but what Indians perceived as the intrinsically valuable goals of political and economic self-sufficiency through nonviolence. The goal of John F. Kennedy was not merely creating the Peace Corps (instrumental) but inspiring people to ask themselves what they could do for their country (namely, something intrinsically valuable). The goal of Abraham Lincoln was not merely to win the Civil War or save the union but to create a new birth of freedom in his country.

Transformational leaders typically present their goals as larger than any particular task or organization or time-bound objective. When they succeed, the goal can survive the severance of the relationship between leader and the institution in which it was formulated. Thus Abraham Lincoln can be assassinated, but his vision of a nation pursuing a new birth of freedom lives on. John F. Kennedy can be shot, but his vision of changing race relations in the United States is implemented by his successor. Martin Luther King Jr. can be murdered, but a whole nation continues the work that he started. Steve Jobs can be fired from Apple Computer, but his vision of producing cool electronic tools lives on in the minds of both staff and customers, who are such passionate evangelists for the vision that his successors are unable to change it. Toyota's purpose of enriching society through the building of cars and trucks isn't dependent on any individual executive; it pervades the entire organization.[19] When parents and teachers succeed as leaders, their children and students adopt their values throughout their entire lives, even long after their parents or teachers are gone.

Goals that are articulated as worthwhile in themselves enhance the possibility of sustained enthusiasm, and hence the possibility of transformational leadership. Of course, articulating the goal as worthwhile in itself doesn't mean that listeners will necessarily see it in this way. Opponents, cynics, and skeptics may perceive ulterior motives and interpret the professed pursuit of a worthwhile goal as a superficial, deceptive mask, mere public relations, hiding personal ambition, political manipulation, or worse. And if indeed this turns out to be a correct assessment of the leader's actual motivation, or is revealed in the firm's actual conduct, then that fact is likely to become apparent all too soon and in due course undermine any enthusiastic commitment. But when leaders themselves embrace the goals they have articulated and embody the worthwhile goal relentlessly in their own behavior, then they turn themselves into an unstoppable force for change. This is because the opponents, critics, and skeptics are no longer fighting a person: now they are fighting an idea.

When people pursue a goal for its own sake, they may experience advances ("wins") or setbacks ("losses") along the way, but in a larger sense, they don't win or lose. This is because there is no ultimate winner or loser: when an activity is pursued for its own sake: *the activity never ends.* Since the activity is valuable for its own sake, participants do their best to continue the activity and to reach new standards of excellence.

They encourage others to join the activity and the effort to attain new levels of excellence. The activity is usually not bounded by any preestablished set of rules or limits, or even any particular institution. The activity and its rules are always evolving, flowing through networks and across institutional and other boundaries. In this way, participants anticipate and welcome surprise and change. The work may be perplexing, backbreaking, and tedious, and yet participants see the effort and the difficulties as a challenge, worthwhile in itself, and an opportunity to do better.[20]

Setting Priorities Among Goals

Not having a clear and inspiring goal is one common failing of leadership. Another is having too many of them. Many people—and corporations—see a plethora of goals that they could be pursuing, but haven't made up their minds which goals to pursue with a single-minded focus.

Indeed, given the infinite number of problems to be solved in the world, the number of goals that could address them is also infinite. If we sit staring at the cornucopia of possible problems that confront and confound us and the possible actions we could take, we will never generate lasting change. Then like Hamlet:

> The native hue of resolution
> Is sicklied o'er with the pale cast of thought,
> And enterprises of great pith and moment
> With this regard their currents turn awry,
> And lose the name of action.[21]

When people try to tackle a large number of goals, they fail in all. Leadership is such a demanding activity that any one individual can probably pursue no more than a couple of significant change ideas at any one time. Priorities must be set.

We always face simultaneous leadership challenges in multiple domains, whether it's an organization, or a community, or a family, or a town, or a country, or even the planet.

An organization generally offers multiple grounds for improvement. Maybe it's the entire organization, which perhaps has no clear, inspiring purpose. Or maybe it's just one aspect of the organization that has become a drag on performance. Maybe the values of the organization aren't reflected throughout the organization as they should be. Maybe knowledge isn't being shared. Maybe innovation isn't happening as rapidly it should. Maybe the organization isn't adapting fast enough to the dramatic changes now taking place in the world economy. Maybe the global marketplace is unaware of the genuine excellence of the firm's products and services.

The change could concern one's community, which may have a few unattractive wrinkles. Or maybe it's the family: perhaps it's a teenage son who needs to rejoin the human race. Or a teenage daughter who constantly snaps back. Or a spouse who is acting distant. Or excessively intrusive in-laws. Or it could be the town, which has a few potholes in need of fixing. Or maybe the country: perhaps it's a longing for peace and security, with widespread prosperity and the budget in balance, and honest public servants pursuing the public good. Or it might be some grander, global challenge, like addressing global warming, coping with international terrorism, or ending world poverty.

No one can be a successful leader in all these domains simultaneously. In most areas, we will necessarily have to follow the lead of others. Selecting a goal, or at most several goals, and then persevering relentlessly in their pursuit is a sine qua non for success as a transformational leader.

To illustrate the power of single-mindedness, one need only glance at the presidency of Ronald Reagan. To some, it is a mystery how such a man could combine the roles of leader and politician. Clark Clifford labeled him "an amiable dunce." Yet Reagan handily won two terms as U.S. president and launched the conservative revolution in the United States of aggressive pursuit of the cold war, smaller government, and lower taxes. One key reason for Reagan's success is that he had the single-minded focus of a leader. He had a relatively small number of goals—defeating the Soviet Union and reducing taxes and the size of government—and he pursued them single-mindedly.

Timing will also play a role in the decisions as to which goal to pursue. "Ripeness is all," wrote Shakespeare. Launching a leadership activity prematurely, before it has any realistic chance of success, is one way of preventing the activity from ever coming to fruition. On the other hand, permanently waiting for the right moment will also ensure that the change never takes place. The challenge is to achieve the appropriate balance between doing nothing and choosing at least some leadership domains where progress can be made.

It is one thing to articulate a clear and inspiring goal. It is another to embrace it. Selecting a goal will have little effect unless and until the leader makes a whole-hearted commitment to it. It is to this issue that I turn in Chapter Three.

3

THE LEADER'S OWN STORY

Committing to the Goal

> " That a man may be scarce less ignorant of his own powers, "
> than an oyster of its pearl, or a rock of its diamond; that he
> may possess dormant, unsuspected abilities, till awakened
> by loud calls, or strung up by striking emergencies, is
> evident from the sudden eruption of some men, out of
> perfect obscurity, into public admiration, on the strong
> impulse of some animating occasion, not more to the
> world's great surprise than their own.

—Edward Young[1]

Abraham Lincoln did not begin his presidency as a transformational leader. In his first inaugural address, on February 23, 1861, Lincoln stressed his intent to maintain the status quo laid down in the U.S. Constitution. He was explicit in declaring that he had no intent to abolish slavery, referring to his earlier speeches as a candidate for president:

"'I have no purpose, directly or indirectly, to interfere with the institution of slavery in the States where it exists. I believe I have no lawful right to do so and I have no inclination to do so.' Those who nominated and elected me did so with full knowledge that I had made this, and many similar declarations and had never recanted them. . . . I now reiterate those sentiments."

Lincoln's explicit goal was to preserve the Union. For a prudent politician, this made perfect sense, since there was no consensus for abolishing slavery. So Lincoln was assiduous in asserting that he had no such plan. Because many influential northerners were not in favor of military action to deal with the South, Lincoln used the outbreak of hostilities at Fort Sumter when Congress was not in session to initiate military action. Lincoln declared martial law, suspending the writ of habeas corpus among other questionably legal acts. In this way, he was able to present the seceding southern states as having launched the Civil War by preventing the federal government from implementing the Constitution.

In due course, Lincoln came to the view that the Union couldn't be preserved without abolishing slavery. When he assembled his cabinet on July 22, 1862, he surprised them by reading a preliminary draft of a proclamation promising emancipation for all slaves.

Privately, he continued to argue that his goal remained the pragmatic one of preserving the Union. But publicly, Lincoln became a leader in a moral cause. His plan cost him the backing of moderate Republicans—without bringing him the full support of the radical Republicans, who wanted a more definitive legal step unlimited in time and geography.

On December 1, 1862, he made the case for change in his Annual Message to Congress:

> We say we are for the Union. The world will not forget that we say this. We know how to save the Union. The world knows we do know how to save it. We—even we here—hold the power, and bear the responsibility. In giving freedom to the slave, we assure freedom to the free—honorable alike in what we give, and what we preserve. We shall nobly save, or meanly lose, the last best hope of earth. Other means may succeed; this could not fail. The way is plain, peaceful, generous, just—a way which, if followed, the world will forever applaud, and God must forever bless.

In this new moral language, Lincoln the transformational leader has emerged from the chrysalis of Lincoln the politician. In his earlier speeches, including the first inaugural address, Lincoln had justified his actions on instrumental, legal grounds. Now he puts forward a new vision of the future, based on moral grounds, something worthwhile in itself. Lincoln asks his listeners to move beyond their limited worldviews and embrace a different kind of future.[2]

The case for change became even more explicit in his Gettysburg address on November 19, 1863, where he calls for "a new birth of freedom" for the nation:

> It is rather for us to be here dedicated to the great task remaining before us, that from these honored dead we take increased devotion to that cause for which they here gave the last full measure of devotion; that we here highly resolve that the dead shall not have died in vain, that the nation shall, under God, have a new birth of freedom, and that the government of the people, by the people, and for the people, shall not perish from the earth.

In his insightful book, *The Eloquent President,* Ronald White points out that Lincoln was here "no longer, as in his inaugural address, defending an old Union, but proclaiming a new Union. The old Union contained and attempted to restrain slavery. The new Union would fulfill the promise of liberty, the crucial step into the future that the Founders had failed to take."[3]Lincoln thus assumes the mantle of transformational leadership, stimulating people to want to do something different, inspiring them to higher levels of aspiration and conduct.

Viewed as a leadership speech aimed at sparking change in the immediate audience seated in front of him, the Gettysburg address had no discernible effect. It followed an oration by Edward Everett that lasted two hours and eight minutes. Lincoln's address lasted only three minutes. The audience was still dazed by Everett's marathon performance and no doubt expecting a much longer speech from Lincoln. The address ended even before the official photographer could take his photograph. It is probable that Lincoln was sitting down again even before he had got the audience's attention: if the speech had not been written down and reprinted, it would have had little if any impact.

Even in print, initially the speech passed unnoticed. Most newspapers included the text of Lincoln's speech after Everett's without comment. It was only the next day that some editors began to point to the extraordinary nature of what Lincoln had said: Josiah Holland, writing in the *Springfield Republican,* called it "a perfect gem," and James Burrill Angell wrote in the *Providence Daily Journal* that it was a speech "of the very highest eloquence."[4]

Meanwhile, Lincoln's opponents criticized it viciously. The *Chicago Times* wrote of its "silly, flat and dishwatery utterances." The *Harrisburg Patriot and Union* hoped that "the silly remarks of the President . . . shall no more be repeated or thought of."[5]

The opposite was of course the case. The speech had its impact through endless repetitions and recitations in families, schoolrooms, churches, courthouses, and legislatures, as the idea of "government of the people, by the people, for the people" came to represent a vision of what the United States should stand for, an idea that continues to stimulate the desire to bring it to fruition.

Politicians as Leaders

Although it is often said that we look for leadership in our politicians, the actual practice of modern politics has little overlap with transformational leadership. Modern politics is characterized by a sharp focus on the acquisition and retention of political office rather than on appealing to people's higher moral values and inspiring people to undertake enduring change.

The reasons that this is so powerful and practical are: for the most part, politicians who are not sharply focused on the acquisition and retention of power either don't acquire office in the first place or, if they do manage to acquire it, don't survive for long.

The fact is that politics has different goals, different dynamics, different modalities of action, and different measures of success from those of transformational leadership. Successful politicians are the ones who are elected and reelected. The means by which they acquire and retain political office are different from leadership. The relevant principles are not too different from those described by Machiavelli, some five hundred years ago.

The successful politician is one who is *willing to fight,* to attack the established order and be ruthless in the pursuit of power. Those without the stomach for such fights, who are often the best people, never make it to high office.

The successful politician needs to be *well armed,* which in the modern setting means "well funded." Being well armed with financial resources is a sine qua non of political success, and enables candidates to conduct the vigorous campaign necessary for winning elections. As Machiavelli said, "Among other ills which ensue from being disarmed is contempt."[6]

Politicians must be willing to *play hardball.* This means going as close to the edge of the law as is possible without actually being convicted of illegality, and where necessary, bending the law to their own advantage. Attack ads, the release of damaging information about opponents at the most inopportune moment, secret charges, innuendo and rumor—these have become the standard modus operandi of the modern politician. The most skillful exponents do all this without leaving fingerprints: no traces of the candidate's hand show in the brutal tactics that are used to accomplish the victory.

A politician must be *flexible* and adjust the agenda to reflect unpredictable shifts in the situation. This may mean a willingness to break campaign promises, which in any event tend to be vague and general, in order to preserve flexibility. This is at odds with the commitment needed for transformational leadership—where a sharp, explicit, laser-like focus on a worthwhile goal is paramount. A politician who tries to act as a leader based on an unchanging goal risks being labeled as a doctrinaire ideologue: dogmatic, impractical, stubborn, and unrealistic.

Despite the hardball tactics actually practiced to win elections, which may involve amoral behavior like breaking one's word or practicing character assassination of opponents, the successful politician must endeavor to preserve a public image of being *honest, compassionate, moral, and devout.*[7] Often this entails using underlings to do the dirty work of getting elected.

A successful politician typically pursues *those issues on which there is already a consensus in the electorate,* rather than those on which people have to be persuaded to do something different. This is because, as Machiavelli famously explained that the innovator "makes enemies of all those who derived advantage from the old order and finds but lukewarm defenders among those who stand to gain from the new one."[8] On occasion, politicians may be able to find issues that have a hidden consensus and put together new coalitions, but they tend to avoid the heavy lifting of leadership, namely, persuading people to raise their moral sights and agree to do something fundamentally different.

As a result, retaining power is principally about *listening to the electorate*. "If you want to get elected, learn to speak," said Tom Daschle, former Democratic leader in the U.S. Senate. "If you want to stay elected, learn to listen."[9] The great shifts in power in the United States—in 1994, from Democrat to Republican, and in 2006, from Republican to Democrat—were both reactions to the abuses of the party in power and its seeming indifference to the interests of the voters. As the journalist Matt Bai has written, "Ruling parties and presidencies are almost never felled by issues alone. Rather, it is the more general perception of a creeping chaos—the sense that leaders no longer have a firm grasp on events or the credibility to unite disparate constituencies—that causes political powers to come undone."[10]

As a result, politicians are typically *ambiguous about their commitment to change*. To the extent that political candidates present themselves as "candidates for change," they typically define the change either in terms of some existing consensus or in such general terms that it is hard to know what exactly is promised. They say, "get this country moving again" or "clean up the mess of the previous administration" and the like. For a politician to urge a specific change for which there is no discernible consensus is to risk not acquiring power in the first place. Hence few successful politicians make explicit commitments to specific transformational change.

It is common to criticize modern politicians for their "frequent failure to rise to the full need for leadership."[11] But should we really be surprised at the lack of leadership in politics? Nothing in the terminology of politics suggests that the people are electing "leaders." Thus the top politician is elected to become, not a "leader," but rather the "president," that is to say, someone who *presides* over the body politic, without any implication of change.[12]

Similarly for those countries where the number one politician is called a prime minister: a minister is someone appointed or elected to some high office of state, especially the head of an administrative department. The prime minister is the minister who heads the entire government. Here again, no concept of change or leading change is inherently built into the concept.

Equally, the members of Congress are elected to the House of Representatives, that is, they are the people who *represent* their districts. Senators are elected to a body whose function is to *advise and consent*. Again, nothing in the explicit language of politics suggests that political activity has anything necessarily to do with leadership.

In practice, those who hold office—president, mayor, governor, senator, representative—have to deal with myriad issues. If they are single-mindedly focused on a narrow set of issues as a leader, what is going to happen to the other issues that clamor for attention?

In any event, politicians who are not leaders can perform a useful social function by holding the body politic together. Successful politicians contribute by setting boundaries and establishing values, norms, and regulations. They build on the status quo and hold the space in which many different types of energy can flourish—those who pursue change as well as those who defend the existing values.

They can invite different voices to have a say in defining problems and solving them. They can contain conflict so that it may be resolved. They can guide the forces of change by giving them direction, value, and purpose, while providing a sense of stability to help frame the change being promoted. These are not qualities to be sneezed at, even though they are not necessarily the qualities of a transformational leader.

CEOs as Leaders

When Alan Klapmeier, who co-founded Cirrus Design, a Duluth, Minnesota–based manufacturer of private aircraft, went to air shows and began telling people about a new flight panel display that made piloting an airplane more intuitive and safer—an innovation that he believed would change the industry—his own board of directors tried to stop him from introducing it. They had good reason: Klapmeier had just completed a market research study that showed that, of all the product development ideas surveyed, a new flight panel display was the one that elicited the least interest.

Klapmeier argued that the results of the market survey were deceptive: "You can't ask a question of somebody who doesn't understand the question and make a decision based upon their answer. They don't know how good this stuff is going to be—how it will change the way they fly, change safety, change utility. They're just wrong."[13]

In due course, Klapmeier convinced his board of directors: the innovation was introduced and it turned out to be a commercial success. The directors had done their duty to the organization and its shareholders: as for all boards of publicly owned corporations, the decisive issue for them was not whether the innovation was inherently worthwhile; it was the overriding institutional preoccupation: Would it help the company's bottom line?

While traditionalists like Milton Friedman have lamented the political necessity for publicly owned corporations to show responsiveness to the inherent value of what they do under the heading of "corporate and social responsibility," even if only to fend off insurgent stakeholder campaigns, strategists like Michael Porter have spotted in examples like that of Klapmeier the possibility of competitive advantage for a corporation. If a firm can focus its efforts on activities valuable in themselves where it has, or can develop, an edge over its competitors, social responsibility can become not a drag on the firm's profitability but rather a strategic business opportunity. Companies can do well while doing good.[14]

However, the fact that ingenious and courageous leaders like Klapmeier or brilliant theorists like Porter can devise goals that are both worthwhile and profitable doesn't remove the inherent tension between the pursuit of worthwhile activities and the goal of enhancing the bottom line. In the world of publicly owned corporations, businesses tend to be fair-weather corporate citizens. When they are pursuing activities that are both worthwhile and profitable, they can present themselves as good corporate citizens. But when the firm faces a conflict between the two, Wall Street insists that the bottom line take precedence. If Klapmeier's innovation had failed in the marketplace, he would have been out of a job.

As a result, leaders who single-mindedly pursue a worthwhile cause from within a publicly owned corporation frequently find themselves encountering abrupt involuntary severance. If they are merely managers when the severance occurs, this really is the end: the organization turns the page and moves on with someone else at the helm; the manager's tenure is inherently forgettable. With genuinely transformational leadership, by contrast, severance from the institution is typically just the beginning. Typically other leaders who have been inspired by the vision step into the breach and carry on. Or the leaders themselves may carry on the vision in a different institution.

Given that, in the current climate, publicly held corporations are under continuing pressure to grow and do whatever is profitable, regardless of corporate purpose, it is usually easier to pursue an inherently worthwhile purpose in a privately held corporation. Thus the fourteen corporations discussed in Bo Burlingham's book, *Small Giants*, which are pursuing what they perceive as worthwhile goals, all found that closely held private ownership was an important, even essential enabler. Some owners, such as Gary Erickson of Clif Bar (a maker of organic energy bars and other health foods), had the opportunity of making more money by selling their company; they ultimately decided to keep the organization private to pursue what they saw as a worthwhile purpose. Private ownership can help keep the focus on a purpose, provided of course that the shareholders agree. Where they don't agree, then either the shareholding or the company may have to be broken up. In the case of Clif Bar, one of the two co-owners didn't agree to keep the company private, and so the other co-owner bought her out, at a cost of $65 million— a striking example of an individual—and a company—adhering to a worthwhile purpose.

Speaking to the CEO

For any major change to take hold in an organization, eventually the very top of the organization will have to support the change. How is that accomplished? How does one communicate strange, disruptive new ideas to people with great power and get them to listen? This is one of the toughest leadership challenges. Often powerful people appear overbearing, intimidating, with no time to listen. How can they be persuaded to change?

People with immense power—CEOs, senior managers, presidents, senators, representatives, whatever—all have different personalities, styles, and approaches. Nevertheless they tend to share some common characteristics, stemming from the nature of the burdens of office.

In discussing people with great power in this section, I'll call them by the generic term, "CEO," on the understanding that what I am saying applies to anyone with significant power, regardless of the specific job or title.

As with all communications, the first step in communicating with CEOs is to understand *their* situation. This can help overcome the tendency to interpret apparently threatening behavior as aimed at you personally, rather than as the normal accompaniment of having great power.

The reality is that it's tough being a CEO. If you put yourself in the shoes of CEOs and understand their stories, you can begin to understand their behavior. CEOs bear responsibility for an organization's success or failure, but many of the key determinants of success lie outside their control. They have more power than anyone else in the organization, but actually using that power can be counterproductive. Although swamped with information, they have difficulty finding out what's really going on. They are deluged with requests for help by people both inside and outside the organization. Worse, they're not even the final decision makers: they have board members scrutinizing what they do. And they have to deal with an array of investors, shareholder advocates, regulators, attorneys general, and nongovernmental organizations who all want a say in how the organization manages its affairs. They are conscious of lurking journalists on the hunt for news and hungry for a juicy scoop. So it should hardly come as a surprise that CEOs feel besieged and aren't easy to deal with.[15]

As a result of the pressures on them, CEOs tend to function mostly in the intuitive mode. They have no time for slow, deliberative arguments. They want answers—and they want them now. And they want them in the form that they like to receive them. And they want them from people they can trust.

The apparent aggressiveness of CEOs isn't necessarily personal. They're responding to the difficult situation they face. Often they don't have time to reason, and so they push for action. It's generally not their intention to hurt anyone. Usually they're just trying to get things done.

Learning everything you can about the CEO's individual manners, preferences, hopes, predilections, fears, and fetishes—in effect, under-standing that CEO's individual story—will give you the best chance of making an effective communication and persuading the CEO to change. A recent study by Gary Williams and Robert Miller of some sixteen hundred executives indicates that 80 percent of top executives fall into three groups: charismatics, skeptics, and followers, along with 20 percent who are controllers and thinkers.[16] If you can figure what sort of person you're dealing with, you can adjust the communication to fit that mind-set. The authors suggest that for a charismatic, the boldness of the idea should be featured. A risk-averse follower needs to be reassured that others are doing it. A skeptic may need to hear the message from someone they trust. Controllers and thinkers may need to be given more detail.

Who delivers the message may be crucial. If you are not already a member of the CEO's trusted inner circle, then you may be perceived as either an opponent or part of the irrelevant periphery—not the most promising roles from which to launch a disruptive new idea. It's not impossible to succeed in such a setting, but getting the CEO's attention will be a major challenge. Just think. If you're seen as an opponent, then the CEO is likely to be worried that this is a trap. If you're viewed as part of the periphery, then the CEO will probably not be listening at all. So it may be easier if you can find someone who is already a member of the

CEO's inner circle, someone who is already trusted, to make the case, or at least sponsor the interaction.

Attention getting with normal people is key. With the CEO, it's almost the whole ballgame. To get the attention of CEOs, usually the most promising approach is to focus on issues of interest to them now. CEOs usually won't buy the idea unless it becomes part of themselves. There is often no in-between—it's either the CEO's own idea or it's not worth anything.[17] As noted in Chapter Five, indirect narratives can help the idea become the listener's own—something that's crucial in the case of the CEO.

Being clear on your own story is also important. It can help overcome the feelings of awe that often arise in the powerless when they encounter the powerful.[18] You need to see that it's the truth and authenticity of your own story that gives you moral authority. Rather than trying to persuade the CEO of anything, you are seeking to enable the CEO to see hitherto hidden possibilities. It means helping the CEO view the world and the others in it in a new and more truthful light through the lens of a new story.

The Leader's Own Story

Thus an important foundation of leadership is for leaders to settle on their own story: Are they themselves ready for the challenges of leadership? Are they ready to commit to the worthwhile goal? The answers to these questions are not as obvious as they might at first seem.

Is the Leader Committed to the Goal?

The commitment I'm talking about here is not just a mental commitment but a commitment of mind, body, and soul to making it happen. Committing to a goal in this way is not a trivial undertaking. As David Whyte notes, "A firm persuasion is a kind of self-knowledge. . . . It must be discovered, cultivated and earned."[19]

If the leaders have not achieved sufficient commitment, the goal will seem small and even boring, as though spending energy and effort in accomplishing it will make little difference in the overall scheme of things.

They will find themselves beating around the bush, avoiding issues, saying things they don't really mean.

Once a commitment is made, the goal will seem larger, bolder, and more exciting. Leaders will find themselves saying what they really mean, speaking truth to power, sometimes saying things they didn't know they knew. They now have a sharp focus on the goal: the discussion focuses on why the goal must be achieved, because it's vital for the future.

Once the commitment is made, leaders need to fix on it like a laser beam. They need to see it intensely, even obsessively. They feel it. They hear it. They taste it. They smell it. It becomes part of them, their very identity, because it is something that they are committed to make happen, come what may, whatever it takes.

Commit to Making the Change Happen

Deciding to be a leader is thus a choice we have to make. Leadership isn't something we can be appointed to by other people, like being named manager. It's an inner decision to adopt a stance, an orientation toward the world, to see ourselves as pursuing an activity for its own sake and to set out to induce others to do likewise. Not everyone will make this decision.

For one thing, as noted earlier, becoming a leader can be dangerous. It can put us on a potential collision course with the powers that be, because the traditional function of management is to prevent destabilizing change.

But leaders also face other risks. Becoming a leader can be disruptive for the life of the leader. Leaders may have to undertake stressful new responsibilities. They may have to stop doing things that they know about and like doing, and start doing things they are unfamiliar with. They may have to venture into the unknown, making mistakes and learning from them. They may have to press ahead, knowing that previous change efforts were unsuccessful, without any certainty of success.

Becoming a leader may lead to changes in relationships with others, particularly those not initially supporting the change. Leaders may end up hurting the feelings of colleagues or friends who disagree with them. They may find themselves having to confront the fact that change sometimes gets sabotaged. They may have to consider at least temporarily giving up any friends or colleagues responsible for the sabotage.

Even more painfully, leaders may get no personal recognition for generating the change; they may even be punished for its success. Great change agents induce strong opposition. Being a successful leader may sometimes entail sacrificing yourself to the cause. Even if the sanctions suffered by Gandhi, Martin Luther King Jr., and John F. Kennedy—who were assassinated—aren't a serious possibility, the risk that leaders will not get credit for sponsoring a successful change is significant. Leaders may have to sacrifice their ego, ambition, and pride to make the change happen.

If the change fails, the risks may be even higher. There's a risk of losing managerial perks and privileges, such as the large corner office, the right to hire and fire, and the right to give people bonuses and promotions, a nice income, vacations, health care, business class travel, and off-site retreats at places like Pebble Beach.

In fact, committing to being a leader will sometimes be in tension with having a career. If everything pleasurable, human, emotional, bodily, frivolous is subordinated to one's career, that is to say, to getting ahead in an organization, then no psychological space is left for a thoroughgoing commitment to change. There may be no room to be a genuine leader.

Leadership isn't for the faint of heart. Leaders need to understand these risks—before they enter the fray. It is open to everyone to accept the challenge, but realistically, not everyone will do so.

Potential leaders may thus have to decide: Am I ready to tackle this leadership challenge at this time? Some will decide no, not now. They will decide that they don't want to risk their career, their family, their friends, or their financial well-being at this particular time for this particular issue. So be it. But they should make that decision consciously, fully aware of the implications of the decision they are making.

By contrast, when leaders make a definite commitment to some goal that is worthwhile in itself, the world comes into sharp and thrilling focus. Now they can say what they really believe. They can feel the rapture of being comfortable in their own skin, living a life that is truly their own. It's an opportunity to lift their game to a new level, to get beyond spin and manipulation and diplomacy and careerism. They become their own persons, making mind, body, actions, and values consistent.[20]

Making the decision to be a leader isn't a decision to be taken lightly. Most of the great heroes of history have hesitated when faced with the issue of whether to proceed with leadership or not. Homer's Odysseus hesitated for seven years before leaving the island of Ogygia, where he was living with the nymph Calypso. Hamlet spent forever agonizing over whether to act or not. And Chris Vogler pictures the scene in *The Call to Adventure*: "The tribe is gathered around the campfire. An elder emerges from the smoke and points to you: 'Our Tribe is in danger. You have been chosen to undertake a quest. You will venture your life so that the Tribe may go on. Do you accept the call?'"[21]

John Milton eloquently captures the feeling of what it's like to decide to lead change in his essay *Areopagitica*, published in November 1644, written at the height of the English civil war, when he was making the case for the freedom to print without a license:

> Methinks I see in my mind a noble and puissant nation rousing herself like a strong man after sleep, and shaking her invincible locks; methinks I see her as an eagle mewing her mighty youth, and kindling her undazzled eyes at the full midday beam; purging and unscaling her long-abused sight at the fountain itself of heavenly radiance; while the whole noise of timorous and flocking birds, with those also that love the twilight, flutter about, amazed at what she means, and in their envious gabble would prognosticate a year of sects and schisms.[22]

Committing to the goal is central: immersing oneself and fixating on the story of the change is vital. But the change itself can become problematic if it is not linked to a deep understanding of the audience's story. It is to this issue that I now turn in Chapter Four.

4

MASTERING THE
AUDIENCE'S STORY

> $\textbf{\textit{66}}$ I know that you believe you understand what $\textbf{\textit{99}}$
> you think I said, but I'm not sure you realize
> that what you heard is not what I meant.
>
> **—Robert McCloskey[1]**

On September 5, 2001, Howell Raines took over as executive editor of the *New York Times* with a bold change strategy. He was a man in a hurry and full of justifiable self-confidence.

He had a coherent, comprehensive game plan. As the man in charge of the ancient newspaper known as the "Gray Lady," he knew that it was too complacent. He planned to shake it up and make it not just the authoritative newspaper of record but exciting as well. He planned to "raise its competitive metabolism." The matter was urgent: unless his game plan was implemented, he saw that the very survival of the organization was at risk.

Raines had worked out the details for implementing his plan. He wanted more original stories on the front page, which had become "calcified." He envisaged "big stories" being covered with "overwhelming force." He intended the masthead—the senior editorial staff whose names appear under the executive editor on the editorial page—to have more of a say in shaping and coordinating coverage. He envisaged closer integration between the print edition and the new online media. He intended the *Times* to be first with the news, and to set aside its traditional cop-out: "It isn't news until we say it is." He thought the newspaper should listen more attentively to the real interests of its potential readers in all age groups and geographic areas and cover the top stories in those areas. His aim was that "the world's greatest newspaper" would become as good as it could be.

He had the advantage of knowing the firm and its staff intimately. He had worked there for more than two decades in different offices: New York, Atlanta, Washington, and London, performing different roles as journalist, correspondent, bureau chief, and most recently as overseer of the editorial page.

He had the luxury of time to prepare for his assignment. He learned of his appointment in May 2001 and was able to spend that summer getting to know the newsroom, in the course of many breakfasts and lunches with the managers and staff. Moreover, he had been preparing for this assignment since the early 1990s. He felt as though he had come home. He was expecting to have fun.

He had the strong backing of his boss, publisher Arthur O. Sulzberger Jr., who had seen and liked his aggressive approach to running the editorial page, and had supported him in the face of complaints from President Clinton and Mayor Giuliani. Sulzberger not only endorsed this bold change strategy: he told Raines to implement it quickly.

Raines was given the right to hire and fire, which he used extensively. He was able to push aside his only rival, Bill Keller, who was given a biweekly column and a writing assignment for the magazine. He was able to pick key lieutenants, people who shared his view of what needed to be done, such as Gerald Boyd as deputy managing director. He promoted Andrew Rosenthal as assistant managing director. He named Roger Cohen as acting foreign editor. He brought back Michael Gordon from London. He moved Patrick Tyler to the Washington bureau to write "lead-alls"—stories that brought together the different threads of a news story.

Fate was also kind in giving him a flying start. He took office on September 5, 2001, with the intent of "hunting big game, not rabbits."[2] He had the good journalistic fortune to have the biggest story of them all—the tragedy of 9/11—occur only six days later. It was the perfect opportunity to implement his strategy of covering a story with "overwhelming force." The newspaper won universal recognition for dominating every aspect of that story: the following year, the *Times* was rewarded with an unprecedented seven Pulitzer prizes for its work. Thus in his first year, he was able to show "that a paper that was being driven like an elderly Buick had the horsepower to run at Grand Prix speed."[3]

Raines thus had every managerial advantage. But only a few months later, he and his deputy, Gerald Boyd, were dismissed, with the change strategy in tatters. The publisher decided to placate large segments of the staff by promising to ease up on Raines's strategy of "more, better, faster" and denied that there was any complacency at the *Times*. "Never has been," Sulzberger said. "Never will be."[4]

The catalyst for Raines's dismissal after only nineteen months on the job was the revelation that a young reporter—Jayson Blair—had been found guilty of plagiarism and lying.

But the misdeeds of Jayson Blair were hardly Raines's fault. As executive editor, he had no way of knowing, and no cause to be consulted about, Blair's rapid promotion from trainee to reporter, his lack of professionalism, or his frequent errors. Once the problems were spotted, Raines had insisted on complete disclosure.

The underlying reason for Raines's dismissal is that he had "lost the newsroom."[5] He had failed as a leader to win the hearts and minds of the staff on the *New York Times* to implement his bold change strategy.

Why?

In Raines's failure, many factors were at play, some of which he himself now recognizes. He should have listened more. He should have done something about the look of "an angry hawk" that came across his face when he talked about something important. He should have noticed that his aggressive management style intimidated people. He should have recognized that his constant use of military metaphors and his frequent references to dictatorial football coach Bear Bryant weren't helping. And perhaps his lack of an Ivy League background also counted against him.[6]

But more important than these tactical issues was the fact that Raines failed in the central task of leadership, namely, stimulating a desire in the managers and staff of the *New York Times* to want to become a very different kind of organization. He felt intensely the necessity of expanding newspaper readership and making the newspaper more profitable. Yet Raines was unable to communicate to the managers and staff why their lives as journalists would be better if they started to conduct themselves differently.

Managerial Action Is Less Effective Than We Realize

Raines's strategy was apt and he aggressively applied the tools of management to implement it. But what Raines discovered, like most CEOs, was that the tools of management are not merely ineffective: they actively get in the way of transformational leadership intended to inspire deep change.

One of the hardest things managers like Raines have to learn is that neither the sincerity of their intentions nor the soundness of their ideas can guarantee that their behavior will be perceived as constructive or helpful. The cultural, psychological, and political complications of any power position like that of top management mean that the situation is never innocent. When managers assume that the meanings they intend with their actions are inevitably the ones that their audiences will take from them, they are in for the kind of surprise that Raines encountered.

The first right of a manager is to *give instructions* and be obeyed. Managers speak as the lords of the world, magisterially, insisting on the obedient silence of their staff, obliging them to listen. Raines instituted a daily meeting of the masthead editorial staff and issued orders as to what was to be done to put together the next edition of the paper. However, the orders were often perceived as interference in the intellectual integrity of the journalists and the section editors.

Managers generally have the right to a *corner office*. But that right doesn't necessarily help connect managers with the people they need to lead. In fact, it often takes managers physically and emotionally further away from them. One of the grievances against Raines was that he stayed in his corner office and didn't wander round the newsroom and have conversations with the staff. The area where staff attended the morning masthead meeting became known as "the DMZ," because it separated the newsroom from where the masthead editors had their offices. The physical layout of the office space reinforced the psychological chasm that developed.

Raines was able to exercise the power of the hierarchical manager *to hire the right people.* According to Jim Collins in *From Good to Great,* the first thing a leader should do is to hire the right people. Raines followed the advice and placed his own people in key positions. But for the most part he inherited the staff that he had. And for the people he did select, Raines was accused of playing favorites: he defended his moves by saying that these were the "best people." However, this simply offended the staff even further by implying that they were not the best people, thus further undermining support for his changes.

Raines also had *the right to fire people* and he moved aggressively. But did that help him become a leader and get people to change? Firing people usually ends up by keeping the people who know how to work the system, who know how to play organizational politics—the people with connections, the flatterers, the people who fit into the existing way of doing things, the people who tell the bosses what they want to hear. It was thus no accident that a flatterer like Jayson Blair flourished: he delivered exactly the kind of graphic story that Raines was demanding. The problem was that Blair's stories weren't true.

Then there are *incentives.* Managers get the right to give bonuses or promotions, or what plain folks might call bribes. And if managers do that, people may go through the motions of doing what they're told, but usually they do it unenthusiastically and grudgingly. They tend to feel (and sometimes say), "If we keep our heads down, maybe this too shall pass." Moreover, incentives lead to gaming the system—the nemesis of enterprise ranking, rating, and reward systems since time immemorial. At best, incentives pick up the stragglers, but they don't inspire people. They don't create enthusiastic champions. They don't create the energy, the zest and enthusiasm needed for sustained change.

Hierarchical managers may have other resources to bring to the discussion and can get into a *bargaining* mode with staff under their jurisdiction. The problem with bargaining is that it induces a narrow, cramped, legalistic approach to issues. Negotiating for better performance doesn't spark the generous enthusiasm that is willing to go the extra mile without any reward. And managers find that they quickly run out of rewards to offer for all the things that need to be done to get superior performance. At the *Times*, Raines had immense power but he didn't have enough rewards to offer for all the changes he planned.

So the attributes of hierarchical leaders—ordering, assigning office space, hiring, firing, offering incentives and disincentives—don't necessarily help leaders connect with people and do the most important thing that genuine leaders have to do: instill in people the sustained desire to do something fundamentally different.

Even when managers reach out and act in ways they think of as democratic and respectful, like the many preparatory lunches that Raines held with staff at the *Times* in the summer of 2001, the behavior can be seen as threatening and manipulative.

Audiences Are More Difficult Than They Used to Be

The irony is that once upon a time, the kind of things Raines was doing as CEO at the *Times* would probably have worked.

Once upon a time, people lived and worked where they were born. As a result, they shared common assumptions, beliefs, and values. The world was static—nothing much changed. Men had jobs. Women stayed at home and raised the kids. Within organizations, communication was top-down: people had little choice but to accept the word of those in authority, which in any case was *more of the same*. A few owners of property had control. Bottom-up communication hardly existed: in a static world, there was little need or possibility of persuading one's higher-ups to change. Politics was run by insiders: the task of persuading the populace to accept whatever had been decided was more or less an afterthought. In the marketplace, choices were few: oligopolies ruled. In the family, the parents' word was the law. In this world, those in authority were in charge. Leadership was hardly needed. By and large people did what they were told. Top-down command-and-control methods of communication generally got the job done.

That world is now a distant memory. For one thing, today's audiences are much more difficult than they used to be. Managers are dealing, day in and day out, with people who are tired of being talked at, of receiving choreographed, scripted messages, the latest directive. People are fed up with being commanded, controlled, compelled, directed, pushed, pulled, bullied, and browbeaten. They expect to be treated as adults. They want to be talked to as intellectual equals. And in the modern economy, the workers often have some control over the key means of production—knowledge—so their demands can't always be ignored.

Burgeoning diversity also makes the communication challenge even tougher. It's amusing to read the ancient Greek philosopher Aristotle and find that his notion of a diverse audience is one comprising middle-aged men from Athens and Sparta.[7] By modern standards, those audiences look remarkably homogeneous. Now the audience in the workplace or the marketplace comprises not just Athenian and Spartan men of the same age, but people of different gender, ethnicity, nationality, religion, life-style, age group, and geographical location. Common assumptions, values, and beliefs are the exception rather than the rule. How do you connect with people when they have different views about virtually everything?

Basic Change Is More Disruptive Than We Expect

And the kind of changes we're asking people to undertake these days are much bigger than anything we used to consider possible.

When Howell Raines asked the staff of the *New York Times* to start acting very differently—more rapidly, more collaboratively across organizational boundaries, covering new subjects, for new kinds of readers, with a new priority to online information, with a new priority to timeliness—he was asking for major changes in behavior. The managers and reporters at the *New York Times* had a huge stake in the status quo, which was familiar and comforting. It wasn't perfect, but at least it was stable and safe. There were grievances or irritations, but compared to the terrors of launching into the strange new world that Howell Raines was describing, the status quo looked like a rational, sensible, secure place.

The fact is that leaders often underestimate what they are asking people to do when they propose basic change.

Just think. In 1993, when Lou Gerstner took over IBM, the quintessential computer hardware firm, and told staff that in the future they were going to make a large part of their profits from services by integrating different computer systems, that implied a whole lot of people acting very differently from the past. For those who had been working at IBM for a long time, their very identity was bound up in working for a hardware firm. So when Gerstner came and started telling them that now they were going to be working for a firm that provided services, he was asking them not just to do a different job but also to assume a new role, in effect to take on a new identity. That was a very large thing to ask. Who was Lou Gerstner to tell them what sort of a people they should be?

Or in 2001, when Jeff Immelt came to GE, the quintessential process-driven organization, and told these process-driven people that they were part of a "green corporation" that was going to put "imagination to work," this meant far more than that people would take on different work—it implied assuming a new role and new values. In effect, he was asking the staff of GE to become different kinds of people. That was a large thing to ask.

Leaders Must Understand the Audience's Story

If leaders are to meet these more difficult challenges and succeed in inspiring enduring enthusiasm for more basic changes in more difficult audiences, they need to set aside any idea of imposing their will or moving their listeners to a predetermined position. The task is rather one of enabling the audience to see possibilities that they have hitherto missed. It means creating the capability in the audience to view for themselves the world and their relations with others in a new and more truthful light. It involves pointing a way forward for people who find themselves—for whatever reason—cornered by the current story that they are living. It entails enabling the audience to recognize a new, different, and more promising story that they could be living, which they for some reason have not visualized up till now.

If leaders are going to have any success in prompting the audience to discover this new story and imagine a different kind of future, they first need to understand the current story that their listeners are living. What's going on in that world? How does it hang together? Why does the world that people are currently living in make sense? What is it about their attitudes, beliefs, hopes, dreams, and fears that makes that world fit together in a way that is broadly plausible? There may be some tensions between different parts of their worldview—unrealized dreams, dissatisfactions, inconsistencies between actions and values. But overall, the world coheres. Why? How?

On the surface, this world will consist of the familiar, observable, routine, predictable activities of the human animal. But below this surface of routine and predictable activity is a realm of deeper feelings—of the joy and exhilaration of being alive, of the desire of loving and being loved, of the pain of not realizing deep ambitions, of the dilemmas of balancing personal goals with those of others, of a looming sense of mortality. It is this deeper world that is the source from which all enduring enthusiasm for change will come. And it is this world that leaders must understand.

Since this world is not directly observable, how do leaders get to know it and understand it? To a certain extent, they must proceed by surmise, by guesswork, by hunch, by inference. They must fathom it like an artist. They question. They explore. They intuit. They wander. They mingle. They live in it. They listen. They watch. They exercise the patience of a hunter tracking a wild animal. They get to know the habitat. They become a part of that world. They learn what that world values and scorns. If leaders probe with patience, persistence, and skill, they will eventually find within that world the dignity, the humor, the humanity, the order, and the energy that will laugh at boundaries and find a path through obstacles to a new future.

This is not a matter of gathering data about that world, analyzing it, calculating the percentage of time spent on this or that activity, or doing a quantitative survey. It's not about observing people as a scientist or voyeur, although such data-gathering may provide useful inputs.

It's a matter of imaginatively reaching out and getting inside the subjective world of the people who need to change and getting a sense of what it is like living in that world, so that the leaders feel its logic and power and order and compelling harmony. They are drawn into a relation with that world. As Martin Buber might say, these people cease to be an "It" and become a "You."[8] It's a matter of getting to understand their story.

If leaders succumb to the fundamental attribution error and think of their followers as obstacles, as enemies, as resisters, as opponents, as malcontents, or as stupid or obstinate or irresponsible or ill-willed, the risk of a disconnect will be significant.

So leaders need to understand the world of their listeners in all its peculiarity, its strangeness, its stubborn differences. The best—and perhaps the only—way to do that is to reconstruct the story the listeners perceive themselves to be living. As psychologist Dan McAdams says,

> People carry with them and bring into conversation a wide range of self-stories, and these stories are nested in larger and overlapping stories, creating ultimately a kind of anthology of the self. Although no single story may encompass all of the many narratives that any given person can use to make sense of his or her life, some stories are larger and more integrative than others and come closer, therefore, to functioning as identity formats for a given person. Thus identity may not be captured in a single grand narrative for each person, but identity nonetheless is accomplished through narrative.[9]

We usually spend a great deal of time thinking about what story we are going to tell. But the hard part of communication is often figuring out what story the audience is currently living. If we are to make the imaginative leap and get inside the listeners' stories, we need to have a very different relationship from traditional hierarchical managers. Instead of talking *down* to people we need to talk *with* people. We need to be conducting conversations with the people we hope to lead.

Through conversation, we can learn what's going on in our listeners' world, and figure out what story might be able to inspire new enthusiasm. This will require active interchange with them, rather than detached observation. Detached observation operates as a distancing device. When we are trying to connect with the people we lead, distancing is the last thing we need. Through the mutually shared experience of exchanging stories we discover what's going on in our listeners' world.

Finding and Encouraging New Leaders

In the course of such conversations, CEOs may also be able to find potential leaders within the organization who are already evangelizing and implementing needed change.

When Larry Prusak and Tom Davenport examined how large organizations actually succeeded in implementing major innovations, they found that the impetus for change usually didn't come from the CEO at all.[10] Usually it was people in the middle of the hierarchy, who, often without any formal managerial mandate, became the evangelists for changes that were eventually adopted by the CEO, just as Allard and Sinofsky became evangelists at Microsoft in 1993 for change that was eventually endorsed by Bill Gates in his 1995 Tidal Wave memorandum.

Prusak and Davenport call these mid-level evangelists for change "idea practitioners." In case after case, in companies like Dell Computer, Xerox, Johnson & Johnson, Intel, Hewlett Packard, Bristol-Myers Squibb, Eli Lilly, Société BIC, W.L. Gore and Associates, and the Canadian Imperial Bank of Commerce, the driving force behind new ideas was not the CEO but an idea practitioner—someone below the very top of the hierarchy who believed passionately in the innovation and was eventually able to win support from the hierarchy.

If CEOs can find the people in the organization who are already doing things differently, they can endorse their efforts and encourage others to join them. It will save them the trouble of having to inspire new leaders.[11]

Raines's Mistake

So what should Howell Raines have done? Raines's communications with his staff were mainly one-way tellings rather than two-way conversations. He didn't do enough about "the look of an angry hawk" that came across his face when he was talking about something important. He paid inadequate attention to the way the staff didn't say much at the lunches he held in the summer of 2001, which weren't real conversations. As a result, he never got to understand their stories.

Instead it was Raines who was formulating his view of the future and taking the decisions about who were the best people and which news to give prominence to. He didn't draw on the prodigious talents of the staff at the *New York Times* to contribute to the task of inventing the future. It was Raines who flexed his managerial muscles and made decisions in a hurry. In so doing, he killed motivation by not engaging in a real dialogue with the section heads and staff so that they could contribute to the future. So when a crisis came, he found he had "lost the newsroom" and had no way to get it back. Like so many of his peers, Raines had been so busy being a manager he never got round to being a leader. He was so busy imposing *his* vision on his followers that it never became *theirs*.

Raines needed the staff of the *New York Times* to realize that there was a new, a different, a more promising story that they could be living, which they for whatever reason had not visualized before. But without understanding their current story, how could he know what new story would energize them? How could he inspire them to adopt this different way of looking at the world?

Thus while Howell Raines was complaining about "attitudes of entitlement and smug complacency that pervade the paper" and lamenting that "routine work, too, is praised as excellent . . . and sloppy work is accepted as adequate," he was unable to figure out what would imbue these people with new enthusiasm.[12] For Raines to have been able to craft a message that resonated with those people, he would have needed a deeper understanding of their story.

Understanding the story of the change idea and the audience's story will require a certain degree of narrative intelligence. What is narrative intelligence? How does one acquire it? What are its elements? How does it relate to other ways of changing people's minds? It is to these issues that I now turn.

5

CULTIVATING NARRATIVE INTELLIGENCE

❝ How quick come the reasons for approving what we like! ❞

–Jane Austen[1]

On the evening of Sunday, January 24, 1965, a twenty-four-year-old doctor was driving along a two-lane country road from Sydney to Goulburn. It had been a sunny, pleasant day for him in Sydney, relaxing by the swimming pool with his mother, sister, and brother. Now he was returning to work in a hospital in Goulburn, his first assignment since qualifying as a doctor. It was early evening, and as he drove along, the olive green fields of the Australian countryside were silently dissolving into night. Traffic was light that evening, and he had no particular reason to pay attention to the car that was traveling toward him from the opposite direction. Its headlights were on, and it was easily visible. But when the car was only a few yards away, he suddenly realized that a second car was overtaking it at high speed so that there were now two cars heading straight for him in parallel on the two-lane road. To avoid a head-on collision, he swerved off the main road onto the gravel shoulder. However, just at this point in the road, there was a deep concrete culvert. His car fell into the culvert, struck a cement wall, and came to an instant stop. The young doctor had been wearing a seat belt, but the collision was too much. His aorta collapsed on impact, and he died instantly.

The young doctor was my brother. Naturally, his death was a shock to our family—my parents and my sister and me. The fact that the life of a young man, with everything still ahead of him, could be snuffed out so pointlessly was horrible for us to contemplate. The unexpectedness was devastating.

My mother experienced deep grief for months. But gradually, as she emerged from her despair, she began to think about the issue of traffic safety. She discovered that many young people were being killed on the roads in Australia. Most of the deaths were needless. Safety belts were not compulsory. Speed limits were not respected. Drunk driving was a widespread problem. Many of the roads were not constructed with safety in mind, with hidden concrete culverts waiting to trap unsuspecting drivers in an emergency. Nothing could be done about my brother's death, but, my mother began to realize, something could be done about the lives being needlessly lost on Australian roads.

For the next decade, she devoted herself to traffic safety. It became her passion. She was unstoppable in lobbying to introduce legislation for compulsory seat belts: tirelessly advocating measures to make driving safer, preparing materials, making statements, badgering politicians—no effort was too much.

In this way, a real-world event changed my mother's mind. Although before the accident she had not shown the slightest interest in traffic safety, the loss of her son caused her to become a champion, a leader in a field that desperately needed champions. For the rest of the family—my father, my sister, myself—the event was shocking but not directly life-changing. We were more aware of highway safety than we had been, but we didn't spend the rest of our lives directly dedicated to the issue.

For me, the accident had an unexpected effect. At the time, I was working as an articled clerk in a corporate law office in Sydney by day, while pursuing my law degree at Sydney University by night. The death of my brother did cause me to think: What am I doing with my life? Life is brief. If I were to die now, would I consider my life to have been worthwhile?

In the ensuing months, one incident brought things into focus. In our law firm, I was assigned to help on a case that was going to trial.

Our client was one of the most disagreeable people I've ever met. She was a woman of middle years—morose, critical, intolerant, and unpleasant in the extreme. Nothing was ever right, and she let everyone know that: it was too bright, too dark, too hot, too cold, too dry, too humid, too quiet, too loud. She wore dark glasses at all times. She was the daughter of an extremely wealthy man who had died leaving a reasonable sum to her, but he had left most of his fortune in trust to promote the cause of a system of shorthand that he had invented. She had engaged our law firm to prove that her father had been mentally incompetent when he drew up the deed that deprived her of most of his wealth.

As I read through the old man's letters and papers, it was evident that he had been far from insane. I found occasional non sequiturs in his writings, as one might expect in any elderly gentleman. But he was lucid about his daughter's character. It seemed that he had carefully considered the issue on the merits. He had asked his lawyer to draw up a suitable trust. On the day of the signing, the two men had gone to lunch. They discussed the pros and cons over the meal. They then came back to the lawyer's office, and the deed was signed. By all accounts, the old man's demeanor was calm and deliberate. There was nothing impetuous in his actions. The lawyer had no personal interest in the matter. The old man gave every sign of knowing what he wanted to do. To me, his actions in respect of his estate were practically a guarantee of his sanity.

The law partner in our firm told our client that her lawsuit was hopeless. But she wanted her day in court. Since the legal system is available to anyone who feels aggrieved and is able to pay the legal bills, we continued with the lawsuit, but it was obviously mission impossible.

I joined the case just as it was going to trial, which was expected to last a number of days. Since I was an articled clerk, nobody asked my opinion about the merits of what we were doing. My job was to schlep bags, sort documents, and do minor research.

In the middle of the trial, however, I happened to see a copy of the deed by which the old man had disinherited his daughter. I glanced through it and saw at once that it had a technical flaw: the trust was invalid under an obscure and complex English law known as the Rule Against Perpetuities. The law had been put in place to prevent anyone from tying up property in trust indefinitely. The trust established by the deed exceeded the limits set down by law. The law didn't simply shorten the trust to a period that was legal: instead it invalidated the trust entirely. As a result, the old man's wealth would flow to his daughter rather than to the cause that he himself had chosen. When I pointed the technical flaw in the document to the supervising partner, there was elation at the prospect of winning the case, along with embarrassment at not having spotted it earlier.

It was hailed by all as a brilliant legal victory, although the insight was primarily due to the fact that I was studying this obscure branch of the law at the time, and so the subject was fresh in my mind.

While I was pleased to receive kudos for winning a difficult case, I was also troubled. I had entered the legal profession with two hazy ideas. One was an admiration for the brilliant legal victory of the lawyer played by Charles Laughton in *Witness for the Prosecution*. The other was a diffuse concern for social justice. Now that I had actually won a case that no one expected us to win, I discovered that I wasn't triumphant but dismayed. If I spent my life doing this, I thought, would I not be devoting my life to perverting justice rather than serving it?

With my brother's death still fresh in my mind and the question of how to spend my life still preoccupying me, I decided to get out of the law, but to do what? I had no viable alternative at the time. So I kept on working to complete my qualifications as a lawyer, but all the time I was looking around for something different.

In due course, I completed my law degree and qualified as a lawyer in Sydney, but still no alternative had turned up. So I went to Oxford University in England to earn a postgraduate degree in law. I was getting even more deeply involved in the legal profession, but I was always on the lookout for something worthwhile.

Then one day in Oxford, I overheard a conversation among some fellow students about interesting jobs at an organization called the World Bank that helped developing countries deal with poverty. It was no more than that. Just an odd comment, overheard in the common room in Oxford. At the time, I had never heard of the World Bank, and I had given no thought to a career in international development. But the conversation was intriguing, and so I began to find out all I could about the field. I learned that the World Bank was an international organization that lent money to help developing countries solve their economic problems. It was actively looking to recruit young professional people. So I wrote to it offering my services, and after interviews in London and Paris, I was duly offered a position. Thus began my thirty-one-year career in the World Bank.

What led me to change my mind and leave the legal profession and devote a large portion of my life to international development? In my case, the final trigger was a seemingly insignificant event: an odd comment about interesting jobs at the World Bank. The comment would probably have had no effect, however, were it not for the two previous events: first, my brother's death, which had prompted me to reflect on the meaning of my life, and then the dismay I felt at winning a legal victory that my client didn't deserve to win. All three events led to a process of reflection that led to the change.

Why Do People Change Their Minds?

Understanding why people change their minds is central to leadership. Why do we decide to devote our lives to one thing rather than another? Why do we decide to become champions of one cause and not another?

As I look at my mother's decision to devote a decade of her life to the cause of highway safety or my own decision to devote a good part of my life to international development, I can see that we didn't sit down and make a rational analysis of all the possible things that we could do with our lives, and then use that calculus to decide on a course of action. Rather, our eyes lighted on some particular course of action that caught our attention, and then the reasons why that course of action made sense came quickly.

In fact, people change their minds in three ways—by experience, by observation, and by symbolic learning. They follow the same routes that honeybees use to learn.

WHY HONEYBEES CHANGE THEIR MINDS

Honeybees follow the same three routes of learning as human beings.

Honeybees learn by *experience*. A single bee will visit different flowers in the morning and, if there is sufficient attraction and reward in a particular kind of flower, she will make visits to that type of flower for most of the day, unless the plants stop producing reward or weather conditions change.

Honeybees also learn by *observation*. In experiments, bees have been observed to enter a simple maze with a choice between two paths. One path, which leads to the food reward, is marked with the same color that is used at the entrance to the maze, while the other is marked with a different color. Bees learn to choose the correct path and update their knowledge when there is a change in the marker.[2]

Although it is sometimes suggested that animals can only learn by directly experiencing or observing an event, in fact honeybees can also learn through *symbolic communication*.[3] Bees communicate what they have learned about the source of food and thus recruit other worker bees of the hive to forage in the same area. The communication takes place by means of a strange dance, called the waggle-dance, that honeybees perform when they return to the hive after a successful foraging trip. The nectar-laden bee dances on the comb in a circular pattern, occasionally crossing the circle in a zigzag or waggle pattern. The phenomenon was described by Aristotle in 330 B.C., in his *History of Animals*. In 1973, Karl von Frisch was awarded the Nobel Prize in Physiology or Medicine for his work showing that the runs and turns of the dance were correlated to the distance and direction of the food source from the hive.[4]

Actual Experience

Our actual experience of an event can change our minds, often because the emotions associated with it cause it to have a greater prominence in our lives than it otherwise might. An experience associated with strong emotion will receive more attention while it is occurring, will be remembered more easily and longer than unemotional experiences, and is more likely to have an effect on subsequent decision making.[5]

So it was for me. When I experienced what it was like to be a lawyer and win a difficult case, I found that I didn't feel triumphant in the way that watching Charles Laughton in *Witness for the Prosecution* had led me to expect. Instead, I felt dismay at having contributed to injustice. So I concluded that the legal profession was not for me. In due course, this contributed to a decision to do something different—to pursue international development. The fact that my actual experience of working in the World Bank largely corresponded to my expectations led me to stay on this track.

Observed Experience

We don't have to actually experience real-life events to learn from them: simply observing them can cause the same emotional effect as experiencing them. In the public arena, 9/11 changed the way many people viewed terrorism, in the same way that Pearl Harbor in 1941 changed the way that the United States viewed the threat of Japan and the ongoing world war. My mother and I didn't have to be in a traffic accident ourselves to grasp the impact. Merely observing the traffic accident of someone close to us was enough to shift the course of our lives.

Symbolic Learning

Human beings don't have to go through the complicated steps of the waggle-dance of the honeybee to communicate their learning. They have developed a symbolic means of communication, namely language, that allows for the acquisition of the emotional properties of an experience without needing to have the experience or observe it in person. The physiological reaction of the body to symbolic learning can be similar to that of undergoing or observing the experience itself.[6]

An idea may be introduced to us through language, either by hearing about it from another person or by self-generating the idea ourselves, or a combination of the two.

But the impact of an idea communicated symbolically is usually not as powerful as direct experience. It is one thing to know about traffic accidents in general. It is quite another to go through the experience of inspecting the wreck of your brother's crushed car and having to identify his body in the morgue. As William James said: "An impression can be so exciting emotionally as almost to leave a scar upon the cerebral tissues."[7]

Thus in my mother's case, her observed experience of the death of her son in a senseless traffic accident made a deep impression on her as to how dangerous highways can be. The emotional scar left by the experience led over time to her becoming a passionate advocate for greater traffic safety. In an intellectual sense, she didn't learn anything new from the accident: she already knew that people were killed in traffic accidents. It took the directly observed experience of her son's death to grasp the full significance of those facts. And so she became an advocate for road safety.

In my case, the combination of direct experience (of actual work in a law firm), observed experience (the death of my brother), and symbolic learning (the casual comment about jobs in the World Bank) led to my spending a large part of my life devoted to international development.

Getting Other People to Change Their Minds

Up to now I've been talking about how people decide for themselves to change their minds. How does this apply to getting other people to change? How do we persuade other people to do something different, not just on a one-time basis but passionately, so that they're willing to make fundamental changes to their lives, enthusiastically and with gusto? When it comes to getting people to change their minds, the same three routes are the ones available.

Changing Minds Through Direct or Observed Learning

The more immediately we can involve people in an actual or observed event, the more experiential the learning can be, the more likely it is going to have an impact on them.

As managers, we may be able to change the experiences that people have or observe and so contribute to changing people's minds. This might include acting as role models, so that we embody the behavior that we are trying to induce. It could involve conversations that create interactive experiences that may nudge people to adopt new points of view. It could concern study tours that we can arrange, broadening people's experience: visits to other people or organizations that are already implementing a change we are seeking to introduce can give people a vivid sense of what's involved. It may mean role-playing exercises and simulations, in which people get to experience what it is like to be acting differently: simulations can provide much more frequent feedback than real-life experience; when supported by coaching, they can help participants take corrective action to overcome their cognitive biases.[8] It could involve quick prototyping, which can enable people to experience a roughly improvised version of a new product so that they can get the feel of what it is like to use it.[9] Training can also provide direct experience, by including practice for people in trying out the envisaged change in behavior.

As parents and teachers, we may have a significant influence on the kinds of experiences that our children or students have or observe. Exposing them to healthy, joyful, energizing experiences is a continuing leadership challenge. The role models that we embody as parents and teachers are observed experiences that can have a significant influence on the kinds of adults they become. The kinds of conversations we have with our children may have a profound influence on the way they think.

Active experiential learning—either experienced or observed—has several virtues. For one thing, it involves the emotions, and so has a chance of playing a significant role in people's lives. For another, it allows the participants themselves to make up their own minds, not merely absorb something imposed on them, which increases the chance that it will become part of their own life story, their own passion. And studies show that experiential learning is more effective than passive learning.[10]

In terms of leadership, the limitation of experiential learning is that often leaders are in a situation where they lack the power to change other people's actual experiences. As a result, much of the burden of changing people's minds inevitably falls on the use of language to persuade people to change.

Persuading People to Change Through Language

We have four main ways to go about persuading people to change by way of language, as laid out in Table 5.1. One is by giving people abstract reasons.

TABLE 5.1   Methods of Persuading People to Change Their Minds

	Abstract	Narrative
Direct and explicit	Appeals to reason through detailed evidence and arguments	Narratives in which the object is to have the listener live the story as fully and movingly as possible
Indirect and implicit	Appeals to intuition, through cues, signs and heuristics, and manipulative tricks	Narratives in which the object is to stimulate a new story in the mind of the listener

A second is by giving people indirect cues or rules of thumb as to why they should change. A third is by involving people directly in a story. And the fourth is by inducing people themselves to generate a new story. I discuss each of these methods, examining their various strengths and weaknesses.

Appeals to Reason   The traditional approach to persuasion is the royal road of reason. Give people reasons and they will do what you say. In the modern world, this is the default assumption about how to persuade people to change. The approach has a long lineage going back to ancient Greece. It was the pride and joy of intellectual giants like Plato, Descartes, and Kant.[11] The essence of this approach: "To obtain the best results, emotion should be kept out: rational processing must be unencumbered by passion."[12]

The approach has a number of advantages. It is honest. It is open. It isn't manipulative. It ties in with the idea that human beings should be rational in their decision making.[13]

But when it comes to inspiring enduring enthusiasm for changing behavior, it is worse than ineffective: it can be counterproductive. Research shows that when people are presented with reasons to change their behavior in a fundamental way, the confirmation bias kicks in. As discussed in Chapter One, in difficult, skeptical audiences, the emotional brain tends to dismiss or reinterpret reasons for change so that they present no threat to preexisting points of view. People become more entrenched in their current viewpoint, not less.

Even when reasons change opinions, they don't necessarily lead to action. For instance, the field of research on changing life-threatening behavior related to HIV infection has offered a perfect laboratory for a rigorous examination of what works and what doesn't work when it comes to changing behavior. An exhaustive review of 354 separate interventions from 1985 to 2003 aimed at increasing condom use found no significant increase in condom use from abstract reasons alone. It was only when appeals to reason were combined with more active approaches that any significant change in behavior was observed.[14]

Appeals to Intuition   The fact is that most decisions made by human beings aren't made on the basis of conscious reasoning. They are based on intuitive thinking. Intuitive thinking is fast, automatic, effortless, associative, natural, and often barely conscious. By contrast, the operations of reasoning are slow, serial, deliberate, and effortful. It's true that intuitive thinking is prone to a set of cognitive biases that are difficult to eliminate or even modify, like the confirmation bias or the fundamental attribution error, but for most decisions, most of the time, intuition is good enough. Efficiency is more important than accuracy. In fact, if we were to try to apply conscious reasoning to every decision we had to make, we would never get out of bed in the morning, let alone get anything done.

Intuition operates by using more rapid pathways based on context and similarity rather than the conscious use of logic and evidence. It efficiently incorporates emotions and feelings. Intuition, suffused with emotion, points out things we should quickly focus on in order to take action. It guides attention and keeps us focused on things to do and things to avoid.

The incentives and disincentives of the traditional workplace also function as cues for decision making. "Do this and you'll get a bonus." "Do that and your career is over." These cues don't invite people to examine the reasons why this makes sense or that doesn't: instead, they aim to invoke an intuitive decision to do what the system rewards and avoid what the system punishes.

The fact that intuition is prone to a number of biases means that it is apt to be exploited by those who want us to change our minds.[15]

- *Hype:* Multiple voices exaggerating the virtues or benefits of something can cause us to pay attention to it and have a more positive view of it than we otherwise would.

- *Halo effect:* The perception of one kind of trait can lead us to infer the presence of similar traits. Attractive people are often judged as having a more desirable personality and more skills than someone of average appearance. Celebrities are used to endorse products that they have no expertise in evaluating.

- *Spin:* The offering of positive interpretations of events may cause us to have a more positive understanding of what is going on than is warranted by the facts alone.

- *Bait and switch:* If people agree to do something, they are more likely to honor that commitment, even if the incentive or motivation is removed *after* they have already agreed. For example, in car sales, unexpectedly raising the price at the last moment can be effective because the buyer has already decided to buy.

- *Groupthink:* People will do things that they see other people are doing. In a bookstore, we pay attention to bestsellers because other people have bought the book. This phenomenon is commonly used in the marketing of products, as with customer testimonials.

- *Imposition of authority:* People tend to be submissive toward authority figures. The Milgram experiments in the 1950s showed that participants were willing to apply apparently lethal electric shocks to subjects on the instructions of those in charge. The politics of war shows how easy it is for governments to pressure people into supporting military action.

- *Celebrity pressure:* People are more easily persuaded by other people that they like or admire. If we like Tiger Woods, we may be inclined to consider buying a Buick if we believe he drives one.

- *Artificial scarcity:* If something is in short supply, that fact alone can help generate demand. For example, making offers for goods that are available for "a limited time only" may encourage sales.

Appeals to intuition have several strengths in terms of getting people to change their minds. They require little effort from participants. When they work, they work rapidly. They are effective for low-involvement issues where people don't care much one way or the other, such as which brand of toothpaste to buy.[16]

But as a leadership tool, appeals to intuition suffer from several weaknesses, in addition to their vulnerability to cognitive biases. They may require extensive financial resources or power to put in place the relevant cues and rules of thumb. They are better for establishing attitudes in the first place than for changing behavior in face of established attitudes, which tend to resist appeals to intuition. Moreover when managers offer quid pro quos in exchange for compliance, they may run out of quids to offer for the quos. And once they start offering incentives, they risk getting on an incentive treadmill, where people become unwilling to do anything without incentives. Furthermore, such methods often generate pushback and cynicism, as people become aware that they are being manipulated. In the marketplace, people have become hype-resistant and cynical about big business. In the workplace, people don't always trust managers, and may resent changes if they don't see the point.[17]

Moreover, cues don't work in any consistent fashion. Thus, a synthesis of more than 350 real-world experiments on the effects of television advertising revealed that increases in the amount of advertising did not yield any simple increase in product sales. Even commercials that were effective (as assessed by consumers' successful recall and reports of persuasion) did not strongly correspond to consumer purchases as reflected in sales.[18] In the workplace, studies suggest that major change programs implemented solely by diktat rarely work.[19]

The best role for appeals to intuition may be a limited one, as a support for other communication tools. Cues can help pick up the laggards and the resisters and give them a nudge, but cues are unlikely to be the engine of change that transformational leaders need: appeals to intuition don't generate new champions. Even where they generate change in behavior, they usually don't generate sustained enthusiasm for change.

So if appeals to reason don't work, and intuition doesn't lead to passionate action, how do leaders go about generating enduring, passionate behavioral change?

Direct Narrative One clue comes from another branch of psychology, where the difference between abstract and narrative thinking has been highlighted. Thus the eminent psychologist Jerome Bruner writes in *Actual Minds, Possible Worlds* that there are two modes of thought, that is, "two distinctive ways of ordering experience, of constructing reality":

> They are complementary but irreducible to each other. . . . Efforts to reduce one mode to the other or to ignore one at the expense of the other inevitably fail to capture the rich diversity of thought. . . . A good story and a well-formed argument . . . can both be used as means for convincing someone of something. Yet what they convince us of is fundamentally different: arguments convince one of their truth, stories of their lifelikeness."[20]

Clearly stories have been hugely important throughout human history as tools for changing people's minds. It is notorious that the great religions have been built, and the great wars have been launched, using story as the principal communications tool. One reason is that narrative is integral to the way we make decisions. Rather than making decisions by careful intellectual effort or following cues, we make most of our conscious decisions through narrative. We cannot decide what to do until we decide what story or stories we see ourselves as living. If we want to change the way people act, we need to change those stories.[21]

Acceptance of the use of narrative in organizational leadership has been slow in coming, in part because of strong faith in the power of reason. The incessant corporate mantra has been *analytic is good; anecdotal is bad.* Yet it is increasingly recognized in business that storytelling is what effective leaders actually do. Thus in 1997 Noel Tichy said, "Business leaders need a teachable point of view—a set of ideas about success in the marketplace and a set of values based on personal and organizational success." The best way to communicate that point of view is through a story. The winning leaders profiled in his book "all lead through stories."[22] Some academic journals are devoted exclusively to the understanding of narrative.[23] And business journals have begun to publish articles recognizing the central role of storytelling in leadership.[24]

But how does a story persuade people to act? In some sense, we all know what a story is. But for all that, story is still something of a mystery. People tell many stories to each other every day. But it's rare that stories ignite enthusiastic changes in behavior. When we watch a great film or read a great novel, we don't typically rush into action. Why do some stories spark action and others don't? What is it about some kinds of stories that cause people to change their minds and behavior?

Some psychologists have suggested that the underlying mechanism for stories that spark change is what they call *transportation*.[25] Thus when readers follow a story, they go on a kind of journey. They are transported—virtually—by the storyteller into a different world. The listeners project themselves into a different mental location—the place where the story takes place—even though they have never physically left their static sitting position. The imagined reality they visit is a world elicited by a storyteller who stimulates this mental world into existence. The listeners give up their groundedness in the here-and-now to project their new existence in the mental elsewhere of the story. The more fully the listeners can accomplish this transition, the more effective the story is as a story. When the story is very powerful, the listeners may return to their real world as changed persons. They change as a result of the experiences they have had on their virtual journey, the characters they have met, and the feelings they have experienced. They may be "mentally scarred." As a result, they may have very different attitudes to the subject from those they held before they heard the story and so may act differently in the future.

In the transportation model of narrative, the narrative immerses the listeners as fully as possible in the story. The listeners are (mentally) transported from the real world to the narrative world that the storyteller has created. The story operates like real experience so as to influence attitudes. Immersed in the story, the listeners may experience almost the same feelings as if they were living the story for real. They may become attached to the characters in the story and develop feelings toward them. By this process, the listeners are engaged; attention and interest are fostered. If all goes well, the imaginary story becomes the story in which the listeners decide to live. In this transported mode, the audience may be less likely to raise counterarguments. The more absorbing the story, the more effective it is.[26]

The strengths of direct narrative are numerous. It draws on the natural affinity of human beings for stories. Even the strongest critics of stories, such as Plato and Descartes, were adept in using stories to make their case. Stories tend to be more interesting, fresh, and entertaining than abstract argument. Stories fit the way people think and make decisions. Story weaves in emotion in a way that rational argument can never do. Story is flexible. It may be a grand narrative like the stories that are used to win support for religions or wars. Or it may be a smaller story, such as an ad for car insurance. "Imagine you have just had a car accident. . . ." If the story is powerfully told, it can overcome lack of credibility on the part of the speaker and lack of evidence supporting the story.[27]

We also know that stories appeal to diverse groups: As Howard Gardner said in 1995:

> Some storytellers are so skilled, however, that they are able to create narratives that appear to satisfy both parties to a controversy. Or to operate effectively at more than one developmental level. Through choice of words, through selection of examples, and through the use of nonlinguistic cues, a leader may be able to convince adherents of each perspective that he or she is on their side. The delivery of stories . . . can be sufficiently polyphonic so as to please individuals of different ages, persuasiveness and sophistication.[28]

And yet persuasion by direct narrative, it must be said, also has some drawbacks. It can take time to tell a story that fully transports the listener to another world: today's hard-pressed listeners rarely have the patience for such epics. And to get the story to stick, substantial financial resources, coordination with multiple storytellers, and exercise of power may be needed.[29]

Indeed, the difficulty of getting a direct narrative to stick often leads to a tendency to exaggerate the story, overstating benefits and demonizing opponents. Stories that are partially fabricated or exaggerated can unravel once the audience gets an opportunity for an evidence-based examination of the underlying facts.

Indirect Narrative   A way of overcoming the drawbacks of direct narrative is the indirect narrative. Here the story is told not so much to engage the audience so fully in the storyteller's story that each listener returns a changed person as to spark a new story in the mind of the listener. The presenter's story is deliberately crafted to be less than all-absorbing: the idea is that the listeners not only hear the presenter telling the story, they also hear their own silent voices within, as their minds ponder the implications of an analogous story for their own lives.

The distinction between direct and indirect narratives is important. They involve two fundamentally different mechanisms for getting results. In the direct narrative, the emphasis is on absorbing listeners in the richly told story of the storyteller—mentally transporting them to another world. In the indirect narrative, the emphasis is on stimulating a new story in the minds of the listeners. In the indirect narrative, it's the listener's story that's key.

The Biblical parables are examples of indirect narratives. In a parable, the interest of the story isn't in the story per se: the characters are not richly drawn. The events are described sketchily. The teller makes no effort to transport the listeners to a different world by evoking the sights and the sounds and the smells of the context so that the listeners imagine themselves transported to that context and return emotionally scarred by the experience. Instead, the object is to spark a new story in the mind of the listener about a similar issue that the listener may be facing. The parables are a long way from being well-told stories. And yet they continue to be effective after thousands of years, because they generate new stories in the minds of the listeners.

For the exponent of direct narrative, anything less than 100 percent listener concentration on the story itself is a shortfall and a cause for concern. But in indirect storytelling, less than 100 percent absorption of the listener in the story is actually the goal: here the object is to have the two voices of the listener and the storyteller continue in a kind of parallel conversation. The storyteller deliberately tells a story in such a way as to allow mental space for listeners to forge their own thoughts, with the explicit objective of having the listeners invent analogous stories of their own, in parallel to the storyteller's explicit story.

In indirect narrative, the storyteller's story is not necessarily very interesting as a story: instead, it serves as a springboard, a point of departure for new stories that the listeners will generate in their own minds, from their special contexts, from their own experience of problems. What is memorable for the listeners on such a journey isn't the storyteller's story but rather the virtual journey that they make of their own accord with the story they tell themselves.

The distinction between direct and indirect narrative parallels the distinction between abstract reasons and intuition. Direct narrative occurs openly in the explicit spoken word that can be heard and recorded and written down. Indirect narrative operates intuitively, spontaneously, quickly, and silently in the mind of the listener.

Indirect narrative is a principal route by which transformational leaders stimulate desire for change. Thus when Al Gore's movie, *An Inconvenient Truth,* tells the story of the success in repairing the hole in the ozone layer by concerted international action, he doesn't try to tell a well-told story. He doesn't try to immerse the listeners in the sights and sounds and smells of what was going on when people were taking steps to fix the hole in the ozone layer. His story doesn't transport listeners to that different world. Instead, his telling of that story is minimalist in style. His story may nevertheless succeed if it sparks a new story in the mind of the listener: "We solved the problem of the hole in the ozone layer, so maybe we can solve the problem of global warming!"

When telling the story of how AMP had helped the man with the multiple sclerosis, Craig Dunn is successful if he succeeds in sparking a new story in the minds of the listeners: "If we save this firm, we'll be doing worthwhile things like this for our community!"

When telling his stories about how the Internet was being used at Cornell University, Steven Sinofsky helped spark new stories in the minds of his listeners: "The Internet will be central to everything Microsoft does!"

The indirect narrative has drawbacks. It doesn't work on everyone: any fair-sized group includes incorrigibles who resist any effort to imagine a different future. And it requires a certain amount of narrative intelligence to know how to craft such a story.

But it also has major strengths. It is quick and powerful, drawing on the intuitive side of the mind. When it succeeds, the listeners' stories are self-generated, and it's much easier for people to believe their own stories than someone else's. It takes advantage of the way stories fit the way people think and make decisions. It is mainly based on telling true stories—stories that actually happened. Hence it avoids any charge of manipulation or deception. And because it is about something that actually happened, it is difficult for skeptical, cynical, or hostile audiences to satirize or undermine. Moreover, it's relatively easy to tell a story about something that has already happened: it doesn't require elaborate performance skills. Because it's quick, it's suited to many different contexts—business, politics, family, whatever. When successful, the indirect narrative can generate enduring change that is free of cynicism. Because it generates the listener's own story, the change is espoused with energy, gusto, and enthusiasm.

Three basic principles of persuasion for the purposes of leadership emerge from the review of the routes open to leaders wishing to create enduring enthusiasm for change by way of language:[30]

- *Experiential methods* are more likely to be effective than nonexperiential methods, because the emotional imprint of a live experience is usually more pronounced than that of a virtual experience by way of language.

- *Narratives* are more likely to be effective than abstract communications, because this is how human beings think and make decisions, and because it simulates the emotional significance of experiential learning.

- *Indirect methods* are more likely to be effective than direct methods, because indirect methods leave it up to the audience to make up their own minds rather than having opinions forced upon them.

The Leader as Storyteller

It's a mystery to some how Ronald Reagan managed to combine the roles of leader and politician. Reagan handily won two terms as U.S. president and launched the conservative revolution in the United States.

As noted, one reason for Reagan's success is that he had the single-minded focus of a leader. He had a relatively small number of goals—defeating the Soviet Union, reducing taxes and the size of government—and he pursued them single-mindedly.

But just as important in Reagan's success was the fact that he instinctively understood the language of leadership and effectively mobilized the power of simple stories to defuse tension in areas about which he had no strong views, while communicating his points in areas where he felt strongly. Drawing on his actor's talent for light comedy, Reagan used stories to lighten the "magnificent vagueness" of his political speeches as well as his "banal conversation."[31]

Reagan may have been regarded by his opponents as lacking in intellectual depth, but when it came to leadership, the wider electorate saw in Reagan's storytelling something that was both persuasive and endearing. Reagan's stories helped bring the electorate along with him. In the few areas where he was committed, he used stories to make his point. When it came to the latest congressional or bureaucratic struggle over minutiae of more distant concern, he would remove himself with a bemused shake of the head and a one-liner.[32]

The fact is that Reagan had a talent that all leaders need, namely, narrative intelligence. He knew how to craft and perform a story, with good judgment as to what kind of effect it would have on the audience. In Reagan's case, this narrative intelligence was tacit. He couldn't describe what it was that he knew about storytelling or how exactly he was using it, any more than he could explain how he was able to ride a bicycle. But in practice he was able to use storytelling to great effect in the political arena.

Narrative intelligence can be even more effective when its principles are made explicit, because then other people can learn how to use it.

The Central Role of Narrative Intelligence

In principle, the predominant role of storytelling in leadership communications about change shouldn't strike us as extraordinary, given the role that stories play in the human psyche and decision-making process. When we look carefully at the world, including the world of business and politics, it's easy to see the pervasive role that stories play.

In *The Rhetoric of Economics*, Deidre McCloskey has gleefully exposed the narratives that pervade even the writing of star economists like Paul Samuelson, Gary Becker, John Muth, and Robert Solow. My own book, *The Leader's Guide to Storytelling*, has documented the different narrative patterns available to leaders to achieve a variety of objectives, such as spark change, communicate who you are or what your brand means, get people working together, transmit values, share knowledge, tame the grapevine, generate innovation, or lead people into the future.

Yet there's something profoundly counterintuitive about the whole idea of narrative intelligence. We would all like to believe that it's substance that convinces, that analytic understanding must surely be more effective than any mere story, particularly a rudimentary story without rhetorical flourishes. It's hard to accept that something as primitive and old-fashioned as a bland narrative can be more powerful than analysis in the sophisticated business world of the twenty-first century.

What is even more challenging, though, is how far the idea of narrative intelligence may extend. What if storytelling was not only one communication tool among many but also a criterion for judging the effectiveness of all forms of communication directed toward action?

Many books discuss different ways to persuade. For instance, some books address using questions, like Michael Marquardt's *Leading with Questions*.[33] Other books suggest that the key to persuasion lies in using metaphors, like Anne Miller's *Metaphorically Selling*.[34] Other books, including Edward Tufte's *Visual Display of Quantitative Information*, suggest that the key to communication lies in the clever presentation of images.[35] Still others, including Susan Scott's *Fierce Conversations,* argue that conversations are the way to go.[36] Yet again, other books, like Mark Joyner's *The Irresistible Offer,* suggest that the secret to changing people's minds lies in making an extraordinary offer.[37] And some books extol the virtues of story, like Annette Simmons's *Story Factor.*[38]

Each of these books offers valuable insights for the particular communication tool under discussion; more on them in later chapters. Yet as we read these books and hear each author argue that this or that communication device is "the key" to persuasion, we are tempted to wonder if they aren't overstating the case for their chosen tool. Clearly, all these tools are useful in varying degrees in different contexts. But which context is appropriate? And why are these tools effective in some settings but not in others? Is there any principle, or set of principles, that could make sense of this smorgasbord? Is there some element, some organizing principle, something else that could start to make sense and give some coherence to this marketplace of competing vendors?

I believe the answer isn't too hard to find. If it's true that people think in narratives and make decisions in narratives, then should it be surprising that questions, metaphors, offers, images, and the like are effective to the extent that they generate a narrative in the mind of the listener? And would it not be plausible that the ability to gauge the likelihood of a suitable new story's being generated would be an important capability for anyone seriously engaged in trying to inspire change? If this is true, then we can start to get an idea of the real importance of narrative intelligence for leaders.

The concept of multiple intelligences was put forward in 1983 by Howard Gardner in *Frames of Mind: The Theory of Multiple Intelligences.*[39] Initially, he identified seven core intelligences: linguistic, logical-mathematical, spatial, bodily-kinesthetic, musical, interpersonal, and intrapersonal. More recently, an eighth—the naturalistic intelligence—has been added; work also continues on whether to add an existential intelligence. In addition, the concept of emotional intelligence originated with Wayne Payne in 1985, and was popularized by Daniel Goleman in 1995.[40] None of these intelligences cover what's involved in narrative intelligence, that is to say, an understanding of and a capacity to navigate through a world of interacting narratives.[41]

But what exactly do I mean by *narrative intelligence?* It's about understanding the world in narrative terms and grasping the pervasive role of narratives in all aspects of human existence. It concerns knowing the different components and dimensions of narratives. It's being familiar with the different patterns of stories that exist and knowing which narrative patterns are likely to have what effect in which situation. It's knowing how to overcome the fundamental attribution error and understand the audience's story. It's having the capacity to anticipate the dynamic factors that will determine how the audience will react to a new story. It's being able to judge whether a new story is likely to be generated in the mind of any particular audience by any particular communication tool.

How much is known about narrative intelligence? Even though there's not as much research as the topic could use, some of the basics are in place. Recognition of the foundational role of narrative in human behavior has been the subject of a rapidly growing body of psychological research.[42] The central role of narrative in leadership is confirmed by studies that show that stories are more effective than analytic reasons at persuasion.[43] And studies in social psychology show that information is more quickly and accurately remembered when it is first presented in the form of an example or story, particularly one that is intrinsically appealing.[44] There is also evidence that whereas abstract presentations depend on the credibility of the source of the material, effective stories tend to operate independently of the source's credibility. Once the audience is engaged by a compelling narrative, the perceived credibility of the source has diminishing influence.[45]

Do we have all the studies we need? Clearly not. More research is needed. The fact is that for a very long time psychologists tended to ignore storytelling because the dominant paradigm for research was that of the human brain as an abstract information processor. That view has been changing over recent decades. But we still have much to learn on many aspects of the subject, particularly on the different kinds of narrative patterns and the differential effects that they have, compared to each other and to other communication tools. But there's no need to wait for the further research before we get on with enhancing our own communications through narrative. Enough is known to make a dramatic difference in the impact of leadership communications. Overall, cultivating narrative intelligence will be a key enabler if leaders wish to get the full benefit using the language of leadership.

Appendix 3 offers a simple quiz for assessing your understanding of the explicit principles underpinning narrative intelligence.

Narrative intelligence by itself won't work unless it is founded on truthfulness. Al Gore was undone in 2000 in part by his tendency to embellish his stories. Even Ronald Reagan was handicapped by his casual attitude to veracity. What is truthfulness? Is it really necessary? It is to this issue that I now turn.

6

TELLING
TRUTHFUL
STORIES

> " The will to truth which will still tempt us to many
> a venture, that famous truthfulness of which all
> philosophers so far have spoken with respect—
> what questions has this will to truth not laid before us!
> What strange, wicked, questionable questions! "
>
> **—Friedrich Nietzsche[1]**

In the early morning of Wednesday, September 29, 1982, a twelve-year-old girl in Elk Grove Village, Illinois, swallowed a capsule of Extra Strength Tylenol. Shortly after that, she collapsed and died from cyanide poisoning. Within three days, six other people in the Chicago area had also died in a similar fashion. Investigators soon discovered the link between the deaths and poison in the Tylenol. Urgent warnings were broadcast, and police drove through Chicago neighborhoods issuing alerts over loudspeakers.

Since the poisoned bottles came from different factories, and the seven deaths had all occurred in the Chicago area, the sabotage couldn't have occurred at the factories of the manufacturer—a subsidiary of Johnson & Johnson. Instead, the culprit must have obtained Tylenol from stores over a period of weeks, adulterated their contents with cyanide, and then replaced the bottles. In addition to the five that led to the victims' deaths, three other cyanide-laced bottles were discovered.

What happened next has become business legend. Even though Johnson & Johnson didn't cause the problem, the CEO, James Burke, announced that his firm would take responsibility for it. Following its credo of giving first priority to protecting consumers ahead of giving returns to stockholders, on October 5, 1982, only seven days after the first death, Burke announced an immediate product recall from the entire country, which amounted to about 31 million bottles and a loss of more than $100 million.

The company also placed advertisements in the national media telling people not to consume any Tylenol. When it was determined that only capsules had been tampered with, it offered to exchange all Tylenol capsules already purchased by the public with solid tablets.

At the time of the scare the market share of Tylenol collapsed from 35 percent to 8 percent, but it rebounded in less than a year as a result of Johnson & Johnson's actions. Within a few years, Tylenol was the most popular over-the-counter pain reliever in the United States.

A key factor in Johnson & Johnson's decisive handling of the Tylenol crisis was its institutional credo, which gave clear guidance as to the course of action to take, namely, to give first priority to protecting consumers. Given the credo, prompt, full, truthful disclosure to the public and a product recall were obvious steps. As Johnson & Johnson's CEO James Burke said, "I think the answer comes down to the value system. . . . What's right works. It really does. The cynics will tell you it doesn't, but they're wrong."[2]

Even though the legend of the actions taken by Johnson & Johnson to deal with the crisis has been told over and over, the lessons are not always heeded. Thus when Exxon was faced with a crisis when the *Exxon Valdez* oil tanker spilled 11 million gallons of oil into Alaska's Prince William Sound in 1989, the company acted very differently.

When Exxon's spokesman first talked to the press, his answer was "no comment." This gave the impression that the firm was either hiding something or didn't know what was going on. This impression was reinforced when Exxon sent a team of individuals who were not trained in crisis management. It took ten days before Exxon ran an advertisement in the newspapers, and then it was only done locally. It was two weeks before Exxon's chairman, Lawrence G. Rawl, flew to Alaska.

The *Exxon Valdez* accident turned out to be one of the largest man-made environmental disasters ever to occur at sea. Exxon eventually spent more than $2 billion on the cleanup. As of late 2006, litigation on the amount of punitive damages assessed against Exxon for the spill was still continuing.

When you think about Johnson & Johnson's long-established credo, which had guided its decision making for decades, it is hardly a surprise that the CEO responded promptly and truthfully to the crisis, and in the process generated increased trust in both the firm and the brand. Equally, it's easy to see why Exxon leadership, without that kind of explicit and con-tinuously reinforced commitment to values, might improvise actions on the fly and give the impression the firm didn't care much about the envi-ronment or the damage to the tourism and fishery industries in Alaska.

Truthfulness in the Marketplace

In collaborative activities, truthfulness is the normal condition: decep-tiveness, or being less than forthcoming, is aberrational. Thus when the honeybee does her waggle-dance to tell her fellow honeybees the where-abouts of food, the truthfulness of the communication is crucial. Because it's truthful, the other honeybees can follow her directions and find the food, and so the hive flourishes. The beehive, like any collaborative enter-prise, rests on honesty and disclosure as central to its success.

Competitive situations are different. In *The Liar's Tale*, Jeremy Camp-bell reminds us that throughout nature, deceptiveness and nondisclosure are the norm in competitive situations. Does the spider warn a visiting insect of the prodigious stickiness of her web? Does the fox give any sign of feeling guilty about pretending to be dead, when it is very much on the alert, and famished? Does the leopard lying along a branch try to warn passers-by of danger? Throughout nature, in the harsh competition for survival, you can forget fair play and honesty and full disclosure. Decep-tion, dissembling, feints, and bluffs are the name of the game.[3]

Since transformational leadership is in essence a collaborative activity, the relevant model is the honeybee, not the spider, the fox, or the leopard. In leadership, truthfulness and integrity are essential. Lack of forthrightness or deliberate shading of the truth is devastating to trust and credibility: it undermines the possibility of enduring enthusiasm. Even an apparent lack of openness, as in the Exxon case, can be disastrous.

The marketplace presents interesting issues for transformational leadership since it inevitably comprises a mix of collaboration and competition. On one hand, vis-à-vis competitors, participants face a cutthroat struggle for survival. It's a world of one-upmanship, cunning, gamesmanship, outfoxing, outsmarting, or outwitting the competition. Only the toughest manage to survive, let alone flourish.

On the other hand, vis-à-vis customers, sellers aspire to win trust so that people become return customers and even enthusiasts on behalf of the firm, perhaps becoming brand evangelists to recruit new customers.

Problems begin when sellers start applying the deceptive modalities of competition to their relationships with customers. For instance, when sellers use the kinds of manipulative tools surveyed in Chapter Five—hype, halo effect, spin, bait and switch, groupthink, imposition of authority, celebrity pressure, and artificial scarcity—and try to manipulate people by surreptitious means to make decisions they wouldn't otherwise make, the risk of undermining long-run trust is considerable.

In the marketplace, the tension between competition and collaboration is always in play. The dilemmas can be acute for individuals. In leadership workshops, I am asked: "Do we really have to tell the truth? Surely it's advisable, even necessary, on occasion, to be 'economical with the truth' to be successful in selling and marketing? How will we ever make our sales quotas if we are completely truthful? Is everyone else strictly honest? Is this being unrealistic?"

The answer to those questions is both obvious and difficult. It's obvious in the sense that if the objective is transformational leadership, namely, to achieve the enduring enthusiasm of customers, truthfulness is crucial. Leaders have no choice: truth is their currency. Shading the truth may yield benefits in the short run and even result in a quick killing in the sense of a sale and a profit, but it also risks a "killing" in a different sense, that is, the death of trust. The practices of deception—shading the truth, less-than-full disclosure—and the manipulative weapons of influence don't constitute a sound long-term basis for generating enduring enthusiasm for a product, a service, a brand, or an organization. To be a transformational leader and inspire enduring enthusiasm, there's really no choice: truth-telling is foundational.

And yet the answer is also difficult. The temptation in the marketplace to slide into deceptive, dissembling, manipulative practices in order to make the short-run sale is always there. Salespeople say: "If our competitors are doing it, why not us? And if our earnings depend totally on short-term sales, with no reference to long-term impact, how can we not focus on short-term sales and do whatever is necessary to win? It's irresistible." And of course, in a sense, they're right. In the absence of clear, explicit values, continuously restated and reinforced by the management and embodied in their own conduct, as at Johnson & Johnson, it's easy to see how truth-telling can fall by the wayside and how the deceptive, dissembling, manipulative practices of competition can take over.

In the world of branding, the temptation to shade the truth is even stronger, especially now that companies have discovered how consumers can develop strong relationships with their brands in an anthropological sense, despite the lack of any real distinctiveness of the underlying products or services. Marketers don't need a product that is physically different: even pure commodities can become strongly differentiated in customers' minds: soap, flour, salt, oatmeal, even water.

Perpetuating the impression of a meaningful difference can, however, become immensely expensive when there is no underlying difference, because of the need for a never-ending supply of new branding messages to perpetuate the impression. But even so, for many companies, the investment of large sums of money to this end has in some cases appeared cost-effective. Brands relying on a perception of difference based on impressions and associations rather than any real underlying difference may even become the most valuable asset on a firm's balance sheet.

Some marketers endorse such practices and even urge firms to set aside any notion of truth, crafting stories that will resonate with customers regardless of whether they are true.[4] On this view, even trying to tell the truth in the marketplace is a losing strategy. Instead, marketers should tell great stories about their products that play to consumers' self-regard and worldview. Making up stories is justified, because "consumers demand it. . . . It doesn't matter one bit whether something is actually better or faster or more efficient. What matters is what the consumer believes."[5]

Although this approach of saying whatever you can get away with may have short-run gains, in terms of long-term trust and enduring enthusiasm, it is a frequently trod path to disaster. "Doing the right thing pays off. Storytellers who trick consumers get caught. They become inconsistent and sooner or later they get punished."[6]

Authentically Communicating Distinctiveness

Being a leader in the marketplace entails first making a commitment to truth and authenticity—eliminating any untruthfulness inside the firm as well as outside. In terms of marketing, the firm needs to make sure what it's saying is true before it advertises in the marketplace. The task of authentic leadership in the marketplace is not to convince the world that the firm is distinctive when it isn't but rather to communicate a reality that already exists. If the firm isn't already consistently distinctive, then the task is to make it so—before any attempt to communicate that distinctiveness to customers. In effect, companies need to fix the firm *inside* before going *outside.*

Conceptually, there are three ways of communicating distinctiveness in an authentic way. One is to tell *the story of the firm itself.* This is the story of where the firm came from, how it grew, what values it acquired along the way, and where it is heading. Some of the mystique of Apple Computer and Microsoft comes from the stories of the early creation of those companies by Steve Jobs and Bill Gates respectively. Southwest

Airlines is a story of people living life to the fullest, with humor and a sense of fun, being free to "roam about the country" because the airline makes it affordable to do so by providing cheap, reliable, entertaining flights to popular destinations. Its brand narrative is closely linked to the wit and character of its founder, Herb Kelleher. And at Costco, co-founder and CEO Jim Sinegal regularly uses stories of how he has built the firm by a continuing commitment to provide high-quality, low-cost products to customers, rather than raise margins, so as to convey the firm's corporate values and to illustrate how those values are being brought to life throughout the company.

The second way of communicating the brand is something that looks obvious but in fact isn't. It's the *story of the products and services* themselves. If you want to communicate what's distinctive about your products or services, why not just tell people exactly that? Why not simply tell the story of those products and services? The problem here is that in the atmosphere of cynicism and distrust that prevails in today's marketplace, it's hard for any company to tell credible stories about its products and services. Given the track record of firms telling half-truths or quarter-truths or even straight-out untruths, people have gotten into the habit of discounting most of what they hear directly from marketers.

So what's a company to do? One approach is for the firm itself to opt out of trying to tell the story of its products and services, using few advertisements or none. Instead it seeks to rely on its customers' delighted response to those products and services to tell and retell that story. Thus Google is a highly valued and valuable company, not because of its clever advertisements, but because hundreds of millions of people find its software pleasant and easy to use, and they are happy to tell their friends and colleagues about it. And Starbucks is a highly valued company, not because of large sums of money given to talented ad agencies and PR firms or rock stars, but rather because people around the world enjoy its coffee shops and their products, and are willing to pass on that message. These companies spend little money and energy on issuing advertisements for themselves or trying to tell their story. Instead they focus their energies on providing high-quality products and services that consistently delight their customers, who in turn tell the story more credibly than the firm's marketing department ever could.

These companies' objective is not just to make sales, rather to convert customers into enthusiasts so that they share the company's belief that its activities are worthwhile in themselves. Ideally, the customers believe in the company's products or services to such an extent that they feel compelled to spread the word and voluntarily recruit their friends and colleagues on the firm's behalf. Most of this happens by word of mouth, face-to-face. Although there is a lot of talk about the impact of the Internet, blogs, and chat rooms, when it comes to word of mouth, research indicates that around 90 percent of it occurs offline.[7]

Customers are likely to become brand evangelists only if they are consistently delighted by what the company does. This in turn is only likely to happen on a sustained basis if the company itself exhibits the values of truthfulness, constancy, and integrity in its dealings with its customers.

The third way of communicating the brand is even less obvious: to *tell the story of the client*. In *How Brands Become Icons*, Douglas Holt argues that for any strong brand, there is a certain kind of person who loves, or could love, the brand. If the seller can understand the story of this person and tell that story, it can resonate and help turn the brand into an icon.

Thus Volkswagen has a track record of appealing to iconoclasts. When it presented itself as a company that made cars for iconoclasts in the 1960s and 1970s, it was hugely successful. In the 1980s and early 1990s, when it appeared to forget this part of its history and presented itself as a maker of cars for everybody, albeit higher-quality cars, it lost ground in the marketplace. In the late 1990s, when it suddenly remembered that its core clientele had been iconoclasts, it once again prospered.[8]

In a similar vein, Budweiser offers its jokey television ads that suggest that these funny people kidding around and having a good time together are the kind of people who drink Budweiser beer. The implication is that anyone could be as funny, and have as good a time, if only they also drank Budweiser. The ads appear to be successful in promoting the brand, even though the underlying logic is not exactly rock-solid. Although in today's marketplace, the ads can make the sale, the question for the longer term is whether they are building enduring enthusiasm for the brand. At best, the continued strength of a brand based on such evanescent associations will depend on disseminating a never-ending supply of new stories in an effort to perpetuate the "impression" of Budweiser's distinctiveness.

From Sales Pitch to Trusted Partnership

Given the risk of incurring long-term costs by employing less-than-truthful practices aimed at short-term gains and sales, some firms are exploring the possibility of reaching a more stable plane—to shift from making sales pitches to becoming trusted partners. These companies aspire to become reliable collaborators with their clients, so that clients look to them for advice and dialogue about issues of common concern. Here the conversation aims less at achieving immediate sales and more at ensuring that the firm's products and services will receive positive consideration when the time comes to make decisions about purchases. The object is higher margins, more repeat business, lower price sensitivity, and shorter sales cycles. In assessing what's involved in moving from "sales pitch" to "trusted partnership," these companies are having to reflect on what is involved in the phenomenon of trust. What kinds of behavior lead to trust, as opposed to behaviors that lead to distrust?

A sales pitch works in the "exchange economy" and it's quid pro quo. Sellers are typically only willing to do something if there's something of monetary value in it for themselves. In the marketplace, the sales pitch often amounts to saying what you can get away with in order to make the sale. The competitive practices of spin, hype, and the weapons of influence are rampant.

Social scientists have shown that trust is generated by very different, collaborative behaviors. This is sometimes referred to as the "gift economy." In this world, people do things out of a spirit of generosity and make contributions without any clear expectations of a quid pro quo. A scientific community is an example of this kind of interchange. People write papers and contribute to conferences. In doing so, they have no guarantee of getting anything back in return for making those contributions to the community. They may receive eventual benefits: they may win respect and renown or be offered academic positions or be invited to write books or even win prizes. But none of this is guaranteed or agreed or made explicit in advance. Participants make their contributions and they take their chances as to whether or when they will get anything back in return.

In a scientific community, certain behaviors are respected because they lead to trust. Most scientists are transparently honest. They are careful about what is being claimed and what is not being claimed. They are scrupulous not to overstate benefits or to understate costs or risks. They are always on the lookout for alternative interpretations. They are careful to give credit to the work on which they are building. They talk confidently only about what they definitely know. If they speculate or hazard a guess, they explicitly describe it as such. If they don't know, they admit ignorance. Any hint of oversell is anathema in this world; any scientist who engages in it risks being ejected from the community.

Similarly, in the pharmaceutical industry, strict laws and careful enforcement by agencies like the FDA have to a certain extent created analogous practices. Drugs are rigorously tested for effectiveness and side effects before they are put on the market. Drugs that fail to deliver significant new benefits are withheld from the market, even if huge expenditures have been made in their development. Claims made for a drug are required by law to be supported by rigorous scientific testing. Supplementary actions needed to garner the benefits of a drug are made explicit at the time of sale. Risks are quantified and made explicit to doctors and consumers at the time of purchase. Side effects are stringently scrutinized and quantified. Discovered flaws are communicated systematically and promptly to doctors and consumers. Drugs can be withdrawn from the market if newly discovered flaws put in question the original hoped-for benefits. Although the advertisements of pharmaceutical companies are often characterized by use of the weapons of influence, the claims made for any particular product must by law be supported by rigorous, objective evidence.[9]

In other industries, the practices are very different. For instance, in the software industry, products are tested for effectiveness before they are put on the market, but it is normal for bugs to appear after the release of the product, usually to be remedied by subsequent releases of the software. Successive versions are launched, sometimes effectively forcing users to upgrade both software and hardware, even if the incremental benefits to them are not obvious. Claims made for software are not always supported by rigorous scientific testing. "Outstanding" exploitation of the software is sometimes portrayed as what the average user should expect, or even what every user could expect. Significant supplementary actions needed to garner the benefits of software, such as training and support, are not always made explicit at the time of sale. Sales presentations do not always highlight the risk involved in realigning an organization's entire business strategy or in making the major shifts in organizational culture required to realize the promised benefits. Dissemination of information on the levels of failure to generate expected benefits is rare. Flaws, when discovered, are not always systematically and promptly communicated to all users. Software is rarely withdrawn from the market or refunds offered, even if newly discovered flaws put in question the original hoped-for benefits.

The reasons for these practices in the software industry are understandable. The interaction of products with many other types of software and hardware is so diverse that bug-free software is said to be an impossible dream. Users are sometimes more interested in getting timely updates of software than in avoiding risks from flawed product releases. Experienced users understand the level of oversell normal in the industry and are forced to adopt an attitude of "buyer beware."

Nevertheless, the level of trust generated by such practices is unlikely to be high. To the extent that these behaviors are being used to establish the relationship of trusted partner, companies wishing to become trusted partners will need to review their appropriateness. Customers in a "buyer beware" mind-set take everything a vendor says with a substantial grain of salt and are unlikely to view the relationship as a partnership.

Companies may also need to consider when they conduct dialogue with clients with the aim of establishing the relationship of trusted partner, systematically emphasizing and encouraging known trust-building behaviors:

- *Showing real concern for the interests of counterparts:* In trusting relationships, participants show genuine interest in the problems of the people they are dealing with, even if there is nothing in it for themselves.

- *Revealing vulnerability.* Trust entails asking people to put their faith in someone, even though they have no certainty that that faith will be honored. In effect, participants make themselves vulnerable. By contrast, if the party seeking to be trusted holds itself invulnerable, never admitting or risking anything, then the lack of reciprocity may raise a question in the listeners as to whether a relationship of trust is warranted.

- *Sharing something of value early on.* When people visit someone's house for the first time, they may bring a small gift to signify that they come in a spirit of friendship. This behavior encourages trust to develop. Analogous behavior by a company, for example, offering free knowledge or samples of new products, may also help to initiate trust.

- *Meshing with what has gone before.* In making a sales pitch, the emphasis of the storytelling is usually on the "telling": pointing out features and benefits that have been identified by the seller in advance. By contrast, in a trusted partnership, the process begins with "story listening," that is, understanding the customers and their story—their dreams, their hopes, their fears, their current problems, what's making them tick. This means listening to what the customers are saying as well as what they are not saying.

- *Willingness to learn.* Readiness to learn also helps generate trust. In a relationship of mutual trust, participants don't come to the discussion with the attitude: "I'm not interested in what your situation is; I'm here to tell you what you should know." If they do this, it's likely that the behavior will undermine trust. Instead, a willingness to learn from, and understand, the listener's story helps build reciprocity and mutual trust.

Transforming traditional sales practices into trusted partner behavior will be a significant shift for some organizations. Some staff may be ready and waiting for the transition, while others will be more comfortable with the sales pitch. Leadership entails inspiring everyone to adopt the new practices.

Truthfulness in the March to War

Transformational leadership is rare in politics, and when it occurs, it may take us, as with Abraham Lincoln, in the welcome direction of a new birth of freedom. But when presidents become leaders in pursuit of preemptive military causes, the results can be ugly. The sequence is depressingly familiar with wars of choice.

For politicians to persuade a country at peace to become enthusiastic about launching a preemptive war against another country, they usually have to demonize the enemy, exaggerate the offences it has caused, minimize the difficulties that will occur in the prosecution of the war, and exaggerate the benefits that will ensue.

Once the war is launched, the war can be glamorized with celebrations of the bravery of young soldiers. Any who object to the war can be victimized as dishonoring the troops or emboldening the enemy. As the inevitable difficulties emerge, there are calls to stay the course, so that those soldiers who have already died will not have died in vain.

As the reality of the origins of the war and the difficulties of implementation become apparent, recriminations against those who misled the nation into war are muted by a fear of disregard for those who have died in the cause. Calls for victory continue, and vitriolic criticism is launched against those who want to "run up the white flag of surrender" and "admit defeat." As a result, the war often drags on long after the reasons for fighting it in the first place have evaporated.

Most of these phenomena could be observed in the First World War. Although governments had always used various kinds of persuasion to encourage support for wars, it was in 1915 that governments first systematically deployed the entire range of modern media to deploy propaganda and rouse their populations to emotional assent by demonizing "the Hun" and by presenting the war as a transcendent clash between "civilization" and "Prussian barbarism."

Although the term *propaganda* fell into disrepute, its practice to sell wars didn't end. Thus, in 1965, the White House and Pentagon used misleading military rationales to frighten the American people to elicit initial popular acquiescence in the war in Vietnam.[10] President Lyndon Johnson launched the war based on attacks on supposedly nonbelligerent U.S. ships in the Gulf of Tonkin and on the argument that an international communist conspiracy headquartered in Moscow and Beijing was driving the Vietnamese revolutionary movement. Johnson used the rhetoric of "liberation," "freedom," and "democracy" to justify the intervention. Throughout the struggle, the story was told that if Vietnam fell, American prestige would suffer an immeasurable loss and the rest of Asia, and possibly the world, would fall "like dominos" into the hands of the communists.

In the result, after the U.S. departure in 1973, South Vietnam was overrun by North Vietnam in 1975. But the rest of Asia didn't fall like dominos into communism. Instead, the other countries remained staunchly anticommunist. In due course, Vietnam became one of the fastest-growing free-market economies in the world. Although government and political life is firmly controlled by the Communist Party of Vietnam, neither Vietnam nor its neighbors represent any threat to the United States, as confirmed by successive state visits of U.S. presidents in 2000 and 2006. In retrospect, it is now evident that the supporters of the Vietnam War were living the wrong story: they mistook a local civil war for a major international menace.

Now a similar sequence is playing itself out in Iraq.[11] The war was launched by the United States and its coalition partners in 2003, using a set of stories (outlined in Table 6.1) that reflect the communication tools discussed in this book.

TABLE 6.1   Stories of the Iraq War

Getting attention	Stimulating desire	Reinforcing with reasons
Saddam Hussein is an accomplice of the terrorists who carried out the 9/11 attacks.	A preemptive war will be a quick and easy way to exact revenge on the terrorists behind 9/11.	The United States will gain valuable military bases in the region and have access to large oil reserves.
Saddam Hussein's weapons of mass destruction are an imminent threat to the United States, Europe, and Israel.	The war will eliminate an imminent threat from nuclear attack.	Because Iraq has oil, the war will essentially pay for itself.
Saddam Hussein is an unstable dictator who oppresses his people.	A relatively small armed force will be sufficient to liberate the country from the tyrant.	The U.S. forces will be greeted as liberators.

Sadly, most of the stories used to launch the war turned out to be false:

- Saddam Hussein was a vicious dictator, but he had no significant connection with the terrorists of September 11, 2001, and had no weapons of mass destruction.[12]

- While the immediate invasion of Iraq was quick and relatively easy, the subsequent anti-American insurgency proved to be large and difficult to deal with. The occupying armies were soon caught in the crossfire among different Iraqi factions.

- As some military experts had predicted, the armed force used was too small to pacify a country the size of Iraq. Even so, the war turned out to be expensive, consuming around $400 billion by the end of 2006. The prospect of permanent access to military bases and oil became increasingly problematic.

- Popular support in the United States for the war was initially strong, but it faltered in 2005 and collapsed by late 2006, even as fighting continued. In the end, the U.S. invasion had unwittingly turned Iraq into a breeding ground for terrorists—the very objective that the war was intended to prevent.

Should we blame storytelling and the language of leadership for getting the United States and its partners into misguided wars? Certainly the experience suggests that we should be on our guard to verify the stories used by politicians to persuade us into a war of choice.

Storytelling, like any powerful tool, can be used for benign or malign purposes. Vietnam and Iraq show us both the force of storytelling and the consequences of its misuse. Among the many lessons that we can learn are that when a war of choice is being considered, we should verify the stories. Are they true? We should take the time to gather the evidence and pay attention to expert advice on the feasibility of future plans. Examination of risk is critical. What is the best that can happen? What is the worst that can happen? What are the probabilities of different outcomes? What is not known that could affect the outcome? We should be willing to learn from prior experience.

Truthfulness is not just a quality of the mind. It must be reflected in the entire person—mind, body, and soul—and reflected in the body language of the leader. It is to this issue that I turn in Chapter Seven.

7

LEADERSHIP PRESENCE

The Body Language of Leadership

> " It is no surprise that conductors live so long, as they spend their life constantly exercising and bringing into harmony body, emotion and thought. "
>
> **—Peter Brook[1]**

What is leadership presence? Is it something mysterious or magical? How did great actors and great leaders come to possess it? Were they born with it? Can it be learned?

Whatever it is, it's important. Without it, no one listens. Without it, our opinions get no respect. Without it, we're not taken seriously. Without it, it's hard to be a leader.

In their interesting book, *Leadership Presence*, Belle Linda Halpern and Kathy Lubar define presence as "the ability to connect authentically with the thoughts and feelings of others."[2] I've already discussed some of the elements that contribute to presence in that sense: having a commitment to a clear and inspiring goal, while being aware of your own story and being attuned to the story of your listener. But this chapter is concerned with something else—the physical things we do with our body when we are trying to communicate.

If we're able to project our energy so that it energizes others, and so that our thinking, our feeling, our verbal messages, and our bodily movements are all congruent, that can hugely reinforce what we are trying to communicate. If our body language contradicts what we are saying, it will distract from or undermine our intended message.

Why is body language so important? One reason is that listeners are not just fluent readers of body language. They are acutely aware of the slightest bodily cues a speaker gives, wittingly or unwittingly, and can infer immediately what they mean. Remember when President George H. W. Bush glanced at his watch in the middle of a presidential debate in 1992? Viewers immediately jumped to the conclusion: Bush wants the debate to be over.

Whatever leaders communicate through their body language will usually speak louder than their spoken words, because listeners will conclude that the body language is what the speaker really feels and means, even if the words are saying something else. So although this book devotes less space to the body language of leadership than to verbal language, in performance, body language is at least as important.[3]

Some of the more interesting insights on body language from the world of animal trainers. Vicki Hearne's wonderful book, *Adam's Task*, notes that the people who come to visit the wild animals she works with fall into several categories. First, there are the people with super-sized egos, which she calls "Hollywood types": they are self-absorbed and indifferent to where they are. Their pompous strutting is essentially irrelevant to, and ignored by, the animals.

Then there are the "researchers" who are testing abstract propositions on the animals. These people are, she says, "contaminated by epistemology." Around dogs, they are what she calls "bitees," that is, the people most likely to be bitten as a result of the dogs' frustration at their combination of intrusiveness and unresponsiveness.

Finally, there are the "animal trainers," who exhibit soft, acute, 360-degree awareness of who they are and who else is there. In the very way they move, they offer mute acknowledgment of the presence of the animals and fit into the spaces shaped by their perceptions. It's precisely this "soft, acute, 360-degree awareness" that leaders need to exhibit in relation to the people they are seeking to lead.[4]

What Hearne is talking about is the body language of leadership that Cesar Millan teaches to dog owners, which I discussed in Chapter One.

What Millan is good at demonstrating in his amusing program, *The Dog Whisperer,* which can be watched on National Geographic television or on the Web, is the calm assertiveness of leadership.[5] In his program, owner after owner learns to establish "presence" through the calm assertive behavior that establishes someone as a leader.

Millan demonstrates with his own body language the difference between being assertive and being aggressive. The body language of aggressive behavior communicates the risk of some kind of imminent attack on the listener, as when the "look of an angry hawk" came over Howell Raines when he was talking to his staff. I don't believe Raines actually meant any bodily or other harm to his listeners, but that's not what the listeners took away from the encounter. If leaders' behavior looks aggressive, their listeners will wonder what's going to happen next. And they may be aggressive in response, perhaps not immediately, but, as in Howell Raines's case, later on, when counterattack becomes possible. It's not a reasoned response; it's an emotional reaction of the reptilian brain to aggressive behavior.

The calm assertiveness of real leadership implies energy, but energy that has been harnessed, energy that offers no direct threat to the audience. Outward calm communicates an absence of hidden tensions with which the speaker is wrestling, hidden tensions that might break out at any moment and hurt someone. Calm assertiveness means confirming in our outward demeanor that we are in control of our own fears and desires. In acting thus, we show that we are there for the audience, ready to give them full attention, available to listen and to interact with them and to offer an invitation to the future.

One piece of good news from Cesar Millan's work is that the agenda of things a leader has to learn is not huge. It's calm assertiveness, with head held high, square shoulders, appropriate eye contact, and being there for the dog. And what's even better news, once the dog owner does that limited number of things, the dog instantly accepts the dog owner as a leader.

The rapidity of learning that Millan's work demonstrates jibes with my own experience in training executives as leaders of people. In terms of body language, they need only take care of a limited number of basics to establish presence. Those basics can be mastered easily and quickly. With these basics in place, the speaker captures the attention of the audience for the duration of the speech. An audience is always ready to listen to anyone who exhibits the body language of leadership.

Now just doing these few basics won't turn you into Laurence Olivier or Meryl Streep or Winston Churchill. The subtleties and nuances to learn about body language and presence are infinite and you could spend a lifetime steadily enhancing your mastery of them. But the immediate progress that can be made in taking care of the basics of the body language of leadership is enough for most leaders to move from "boring" to "extraordinary."

And What Are Those Basics?

The most important element is eye contact. Leadership is a highly interactive phenomenon, and eye contact is the highway on which the interaction takes place. You look directly at the audience, person by person, not sideways, which may be interpreted as shiftiness. You establish eye contact with all the people in the room, particularly people in the back corners. You symbolize through eye contact that you are ready to converse with everyone who is there.

The second element follows from the first: throw away your notes. You can't have eye contact with an audience if you are reading from notes. They are an obstacle to eye contact. They also symbolize a physical barrier between you and the audience. Any physical thing between you and the audience—even a piece of paper—blocks the flow of psychic energy. Moreover, if you are reading from notes, you can't be fully present. By reading from notes, you are signaling that you aren't speaking for yourself, from your heart: you are a messenger reading a message devised at another time. Perhaps the author was you—perhaps it was another person. It hardly matters: the overriding implication of reading from notes is that you are not fully present for the audience at this moment to interact with them. You have become a mere courier, not a leader.

Next, if you can, get out from behind any podium between you and the audience. Podiums get in the way of direct bodily communication. Like any physical object between you and the audience, they block the flow of psychic energy. Subliminally the audience may see you as hiding from them. Let the audience see you without anything between you and them.

Then make sure that you maintain an open body stance, square shoulders, relaxed, calm, assertive, with a total focus on the audience. By doing this, you signify that you are there for the audience. And if you are there for them, they will be there for you.

You use gesture to signify that it's not just your mind communicating. Gestures convey that your whole body is behind what you're saying. You make sure your gestures are in sync with the content of what you are saying. Gestures serve as a kind of visual punctuation to the words. They should also reflect contagious energy and enthusiasm. Stiff or jerky gestures may be interpreted as inner tension and lack of resolution. Here again, gestures should reflect calm assertiveness, signifying personal mastery of your message.

Finally, you plant your feet firmly on the ground and face the audience squarely and openly. If need be, wiggle your toes to remind yourself not to perambulate, which is massively distracting. In particular, don't walk from side to side across the speaker's platform. The audience will interpret this as restlessness, lack of calmness, and perhaps even a hidden wish to quit the room. If you must move, then move toward the audience to indicate a wish to be closer and more interactive with them. Choose different individuals in the audience and move toward them successively. This will be interpreted as a wish to connect and engage, rather than escape.

These elements may sound mundane, even trivial, but believe me, the difference between someone who is respecting these simple principles and someone who isn't is stark. With these limited number of basics in place, leaders will quickly see a dramatic difference in their impact on an audience.

Beyond those basics, there are of course many more nuances of leadership presence. Those readers who would like to explore the subject in depth might consult some of the many interesting books on the subject, such as *Leadership Presence* by Belle Linda Halpern and Kathy Lubar, mentioned earlier, as well as *The Definitive Book of Body Language* by Allan and Barbara Pease, or the *Book of Tells* by Peter Collett.[6]

Practice, Practice, Practice

We often put so much time and energy into the content of what we are to say that we don't allow time to work on how we are going to say it. We repeatedly overlook the fact that if we don't use the right body language and "sound like we mean it," our presentation is going nowhere.

Why do we make this mistake? It's partly our schooling. But there's more. Deep down, as Malcolm Gladwell points out, "we all want to believe that the key to having an impact on someone lies with the inherent quality of the ideas we present."[7] We want to see ourselves as people of substance, not merely people with a persuasive style. The reality is that how we present our ideas is going to be a huge part of determining whether our ideas are accepted or ignored.

Style can't be separated from the substance. The content of the leader's story is only a part of the impact. What gives it force and meaning for the listener is the leader's calm, energy, and enthusiasm.

In the course of delivering the communication, there is no division between style and content. Leaders are both style and content. Listeners don't get a carton of content and a dollop of style. They get a cocktail where style and content are all mixed in together.

With calm assertiveness, even the simplest, most mundane and everyday things can come to seem wonderful, magical, even hallowed. The stories I've quoted in this book that have inspired others to make fundamental changes in behavior aren't in themselves particularly striking. Craig Dunn's story about an insurance agent who helps an invalid or the stories J. Allard and Steven Sinofsky told about what was happening in Cornell were not inherently mesmerizing. Leaders take ordinary occurrences and invest them with significance. In leadership, it's not the story itself that is striking—it's the linkage the stories have to other things, to the survival of AMP or to the future of software in the world as personified in the performance of the story, that makes the difference.

The people telling those stories felt that they really mattered. By communicating that feeling, they made the stories matter to their audiences. The stories acquired significance in the telling. It wasn't the stories themselves that were extraordinary—it was the psychic energy that the speakers invested in them that made them extraordinary to the listeners.

For the duration of the performance the speaker embodies the idea. When leaders have a firm conviction in their minds, their stories become holistic. When they re-experience and re-tell the story, they become the story: they are at one with the audience, with themselves, and with their message. Their voice expresses. Their demeanor expresses. The way they hold their body expresses. Their tone of voice expresses. The look in their eyes expresses. In this way, leaders communicate their true nature in the simplest, most direct way, as one living being to another.

Performance is a matter of bringing into harmony body, emotion, and thought. It draws on all elements: "on their bodies like athletes and dancers, on their feelings like singers and lovers, and on their minds like mathematicians and thinkers."[8]

And leaders develop this capability by practice. It's practice, practice, practice, and then more practice. There is no end to practice.

At first, progress is generally rapid. To acquire the skills needed to do a modestly competent job of incorporating stories into an effective leadership presentation is not particularly difficult. People already do this effortlessly in a social setting. All they need is to transpose skills they already have to more purposeful settings.

What takes time is going beyond this modest competence and really mastering the art. After their initial rapid progress, leaders realize that they are no longer progressing leaps and bounds. Even though they try very hard, the progress they make is gradual. It's like playing the piano or learning how to speak a foreign language: after moving rapidly through the basics, you begin to make slow, imperceptible progress over long periods of time.

As leaders' skills mellow, their experience becomes deeper and more meaningful, both to themselves and to their audience. They will not be able to say why precisely. But subtle, indefinable elements will enter into the performance, elements that weren't there before. They will succeed in putting more of themselves in what they say. They will find more resonance between themselves and their audiences.

As performers, they will in a sense be getting better, even though leadership isn't really about getting "better." It's about connecting in a single moment with the particular individuals who happen to be in front of them on each individual occasion. To be sincere, speaking the language of leadership from the heart and making a full effort to communicate what you know, may often be enough. The listeners will recognize good intent and help rectify any defects in performance skills by hearing what was meant to be said.

Do Leaders Need Charisma?

The body language of leadership is not to be confused with charisma—a characteristic that some writers wrongly suggest is an essential element of leadership. Charismatic leaders, it is said, appear "so extraordinary, due to their strategic insight, strong convictions, self-confidence, unconventional behavior and dynamic energy that followers idolize them and want to become like them."[9]

We've been living for a long time with the legend of the born leader, the colorful charismatic, the innate firebrand who walks into a room and electrifies everyone with sheer physical presence. The fact is that the charismatics—Gandhi, Martin Luther King Jr., Steve Jobs—lacked any particular physical characteristics that made them charismatic. Such people do exist in the world: the film star good looks of John F. Kennedy come to mind. But they are rare. The brute fact is that most successful leaders are quite ordinary in physical appearance. Overall, the idea that some kind of innate physical charisma is required for leadership is a pernicious myth.[10]

Take one of the most charismatic individuals of the twentieth century: Mohandas Karamchand Gandhi. (*Mahatma*, meaning "great soul," was an honorific title he acquired.) Gandhi led an extraordinary life, fusing the ascetic ideals of the ancient Hindu religion and culture with some revolutionary ideas for generating political change through *satyagraha:* "force born of truth and love or nonviolence." His efforts were successful in mobilizing the Indian population of South Africa and then in leading the entire Indian nation to independence. His example, preaching truth and nonviolence, inspired leaders in many countries around the world to emulate his example. When he was assassinated in 1948, practically the whole world mourned him. He was compared to Socrates, to Buddha, to Jesus and St. Francis of Assisi.

His life has been the subject of hundreds of biographies. Jawaharlal Nehru has written: "No man can write a real life of Gandhi, unless he is as big as Gandhi." He was a man "whose eyes were often full of laughter and yet were pools of infinite sadness." He was "a pilgrim on a quest for Truth, quiet, peaceful, determined, fearless, who would continue that quest and pilgrimage, regardless of the consequences." Gandhi "invested many of his gestures with special symbolic meaning, and at one point or another somebody has sanctified his every action and utterance, so that today in India— and elsewhere—there exists not one Gandhi, but hundreds of Gandhis."[11]

Yet the extraordinary charismatic qualities that were so obvious in Gandhi after his achievements were apparently invisible to others before those achievements. He was a short, thin, and sickly child. He was an indifferent student who found schoolwork hard. He envied the big, strong boys who were good at sports like cricket and gymnastics, at which he performed poorly. A photo of him at the time shows not so much eyes that were pools of infinite sadness as eyes displaying a hunted, apprehensive look. With his large nose, he was an ugly young man, something that he eventually became proud of, claiming to be "the ugliest man in the world." He was married by his parents at the age of thirteen to a girl his own age, and, already demonstrating a healthy sexual appetite, consummated the marriage that night. He was a jealous and imperious young husband, forbidding his young wife to go anywhere, while declaring that he found her company tedious.

Having decided to become a lawyer, he opted to pursue, not a rigorous legal education in India, but the path of an expensive dilettante, reading for the English bar in London, an approach that required no coursework and involved passing simple examinations that were practically a formality.

In England, Gandhi set out to become an Englishman. He bought Western clothes. He took up ballroom dancing. He took up elocution lessons for a while, but eventually concluded that his efforts to become an Englishman were futile. Instead he spent much of his time pursuing various vegetarian causes, "to the irritation of practically everyone, Indian or English, whom he came to know."[12]

After three years in London, he returned to India, and he set up a legal practice, first in Rajkot and then in Bombay. When he finally obtained a case to argue, he stood in front of the court and couldn't think of a single question; he had to sit down and give the brief to a colleague. After that, he didn't get another case.

On one occasion, he interceded on behalf of his brother, who was angling for the prime ministership of the tiny princely kingdom of Porbandar. Apparently his brother had offended the British political agent on whom his career depended, and so Gandhi, who had casually met the agent in London, took up his brother's cause. The agent told Gandhi that if his brother felt that he had been wronged, he could apply through the proper channels. When Gandhi persisted, the agent told him to leave. And when Gandhi continued to argue, the agent had his servant take hold of Gandhi and throw him physically out of his office.

At this point in his life, Gandhi was the very antithesis of charisma. He was unattractive in appearance. He was graceless in manners. He was lacking in tact. In private, he was annoyingly persistent. In public, he was too shy to open his mouth. He was unable to earn an income as a lawyer. If his eyes were "pools of infinite sadness," there is no record of people noticing it at the time.

The fact is that Gandhi's charisma was the result, not the cause, of his accomplishments. No one sensed an inkling of charisma until after he had made up his mind what he wanted to do with his life, which occurred after an incident of racial discrimination in South Africa: he was holding a first-class ticket, but he was thrown off the train by a white guard at the request of a white man, and left shivering in a dark waiting room. Within a week of the incident, he convened a meeting of the Indians of Pretoria and delivered an address on white discrimination. It was his first public speech. Passion for the cause dissolved his shyness. He found the words needed to communicate his commitment. And so began a long journey as an agent of change, first in South Africa and then in India. It was only *after* he had success in influencing people that people began to think of Gandhi as having charisma.

Academic research confirms the same phenomenon at more mundane levels. For instance, Nancy Roberts of the University of Minnesota has written movingly of a highly successful school superintendent of a district in the Mid-West. When she was appointed to her position, the superintendent was not perceived as charismatic. It was only after she had been in the position for several years and the change process that she launched was well under way that people began to think of her as charismatic. This wasn't the inevitable result of extraordinary personal qualities but rather the result of her handling of the problems that the school district faced at the time.[13]

Similar findings come from a five-year study by Warren Bennis and Burt Nanus of sixty top-level corporate leaders and thirty leaders of public sector organizations. Few of the individuals studied fitted the stereotype of a charismatic leader. They were not larger-than-life individuals. Most of them were very ordinary in appearance, personality, and general behavior. They were, however, strongly committed to a vision and reflected that commitment in their decisions and behavior.[14]

Charisma is thus usually a consequence of leadership, not the cause of it. Once leaders have accomplished something, they appear to acquire qualities that no one noticed in them before. They seem to grow in size: people begin to look up to them and start talking about their charisma.

Can Leaders Use Written Stories?

Most of this book concerns oral communication. Can leaders use written communication to inspire enduring enthusiasm?

It's not impossible, as Lincoln's Gettysburg Address demonstrates: a speech that was ineffective when delivered had profound and lasting effect in written form. And books have obviously had transformational effects over time.

But in practice, in the hectic modern world where people want results now, reliance on the written word will generally be insufficient to inspire the kind of skeptical, cynical, or hostile audiences that one finds in today's workplace or marketplace to enduring enthusiasm for a cause. To engage these kinds of audiences with strange, new, transformational ideas, I have two words of advice: be there!

If leaders are physically present with those people, face to face, eyeball to eyeball, with a powerful story to tell, a story they deliver with energy and passion, then there is a chance that they will connect with a good portion of the audience. Merely sending out an e-mail message, or an article, or a book, or inviting people to go to a Web site won't get the job done.

Of course, once leaders have got an audience positively excited about the idea they are trying to communicate, then all those forms of communication will be helpful and should be used to reinforce the message and continue the conversation: e-mail messages, articles, books, Web sites, podcasts, and videos all come into their own. That's because now the listeners *want* to find out more. Now they're interested. Now they're excited. Now they're keen to find these materials and learn.

This is not to say that books can't have an impact in changing people's minds. Obviously, down through the centuries, books have introduced major changes in the world. But books and reading take time. It might take someone eight hours to read a book. These days busy people don't have eight hours to spare. They're only going to read the book if they're already motivated. Getting them motivated is why oral storytelling plays such a central role in leadership.

Should Leaders Use PowerPoint?

While it's common to rail at PowerPoint for causing excruciatingly boring presentations, this is analogous to complaining about the English language. PowerPoint is a powerful, infinitely flexible graphics program. The only practical limit on adapting it to any need is the imagination of the presenter.

This is not to deny that PowerPoint causes problems. In the 30 million or so PowerPoint slide shows that take place each day around the world, most are filled with illegible text and boring images and bland abstractions. It's these unsound practices that account for the dazed looks on the viewers' faces, not PowerPoint itself.

Should one forgo PowerPoint slides? It's true that the occasional speaker can mesmerize a crowd without any visual aids. The atmosphere can become like that of a circus tent. All eyes are on the presenter, who turns into a performer. The medium encourages the speaker to use theatrical tricks to keep the audience's attention. It can be an effective performance. But it is less likely that the message sticks as well as one that combines words with images.

That's because some people simply respond better to images than words, while other people respond better to words than images. The evidence is not gender neutral, that is, the bell curves of men and women don't overlap. On average, women respond better to words than pictures. On average, men respond better to pictures than words. Obviously there are exceptions—verbal men and picture-oriented women—but on average, that's what the data shows.[15] As a result, if you want to reach the whole audience, it is a good idea to use both words and images.

My Web site offers a number of basic principles that can help avoid the worst pitfalls in preparing PowerPoint slide shows.[16] Most of the principles are little more than common sense. Use text that's legible. Make sure images are relevant to your message. Use slides that are self-explanatory. Following these simple principles of visual hygiene can help harness the immense capabilities of PowerPoint to transform boring, abstract slides into compelling, memorable presentations that lead to action.

Part Two of this book has explored the enabling conditions of the language of leadership. The elements that can ensure that the language of leadership has its maximum effect include articulating a clear and inspiring change idea, committing to the story of change, mastering the audience's story, using narrative intelligence, telling the truth, and deploying the body language of leadership.

With those elements in place, Part Three explores ways to proceed step by step in using the language of leadership: getting attention, stimulating desire, reinforcing with reasons, and continuing the conversation. I begin with getting the audience's attention.

[PART 3]

THE LANGUAGE

OF LEADERSHIP:

KEY STEPS

8

GETTING PEOPLE'S ATTENTION

> *No fresh and new experience is possible if there isn't a pure, virgin space ready to receive it.*
>
> **—Peter Brook[1]**

Quick. Complex. Interconnected. Confusing. The world today is such an unpredictable kaleidoscope of shifting information, activities, people, places, stories, and goals, all vying for a place in our minds, it severely tests our ability to concentrate on anything in particular.

Is it any wonder, then, that attention has become a scarce resource? Or that modern audiences usually aren't listening when leaders start to speak? Listeners may be physically present, but mentally they're often somewhere else. Before any meaningful communication can occur, the speaker needs to clear the way and create an open space for the audience so that their minds can consider something different. The most important function of getting attention isn't taking information in, but preparing listeners' minds for something new.[2]

And the attention I'm talking about here is front-of-the-mind attention: conscious, focused, explicit, intense, and undivided. It's the kind of attention we apply when solving a problem, writing a letter, or watching an exciting movie. While this is happening, our brains may be paying back-of-the-mind attention to many other subjects—subjects that will never come to conscious attention unless something unexpected occurs, such as a cry for help, the smell of burning, or a ringing doorbell.

Getting attention means diverting the audience's focus from any external sensory signals—the squeaking of chairs, the noise of the streets outside, the chattering at the back of the room, or the weird tie that guy is wearing.

Equally important, the internal meanderings of the mind need to be suppressed. What happened at dinner last night? Did I really turn the car headlights off? Is my career heading in the right direction?

But most important is the need to generate a sense of expectancy that something significant is about to happen. In a theater this is accomplished by the physical arrangements: the seating, the stage, the curtain, and the lights, which together create the sense that something interesting is imminent. In most leadership situations, an analogous effect must be achieved by what we say.

Six general principles govern efforts to get attention:

First, attention is attracted to what is *unexpected*. Routine, run-of-the-mill occurrences are relegated to back-of-the-mind attention, or what psychologists call "automatic attention." Most of what we do during the day is handled in this fashion, thus freeing up focused attention for more significant issues. It's the unexpected that gets front-of-the-mind attention.

Second, attention is engaged by *the emotions*. Emotions serve as markers. Emotion slows down the process of analytic thinking, thus making the object "interesting."[3] To elicit emotion, it helps to be specific. General notions and abstract schemes have little effect on the emotions or the imagination: people may be unmoved by the slaughter of tens of thousands of people in a foreign conflict, while the picture of a single child burned by napalm can stick in their imagination forever. The more specific and concrete, the sharper the image people retain.[4] Master communicators find and describe the telling detail, such as when Leo Tolstoy's heroine, Anna Karenina, notices for the first time how large her husband's ears are, once she has begun her adulterous affair.

Third, attention is engaged by what is *personal to listeners themselves.* The more things have to do with ourselves, the more they are likely to be of interest. As Tom Davenport and John Beck point out in *The Attention*

Economy, if you want to get attention, you've got to give attention. People are more likely to pay attention to you if you attend to what's important for them. "As much as possible the theme has to be, What's in it for me? How does this information tell me what I need to know? How is it tailored to my situation?"[5]

Fourth, from a leadership perspective, it's important that whatever is used to get attention is *relevant* to the subject at hand. It should point to the overall direction of the leader's eventual theme and avoid introducing a distraction from what is to come. Thus if speakers in an organizational setting were to take off their shirts or stand on their heads, it would certainly attract attention, but it would also launch trains of thought that could be highly distracting from what they were about to say. Thus the stories that Al Gore used in his 2000 presidential debate drew attention to problems that had arisen under the administration of which he was a part, rather than to the solutions that he wanted to propose: as a result, the stories got attention, but from Gore's perspective, they focused attention on the wrong questions.

Fifth, the communication tool should be *proportionate* to the scale of the task in changing minds. If the audience is already hugely distracted and the behavior change aimed at is major, then speakers may need to spend a great deal of effort getting attention. By contrast, if speakers are in the lucky position of having an audience that is already curious, inquisitive, and open to the message, then the speakers can pass quickly on to stimulating desire for change. However, given the tendency of leaders, particularly hierarchical leaders, to overestimate the extent to which their audience is listening, it's generally better to err on the side of caution and assume that at least some members of the audience are not paying attention.

Finally, and perhaps most important, attention is engaged by what is *negative*. Psychological studies show that human beings give more weight to losses than to gains, to pains than to joys, to negative events than to positive events. And negative events are more attention-getting.[6]

Preferential attention to the negative is hardly surprising from an evolutionary perspective. Averting danger, such as preventing loss of life or limb, often requires an immediate response. Positive activities, like eating and making love, though crucial for long-term survival, are less pressing. Overall, pain is more urgent than pleasure.[7]

Psychological studies suggest that we have an *automatic vigilance mechanism* that serves to direct attention to undesirable stimuli. As we look around the world, we make a primary appraisal of whether what we see is "good for me" or "bad for me." We do this easily, readily, and quickly, and sometimes even without conscious thought. When our attention is elsewhere, undesirable stimuli are more likely to attract our minds.[8]

Thus the main task of the speaker in getting the audience's attention is to evoke emotion in a relevant, unexpected, personalized way, if possible while directing attention to the subject at hand. And generally this is most easily accomplished by accentuating the negative.

Which methods work best? In what follows, the possible communication tools are sorted into three broad categories: tools that are generally effective, those that are moderately effective, and those that are generally ineffective. Much depends of course on the skill with which the tool is used and the context. Used unskillfully, all of these tools will fail. Applied with flair and imagination, any of the tools can work to some extent. The ranking here reflects the ease of getting the tool to work at all and the intensity of the impact it is likely to have when it does work. More detailed, quantified research is needed in this area. The ranking offered here is no more than a first step toward some sense of the layout of the terrain.

Generally Effective Tools for Getting Attention

Here are the methods that tend to work most easily and most effectively:

- Tell a story about the audience's problems.
- Tell a story of how you handled adversity.
- Ask a question.
- Use a striking metaphor.
- Launch an unexpected exercise.

- Issue a challenge.
- Share something of value.
- Admit a vulnerability.
- Give a musical performance.

Tell a Story About the Audience's Problems

If leaders have done their homework and know what the audience is worried about and what keeps them awake at night, then often the most effective way to get their attention is to begin talking about those problems and demonstrate greater understanding of those problems than those in the audience do. If speakers can show that the problems are serious, perhaps even more serious than the audience imagines, the audience will experience concern in an area that is personally relevant to them. By concisely demonstrating competence, leaders also have an opportunity to enhance trust.

If the resistance of the audience is considerable, then a large number of stories may be necessary to get the audience's attention. Al Gore's *Inconvenient Truth*, for instance, is mainly composed of negative stories about the impact of global warming. He's trying to wake us up to the magnitude of the dangers we are facing, so that we start to pay attention: ladies and gentlemen, this is serious!

Tell a Story of How You Handled Adversity

Another effective way to get the audience's attention, particularly where speakers are unknown to the audience, is to tell a brief but moving story about how you handled some adversity in your life. A concise story about a significant turning point in your life, particularly one that is in some way related to the change under discussion, can be emotionally stimulating to an audience and personally involving if the listeners project themselves into the story. By leveling with the audience, the leader can also build up trust. Thus Al Gore, in talking about his family tobacco farm and the death of his sister from smoking, reveals a side of him that is surprising, affecting, and attention-getting. The Preface to this book reflects a similar effort to get your attention.

Ask a Question

Questions are the staple of advertising's efforts to get attention because they succinctly force attention on a set of issues selected by the communicator.

With *"Where's the beef?"* Wendy's was able to suggest that there was more to its fast food than that of its competitors.

When *"Got milk?"* was combined with arresting images of celebrities with milk on their upper lip, it helped draw attention to a familiar but forgotten drink.

"Is it live or is it Memorex?" drew attention to the fidelity of Memorex recording tape.

"Where do you want to go today?" helped Microsoft draw attention to the multiple uses of its software.

"Do you want to spend the rest of your life selling sugared water or do you want a chance to change the world?" Steve Jobs famously asked this question to draw attention to the possible reason why John Sculley might want to leave a secure, high-paid position at Pepsi to join a bunch of young computer geeks in California.

Questions are also pervasive in political campaigning: *"Are you better off today than you were four years ago?"* helped Ronald Reagan set the agenda for the 1980 presidential campaign. By contrast, Al Gore didn't dwell on the analogous question in his 2000 campaign: *"Are you better off today than you were eight years ago?"* In 2000, most people in the United States actually did feel better off, and the question, had it been pressed, might have reminded them of that.

In using a question, it's important to think through what sort of answer may be expected. An inappropriate question may direct attention to issues that are unexpected or irrelevant to the speaker's message. If listeners look for the beef and find it's missing, or conclude that they are not better off today than four years ago, the question will have the opposite of its intended effect. Equally seriously, if the underlying assumptions of the question are false the question may backfire: asking "Where's the beef?" may not work on listeners who are vegetarians.

Use a Striking Metaphor

"Metaphor," said José Ortega y Gasset, "is perhaps one of man's most fruitful potentialities. Its efficacy verges on magic, and it seems a tool for creation which God left inside His creatures when He made them."[9] Metaphors can help speakers shine light into darkness and ignite their listeners' minds with celestial fire.

Unexpected metaphors can forcefully grab our attention. For instance in November 2005, as part of the ongoing political debate about the implications of the coming retirement of the Baby Boom generation, U.S. Comptroller General David Walker focused attention on the financial risks by referring to "the fiscal hurricane" that was about to "hit the country" as a result of "the imminent demographic explosion": it will be "a retirement tsunami that will never recede."[10] Following a fusillade of metaphors such as those, it's difficult for organizations like AARP to present the coming wave of retirements of well-educated people as a positive opportunity for the U.S. economy. To recapture attention, AARP may have to come up with its own competing set of metaphors.

The best metaphors are subtly effective. With overemphasis, a metaphor can backfire, as Al Gore found during the first presidential debate in October 2000, when he hammered the metaphor of the lockbox in which he planned to deposit the funds for Medicare and Social Security. Gore mentioned the "lockbox" metaphor a total of five times during the debate. The metaphor succeeded in getting people's attention, but it caused as much confusion as enlightenment. In one focus group, a viewer wondered, "What's in the lockbox?" and another asked, "Who's got the key, anyway?"[11] The metaphor also had hints of authoritarian control that showed up in subsequent parodies of Gore's performance. His metaphor became a communication problem rather than a solution.

Finding a single metaphor that encapsulates the whole idea you want to communicate can be difficult. Sometimes the problem can be solved by offending the linguistic purists and mixing metaphors. This is a familiar way of pitching Hollywood movies: for example, if *Alien* is presented as "a combination of *Star Wars* and *Jaws*," its narrative structure may become clear.

If the real-world referents of mixed metaphors are too different, they can jar, as in "He stepped up to the plate and grabbed the bull by the horns." Nonetheless, in the hands of a master linguist like Shakespeare, who frequently took arms against a sea of troubles, a mixed metaphor can sound strangely harmonious.

Launch an Unexpected Exercise

One way to get attention is to have listeners themselves do something unexpected. For instance, when I do workshops on business narrative, I sometimes begin by inviting each participant to tell a sixty-second story to another participant on one of two subjects: either about a time when they discovered what their organization was really good at or about a time when they encountered adversity. Then the pairs switch roles, and the first listener tells a story on one of the two themes. Even without preparation, most participants surprise themselves by performing the task effortlessly and demonstrating some elements of narrative intelligence. The exercise creates a direct experience of the techniques the workshop aims to teach, and it also gets the audience's attention.

Issue a Challenge

"What I am about to tell you is a bit frightening. Sometimes seminar attendees walk out on me as I deliver this material because they're disturbed by what they hear. These are smart people walking out. I don't blame them for leaving. This is the stuff of nightmares." Thus begins a book by Joel Bauer and Mark Levy.[12] It's like a carnival barker's ballyhoo that's used to snare people strolling by. Hokey, perhaps, but it can get attention. In the field of leadership one needs to make sure that the challenge is factual. If people's attention is captured by something that they later discover to be misleading, the backlash can undermine the eventual message.

Share Something of Value

Just as an unexpected gift from a visitor can help generate feelings of geniality and friendship, sharing something of value early on—perhaps an unexpected announcement of some truly good news such as a promotion, a victory, an accomplishment—can capture the audience's attention and enhance positive feelings of trust toward the leader. But again, remember the rules of relevance and truth. If the unexpected announcement is truly extraordinary, it may divert attention from the main message you are trying communicate. Or if you announce an award to the organization for being "one of the best places to work," in a setting where staff don't agree that the award is justified, then the announcement will be distracting rather than attention-getting.

Admit a Vulnerability

One way for leaders, particularly hierarchical leaders, to get attention is to reveal the limits of their knowledge, to concede that they don't know everything and state their interest in learning, or to admit that mistakes have been made, as Craig Dunn did in his encounter with the angry workers of AMP. In organizational settings, such admissions can be unexpected and hence attention getting.

The wording of the admission can be important. Thus in early 2007, presidential candidate Senator Barack Obama was asked about his purchase of land near his home from a longtime friend who was indicted (but not convicted) in 2006 on charges of extorting kickbacks from companies seeking state business.

First version	Later version
"I was stupid."	"It was a bone-headed move."

As columnist William Safire notes, "'Boneheaded' was a good choice: not as condemnatory or self-flagellating as stupid, nor as dismissive as foolish, nor as formal as ignorant, nor carrying a secondary drug connotation as dopey, nor as frivolous as silly, nor as inapt as dumb (considered a slur by the speech-impaired)."[13]

Putting the admission in the form of a simple narrative—"Here's how it happened . . . "—can help show the mistake as driven by situational factors, a one-time error, a deviation from normal prudence, rather than a permanent personal flaw such as stupidity.

Give a Musical Performance

Singing a song or performing a musical instrument can be so unusual in an organizational context that it gets attention. Even if the performance isn't brilliant from a musical standpoint, it may be unexpected enough to wake people up. But keep in mind the rule of relevance. If the musical performance is really extraordinary, or if it has no connection to the subject under discussion, it may be the only thing that the audience remembers. A rap song with lyrics directly related to the topic under discussion might be very effective at getting attention and pointing the listeners to that topic. Much of the effect comes from the unexpectedness. Singing a song once will be a surprise; singing a song every time becomes routine.

Moderately Effective Ways to Get Attention

Here are some things that sometimes work but are harder to manage than the first group:

- Show the real thing.
- Offer a surprise.
- Make an extraordinary offer.
- Talk about an opportunity for the audience.
- Tell a springboard story.
- Tell a joke.
- Show an image.
- Create a frame.

Show the Real Thing

In Shakespeare's *Julius Caesar*, Marc Antony waves the bloody tunic of the murdered Caesar in front of the Roman populace to arouse their interest and sympathy—and get their attention. The risk here is that the real object may have irrelevant elements from which it is difficult to divert the viewers' attention: Caesar's tunic may look nondescript when the live Caesar is not wearing it. So Marc Antony is careful to tell a simple story that focuses the audience's attention on the elements of the tunic that are relevant to his objective, namely, how the murderers' daggers came through the holes in the tunic and entered Caesar's body. Thus stories about the object may be more effective to keep the attention focused on what is relevant than the thing itself.

Offer a Surprise

A surprise—an unexpected announcement, some startling piece of news, an unanticipated prop like holding a live snake—may be momentarily effective in capturing the audience's attention. However this approach is only likely to be effective if the surprise is related in some way to the objective of the presentation. Otherwise it may be difficult to shift the attention from the surprise back to the course of action the leader is aiming to communicate.

Make an Extraordinary Offer

If leaders can summarize what they offer in a concise but surprising statement, this in itself might serve as the attention grabber. In a leadership setting, it can be hard to frame such a statement so that it is relevant to the subject at hand. For instance, announcing, "At the end of the lecture, a member of the audience will win a valuable prize," may get people's attention, but it may also distract the audience's attention from the subject at hand: the audience may spend the rest of the presentation wondering who is to win the prize.

Talk About an Opportunity for the Audience

An alternative to dwelling on the audience's fears is to focus on their hopes and dreams. This can be tricky, since it's difficult to tell a credible story about a future opportunity. Suppose I say:

Imagine that it's two years from now. Imagine that our organization has reached its goal of being the predominant supplier of services in our field. Imagine that our profits are at record levels. Our stock price has soared. We are being featured in *Business Week* and *Forbes*. . . ."

The risk is that such a euphoric future story will elicit the response: "It will never happen here." Future stories are inherently incredible, particularly in organizational settings. If the story is seen as implausible, it can quickly become the subject of ridicule, particularly if the audience is difficult.

Tell a Springboard Story

A springboard story is a story that describes an example in which the change idea that the speaker is proposing has already happened, at least in part. If a leader can find such a story and the story resonates with listeners, it can connect with them at an emotional level and generate a new story in their minds in a way that leads to action. However, because a springboard story is positive in tone, it may be less effective initially in getting the listeners' attention than a question or a story about the listeners' own problems.

Tell a Joke

If leaders know the audience well enough, they may be able to get attention with a well-told joke. As with other devices, this works best if the joke is related in some way to the objective of the presentation. Otherwise it may be difficult to shift attention from the joke back to the idea that leaders want to communicate. And be sure that the joke is indeed likely to be viewed as funny by the audience: since humor often wounds, it is all too easy to attempt a joke that offends some segment of the audience.

Show an Image

If the intended change has an attractive physical appearance or an attractive image associated with it, then that image may be a good way to attract attention. Thus the fashion industry typically uses no more than images to sell its products, without any words: the image itself can be attractive enough to do the entire job of selling. The situation is different with complex ideas, such as knowledge management, the reform of Social Security, or a new business model: it's tough to build an image that succinctly and clearly communicates such ideas. When presenters use an attractive image that isn't relevant to the course of action being proposed (for example, a photo of an attractive woman), the image may get attention—but it may also distract from the purpose of the communication and so diffuse the focus of the presentation.

Create a Frame

A statement that frames a subject and invites an audience to look at it from a certain perspective can be an effective attention-getting device. Thus the Washington, D.C., Democratic mayoral primary in September 2006 ended up being decided on which candidate the electorate viewed as most energetic. By that measure, the thirty-five-year-old Adrian Fenty defeated a field of older, more experienced insiders. Why did energy become the critical issue of the campaign, rather than maturity and experience? Fenty campaigned energetically and repeated the words "energy" and "energized" on every possible occasion. In due course, reporters started writing about energy and describing his campaign as energetic. Here Fenty took advantage of what psychological research has found: it's more difficult to persuade people to change their minds on an issue than it is to invite people to focus on a different issue—the one where the candidate is the strongest.[14]

Framing statements, if widely repeated, can be successful in changing the way people thereafter view a whole of set of issues. They can, however, have an adverse reaction if the audience intuitively rejects the proposed frame. Frames are also vulnerable to being undermined by contrary stories. Thus in the U.S. elections, "the war on terror" was an effective frame for the Republicans in the 2004 election, but it was trumped in 2006 by powerful negative stories of the poor progress in the war in Iraq.

Generally Ineffective Ways of Getting Attention

And here are ways that sometimes work but more often fail or backfire:

- Hype.
- Tell the story of who your company is.
- Just give the facts.

Hype

Repetition of a message may signify that something is important and hence establish a mental frame. Public relations firms and ad agencies try to use repetitious press coverage and media events that lead to an atmosphere of excitement and expectancy. With the same idea appearing in different media at the same time, the object is to generate a sense that everyone is talking about the same subject, so it must be important. In such circumstances, it's hard not to pay some attention. The problem here becomes one of sustaining interest. Hype often generates both excessive expectations and feelings of manipulation, which then cause their own backlash. As a result, hype and the enduring enthusiasm sought by transformational leadership tend to be inversely related.

Tell the Story of Who Your Company Is

In a presentation, speakers often begin with information about the company they work for. Sadly, this subject is usually of much more interest to the speaker than to the audience. These speakers have forgotten the maxim noted by Henry Boettinger in *Moving Mountains:* "Start where THEY are, not where YOU are."[15] In the absence of definite evidence that the audience is interested in some aspect of the organization and why people are interested, speakers will usually be better off talking about the audience and its problems. The firm's own story can come later.

Just Give the Facts

By themselves, without more, facts are not particularly attention getting. Chaim Perelman and L. Olbrechts-Tyteca, in their classic *The New Rhetoric*, describe the phenomenon:

The authors of scientific reports and similar papers often think that if they merely report certain experiments, mention certain facts or enunciate a certain number of truths, that is enough of itself to arouse the interest of their hearers or readers. This attitude rests on an illusion, widespread in certain rationalistic and scientific circles, that facts speak for themselves and make such an indelible imprint on any human mind that the latter is forced to give its adherence regardless of its inclination.[16]

These observations about scientific papers are equally true of a leadership setting. A simple recitation of facts by themselves is likely to be boring rather than attention getting. And if the audience is difficult, reasons may activate the confirmation bias and entrench the audience more firmly in their existing position.

The various methods of getting attention described here obviously aren't alternatives. You might combine several methods, say, a question, a challenge, and a story about the audience's problems. If the audience is very resistant or even hostile, you might need to commingle a number of components to get the audience to listen: indeed, most of your speech may be devoted to the quest for attention. Table 8.1 summarizes the various approaches to getting the audience's attention.

If the audience is already attentive, you may be able to spend little time on getting attention. Instead, you quickly move on to the next (and most difficult) step in transformational leadership: eliciting the audience's desire for a different state of affairs. This is the step where leadership presentations most frequently come to grief, and it is to this challenge that I now turn.

TABLE 8.1 Utility of the Various Communication Devices for Getting Attention

	Communication Device	Example	Value in Getting Attention*	Comment
Generally Effective	The story of the audience's problems	"I know we're facing problems with x and y. And in fact the problems are worse than we thought they were."	High	This is often the best way to get attention.
	The story of how you handled adversity	A concise story about how you dealt with a turning point in your life, which is some way related to the subject under discussion. "Let me tell you how I got into this situation. . . ."	High	Only appropriate where the speaker is relatively unknown to the audience.
	A question	"Do you know how many U.S. women the XYZ Corporation routinely reaches?"	High	This works best if the question or the answer is surprising to the audience.
	A striking metaphor	"We are facing a retirement tsunami that will never recede."	High	Beware of any unintended implications of the metaphor.
	Have the audience do something unexpected.	Ask them to tackle an exercise when they thought they were just going to listen to a lecture.	High	The best exercises are related to the subject under discussion.
	A challenge	"What I am about to tell you is a bit frightening. . . ."	High	Be careful to ensure that the challenge is not misleading.
	Share something of value	"I'm pleased to announce that we have just won the PQR deal that we've all put so much effort into."	High	The news must be unexpected and relevant to the listeners.
	Admission of responsibility	"We all have to face the fact that there were poor management decisions in the recent past. . . ."	High	Leveling with the audience can help generate trust.
	A musical performance that is relevant to the presenter's theme	The presenter sings a rap song with lyrics about the subject under discussion.	High	The risk is that people may remember the rap song, not the message.

	Technique	Example	Rating	Comment
Moderately Effective	The real thing	Display an object associated with the topic and emphasize its importance.	Moderate	It may be necessary to direct attention to the relevant aspects of the object.
	A surprise	An unexpected announcement, some startling piece of news related to the main message.	Moderate	Make sure that the surprise is relevant to the subject at hand.
	An extraordinary offer	"I'll be offering a prize at the end of the talk."	Moderate	The danger is that the offer can be so successful in getting attention that it distracts from the main message.
	The story of an opportunity for the audience.	"Imagine that it's two years from now. Imagine that your organization has reached its goal of being . . ."	Moderate	With difficult audiences, it's hard to make future stories believable.
	A springboard story	Tell a story about an example where the change is already happening.	Moderate	Positive stories are less attention-getting than negative stories
	A joke	"Did you hear the one about the . . ."	Moderate	A joke can work if it is relevant to the subject under discussion.
	An image	A photo of 9/11 can elicit fear of terrorism.	Moderate	It depends on finding an image that arouses feelings and relevant to the course of action.
	A framing statement	"This election is about reenergizing the government."	Moderate	Effectiveness may depend on repetition. It can backfire if the repetition is seen as hype.
Generally Ineffective	Hype	Widespread repetition of positive statements.	Low	It generates mistrust and feelings of manipulation.
	The story of who your company is	"The XYZ corporation has a long and distinguished history . . ."	Low	The company's story is rarely an attention-getter.
	Facts, data, analyses	"The XYZ Corporation has 41,000 employees and sales of over $1 billion."	Low	It can work where the facts or data are surprising.

*The ratings reflect experiential judgments that warrant further quantitative research.

9

STIMULATING
DESIRE

❝ We don't do problems. We do solutions. **❞**

—Amory Lovins[1]

In December 2000, Bob Nardelli became CEO of Home Depot. He arrived with impeccable credentials: he had enjoyed the best operating record in GE, one of the most admired companies in America, and was the runner-up to replace Jack Welch. Home Depot, however, was a mess, and Nardelli set about cleaning it up. He introduced a military-style rule. He fired most of the existing managers and replaced them with his own recruits, many from GE and the U.S. Army.[2] The company even started to look and feel like an army.

He introduced centralized purchasing and a billion-dollar investment in technology, along with sharp reductions in staff and costs. As a result, Home Depot had outstanding financials: Nardelli doubled sales and more than doubled revenues. Home Depot's gross margins also steadily improved.[3]

But in January 2007, Nardelli was fired. Why? The apparent trigger was his unwillingness to lower the amount of his extraordinary pay package. This had become an issue because the stock price was down 7 percent since Nardelli had taken over, while his compensation remained astronomical.

Why had Home Depot's stock price lagged in the face of Nardelli's dazzling financial accomplishments? In short, Nardelli wasn't able to generate sustained enthusiasm for what he was doing in the array of investors, shareholder advocates, hedge funds, private-equity deal makers, legislators, regulators, and nongovernmental organizations who want a say in how a company is run.

Investors were concerned that Nardelli's dazzling financial results, which had lowered service levels in stores, would not be sustainable. He was also pursuing a strategy of expanding into the wholesale building supplies market, and he hadn't been able to convince Wall Street that this move into a low-margin business would be worthwhile.

Nardelli now acknowledges he was "too focused on the idea that you do your job, you take care of your numbers, and the rest will take care of itself."

"I used to play football," he said when asked about the challenges of being a public company CEO today. "In football, you always know the score. Now, it's like we are ice-skating, and you've got a bunch of judges on the sideline shouting out the scores."[4]

The problem for Nardelli, as it is for many CEOs these days, is that this "bunch of skating judges" is now effectively in charge. Even the most powerful CEO can't force these judges to believe what the CEO wants them to believe. Unless corporate leaders can generate sustained enthusiasm for the ideas they are pursuing, their very survival in the CEO role becomes a question.

Generating desire for something different is the most difficult aspect of leadership, because leaders usually have only seconds to make the case for a new idea and get the audience to begin exploring a different, perhaps a radically different, future. The audience will be making their initial decision based on quick, intuitive, feeling-based processes.[5] They will make their decision long before leaders can complete a set of rational arguments in favor of whatever is being proposed.

How can leaders win their audiences over to their way of thinking and get buy-in for a new future even before they have had a chance to present their arguments? How can they get people to see reason when people are making decisions on emotional grounds? On the surface, the problem seems insoluble.

The first step toward solving it is to recognize that the challenge isn't about imposing the leaders' will on the listeners—which, in any event, is impossible. It's not about moving the audience to a predetermined position that leaders—in their greater magisterial wisdom—have foreseen. It's not a matter of a leader's predetermining what is best and then getting people to do it. It's a matter of quickly stimulating desire for change.

General Principles

Eight general principles govern efforts to stimulate desire for change:

First, the underlying idea should be *worthwhile for its own sake*. Leaders will have trouble eliciting sustained enthusiasm for a different future if the goal is merely instrumental and time-limited. Skillful communication may win some short-term gains for an instrumental goal, but enthusiasm is unlikely to be enduring unless the idea is perceived to be worthwhile in itself.

Second, the communication tool must make the idea *memorable*. If the audience can't remember the main elements of the change idea after the presentation, it's going to be hard for them to be enthusiastic about implementing it. Hence catchy phrases or succinct stories that encapsulate the idea may work. Long, complex arguments that are hard to remember won't.

Third, the idea must become *the audience's own idea*. Stimulating desire for change is a subtle process of putting one or more options in front of people and enticing them to co-create a new future. It entails enabling the audience to imagine a different, more promising story that they could be living, a story they for whatever reason have not visualized up till now. It's about respecting the audience's ability to see that for themselves, not about forcing something on them. If the idea does not become the audience's own idea, it will never inspire the enduring enthusiasm that is the hallmark of transformational leadership.

Fourth, the audience needs *room to contribute*. If the audience listens to the idea and sees it as predetermined and predigested, and themselves as passive observers with no say in how it is to be implemented, then sustained enthusiasm is unlikely. This is because no significant change idea can be implemented without adaptation to the context: if listeners are given no role in the process of adaptation, then they are unlikely to see it as their own idea. Instead, it will remain an idea that they regard in a detached fashion, something "out there," something that the leadership owns and they don't. Instead, the audience must get inside the idea, realize that it is unfinished, and see the possibilities ahead of them. As they adapt the idea to their own context, they begin to grasp how it is relevant for them and why it is sensible, logical, attractive, enticing, even obvious. For the idea to become fully adapted to their needs, they must be the ones to customize it, because only they can know their own needs.

Fifth, the idea must be *positive*. Since the sustained enthusiasm of transformational leadership is a positive emotion, the leader's communication of the change idea must be positive. If the leader's speech is negative or neutral, then where will the positive energy come from? If the leader is positive and enthusiastic, this is what spreads. It's the contagiousness of the leader's positive emotion and energy that stimulates desire for a new future.

Sixth, the idea must be *positive for the particular audience*. The communication must lead the audience to see gains for themselves, not just for the organization or for the leader. An idea that makes the company, or even the country, great may inspire people for a short time, but if there's nothing in it for the audience, then enthusiasm will inexorably fade. Hence the communication must make it easy for the audience to see why the change will be good for them personally.

Seventh, the more useful communication tools tend to be *stories*. Stories aren't the only way to stimulate lasting desire for change, but they are certainly among the more useful methods. Some of the other methods that work, such as brilliant aphorisms or word pictures or motivational songs, have the practical disadvantage that they require extraordinary talent to create them. By contrast, telling a story is simple and easy and accessible to every human being. For the kinds of stories that can stimulate desire for change, no unusual talents are needed.

Eighth, communication tools in general are effective *when they generate a new story* in the mind of each listener. This is because people make decisions within a narrative framework. Non-narrative methods of eliciting desire for a different future—questions, metaphors, challenges, offers, and the like—are effective to the extent that they point to a new story in the mind of the listener.

Which methods work best? In what follows, the possible communication tools are sorted into three broad categories: communication tools that are easy to use and generally effective, generally effective tools that require special talents, and tools that generally don't work. Here as elsewhere, much depends, of course, on the skill with which the device is used and the context. Used badly, any of these tools will fail. Applied with flair and imagination, any of them can work to a certain extent. The categorization here reflects the ease of getting the tool to work at all and the intensity of the impact it is likely to have when it does work. In this area, too, more detailed, quantified research is needed. The ranking offers a first step toward giving readers and researchers some sense of the layout of the terrain.

Most Promising Methods

These are the methods that can work most easily with a difficult audience:

- Seeing is believing.
- Tell a positive story.
- Externalize the obstacles to change.
- Use a metaphor that points to a story.
- Tell the story of who we are.
- Tell a "common memory" story.
- Offer a positive challenge.

Seeing Is Believing

Direct experience of the change successfully operating in an analogous context is one obvious way of generating desire for change. If it works there, then why not here? Thus in 1993, J. Allard didn't just tell people what was emerging on the Web. He set up demonstration computers on a folding table in the halls of Microsoft and dragged people there to see the Web in use, to touch it, to feel it. As a result, people could see for themselves.

As noted in Chapter Five, managers, parents, and schoolteachers may be able to create experiences that people have by becoming role models and embodying the behavior that they are trying to induce. They can also organize study tours, role-playing exercises, simulations, or quick prototyping.

In the same way, marketers create experiential learning by embodying the message that they are trying to communicate, by giving out samples and free trials, by offering test drives of automobiles or trial periods for using new software, or doing demonstrations where people can observe the product or service in action.

Tell a Positive Story

Often leaders will not be in a position to confront their audience with the actual experience, particularly when they are trying to lead upward in a hierarchy. The next best thing is often a story about such an experience. A simple story about an example showing where the change is already happening can connect with an audience at an emotional level and generate a new story in their own minds that leads to action.

I first came across this kind of simple but powerful story in my work at the World Bank in 1996, with the story shown in Appendix 1. I found that this particular kind of story had remarkable power to stimulate even skeptical listeners to imagine a different future for themselves, for their organization, for their world.

Since then, I've been helping many organizations craft similar stories with the objective of communicating complex ideas and spark action. I've called this kind of story "a springboard story."[6] Although these stories look simple, crafting them with consistent success requires narrative intelligence: it needs an understanding of the underlying mechanism and some mastery of the relevant narrative pattern to generate the intended effect.

The object of this kind of story isn't to *tell* the audience to implement their change idea: that would lead to an argument. Instead, the springboard story implicitly invites the listener to imagine a new story of which the audience becomes the hero.

This kind of indirect narrative will often be the easiest and most productive route for leaders to stimulate desire for change. It works best when it is told in a minimalist fashion, without much detail. When told in this way, it leaves plenty of mental space for the listeners to imagine a new story. In one part of their mind, the listeners are hearing the speaker's story. But in another part, the listeners are imagining a new story, in which they have each become the protagonist. And in the process, for the listeners, the story they imagine becomes for them a new idea. And because it is their own idea, they don't have to be persuaded of its merits. Pride of ownership helps generate the enthusiasm. "What a great idea! I've just had a great idea!"

The springboard story thus gets its effect indirectly. Unlike a direct narrative, it doesn't try to "transport" the listeners to another world and occupy their whole mental space, so that they become totally absorbed in the speaker's story, and so that their own world totally vanishes. Instead, the story is deliberately crafted so as to occupy the listeners' minds only partially and to leave the rest of their mental space available to imagine new stories in their own context. In effect, the storyteller deliberately refrains from telling a "well-told story" because that would fill the listeners' minds with the sights and the sounds and the smells of the context of the story, leaving no mental space for the listeners' own story.

The springboard story reflects William Gibson's insight: "The future is already here; it's just not very evenly distributed."[7] The springboard story highlights an instance of the change idea already being successfully implemented and prompts an analogous story in the mind of the listener. To achieve this result, the story must have a positive tone: these are stories with happy endings. They show how the idea has already succeeded in another context. If the story succeeded in an analogous context, why not here? The listeners' enthusiasm flows from imagining their own stories with similarly happy endings. Without the happy ending, the likelihood of generating enthusiasm for the change is slim.

But a happy ending by itself isn't enough. The story must satisfy two further requirements:

- *The happy ending must be credible:* If the story appears on the surface to end happily, but the story doesn't ring true, then the audience is likely to be thinking, "It couldn't have happened that way!" When that happens, there is no springboard effect. Instead, there may be increased skepticism vis-à-vis the change idea—and the leader. Thus, suppose the leader aims to win support for a corporate acquisition and tells a story about another example of a corporate acquisition that was successful. Because listeners may know that around three-quarters of all corporate acquisitions are unsuccessful, in the sense that they lose value for the acquiring company, the risk is that listeners will be thinking: this story is incredible. So for a springboard story to work, the speaker will need to give enough detail to show why this acquisition was unexpectedly successful, and different from other acquisitions that failed.

- *The ending must be happy for the audience:* It's not enough for the story to have a happy ending in a generic sense. The story has to be positive for this particular audience. Thus, many leaders in the corporate world tell stories highlighting a success for the company without realizing that the audience may be thinking: "That's fine for the company and for the CEO, but what about the workers who will be laid off? What about the managers who will lose their jobs? What's in it for me?" It's vital, therefore, to tell a story that makes it clear to the audience that a similar story will have a happy ending for them.

Appendix 2 gives a simple template with ten simple steps to assist with crafting a springboard story. While the steps look straightforward, crafting such a story isn't easy. The challenge is to have all the elements in place in the one succinct telling of the story. It's not unlike designing a watch: a number of moving parts have to work together in a tiny space. Successful springboard stories usually require considerable fine-tuning before speakers arrive at a version that works with the intended audience.

Externalize the Obstacles to Change

Another process by which leaders seek to generate enthusiasm for change is to externalize the forces impeding the change. Thus, Abraham Lincoln in his Gettysburg address in November 1863 declared "a new birth of freedom" for the nation. He was no longer defending an old Union, but rather proclaiming a new Union. The "old Union" contained and attempted to retain slavery. The "new Union" would fulfill the promise of liberty. Lincoln here split the ongoing story of the United States into two, the "old Union" and the "new Union." Here the underlying problem is objectified as an alien protagonist, who can be fought against as a kind of enemy.

This is akin to narrative therapists who, for example, use externalization to deal with anorexic patients. "By suggesting that the anorexia is an enemy striving to inhabit one's body, the therapist assists the patient to 'fight' against it. In this narrative, the personification of anorexia as the externalized antagonist allows the client to become the heroine of the story, emerging victorious in a battle against this evil force."[8]

Externalization is often one of the driving forces behind frequent reorganizations and restructurings that occur in business. By creating a new administrative structure, managers hope to objectify some new mode of operating, with new goals and new behaviors. If, however, the new structure is simply a rearrangement of assignments and reporting arrangements, then the existing organizational culture quickly reemerges and the reorganization will fail in catalyzing significant change. It's only if the participants in the new structure begin to live a new story that the new behaviors take and the culture changes.

Use a Metaphor That Points to a Story

Given that a sentence without a metaphor is like a day without the sun, effective speakers make frequent use of metaphor, as well as its less forceful cousin, the simile. The right metaphor loosens the blindfolds that have been covering the listeners' eyes.

Nevertheless, although metaphors can enliven a presentation, they won't stimulate desire for change unless they point to a specific action. Thus, when Senator John McCain described his role as chairman of the Senate Commerce Committee holding polluters accountable as that of "a mosquito in a nudist colony," the metaphor suggested opportunity without pointing to any particular action.[9] Or when Ross Perot said that his role was that "of a grain of sand to the oyster. We've got to irritate Washington a bit," the specific action was unclear. In terms of sparking action, you might say that these metaphors are all hat and no cattle. Or all foam and no beer. Or all missile and no warhead.[10]

By contrast, where the metaphor points to a relevant story, it may be able to stimulate desire for a course of action. For example, in 1999, the *New York Times* reported on the Sonagachi red-light district in India, where Indian prostitutes, who depended on their profession for their families' livelihood and who needed to persuade their madams to insist on their clients' using condoms, said, "If you want to enjoy the fruits of the tree, you must keep the tree healthy."[11]

Tell the Story of Who We Are

Stories about the joint experiences and attitudes of the people within the organization or community and their shared beliefs can also be motivating. At Nike, these would be stories about people who "just do it," with allusions to a kind of rebel force that can cut through the stodginess of the sportswear industry. At Southwest Airlines, they would be stories about how Herb Kelleher and his staff make travel fun and affordable so that people are "free to travel about the country."[12]

Similarly, Shakespeare used "the story of who we are" in his play *Henry V*, in the famous speech in which Henry exhorts his soldiers into battle. He has Henry first offer a safe passage home to those who don't want to fight. But for those who stay, he offers eternal glory.

> But we in it shall be remember'd—
> We few, we happy few, we band of brothers;
> For he to-day that sheds his blood with me
> Shall be my brother; be he ne'er so vile,
> This day shall gentle his condition;
> And gentlemen in England now a-bed
> Shall think themselves accursed they were not here,
> And hold their manhoods cheap whiles any speaks
> That fought with us upon Saint Crispin's day.

The focus of the speech is less on the purpose of why are we here in this muddy field, far from home, fighting this battle against people of whom we know little, and more on the group as a group—these few, these happy few, this band of brothers, soldiers who are about to "gentle" their condition if they win the battle. Shakespeare's magical language may work for a single battle, or even several battles. But the danger in real life is that the question eventually arises: Is it sustainable? The story can unravel if people begin to question: what's the point?

Tell a "Common Memory" Story

A common memory story is one that draws on the audience's shared recall of some phenomenon. It's about something that all, or most, listeners would be familiar with. If the speaker can tell a story that reminds all listeners of a time when they had positive feelings toward the course of action proposed, or something analogous to it, this may be enough to stimulate positive emotion toward the course of action offered.

Ronald Reagan was adept at drawing on stories that elicited common memories and so was able to get many people to believe that it was once again "morning in America." The stories delved into a past world that was simpler and more intelligible than the more complex environment of the 1980s, but the stories were effective in getting people to dream that they could recapture that simplicity and intelligibility.

Offer a Positive Challenge

In the sporting world, challenges are often used in the hope of motivating a team to a higher level of performance: "Let's win one for the Gipper!" or "Let's show the opposition today what kind of players we really are!" If the listeners buy in to the challenge, this may give the team a temporary lift. For sustained enthusiasm, there is a need to elicit enthusiasm for the activity itself, which is unlikely to happen unless the challenge points to an enduringly positive story.

In 1999, Rob McEwen, CEO of Goldcorp, a struggling Canadian mining company, offered a total of $575,000 in prize money to anyone in the world who could come up with the best proposal for finding and recovering new deposits of gold in Goldcorp's 55,000-acre property. In the secretive industry of mining, McEwen took the counterintuitive step of making available on the company's Web site everything that was known about the property and its mining history back to 1948. News of the contest quickly spread around the world and over a thousand geologists, prospectors, consultants, mathematicians, and military officers from fifty countries offered answers to the challenge. Contestants identified more than a hundred targets, of which half had not been identified by the company. Most of the new targets resulted in substantial quantities of gold. As a result, Goldcorp went from a struggling $100 million company to a $9 billion corporation that is one of the most innovative and profitable in the industry. The extraordinary offer not only got people's attention: it stimulated a great deal of action.[13]

Methods Requiring Special Talents

Here are some ways of stimulating desire for action that require special talents to have a chance of success:

- Compose stirring music.
- Invent a memorable aphorism.
- Paint a compelling word-picture of the future.

Compose Stirring Music

The history of "La Marseillaise" shows the power of music to motivate. Written by Claude Joseph Rouget de Lisle at Strasbourg in 1792, under its original name of "The Marching Song of the Rhine Army," the song became the rallying call of the French Revolution. It got its name because it was first sung on the streets of Paris by troops arriving from Marseille.[14] The French Empires of Napoleon and Napoleon III and the German occupation during World War II banned its playing because of its power to motivate. This was illustrated in the famous scene in the film *Casablanca,* in which French sympathizers sang the song to drown out a patriotic German anthem being sung by the Nazi soldiers."[15]

Thus, in principle at least, music can motivate. The practical problem for leaders is that it takes huge musical talent to compose a song with the motivational power of "La Marseillaise." Unless leaders have access to this kind of talent, music may not be a practical option.

Invent a Memorable Aphorism

Abraham Lincoln's idea of declaring a new birth of freedom for the United States would have had less impact if it hadn't been enshrined in the catchy phrase, "government of the people, by the people, for the people." John F. Kennedy's inaugural address also gets much of its force from the memorable sentence: "Ask not what your country can do for you; ask what you can do for your country."

Kennedy's challenge is in the form of what is known in traditional rhetoric as *chiasmus,* that is, an expression comprising two parallel clauses with the same words, but in reverse order.[16] Further examples:

"Let us never negotiate out of fear. But let us never fear to negotiate."

"When the going gets tough, the tough get going."

The fact that these formulations are succinct and easy to remember makes them liable to be repeated by word of mouth. Expressed differently, the same ideas might not have caught on. The difficulty here again is coming up with a memorable aphorism. This requires highly developed linguistic skills, which are rare.

Paint a Compelling Word-Picture of the Future

Some writers like Noel Tichy say that the main function of a leader is to "offer compelling stories of the future."[17] The problem is how to craft such stories. I'm familiar with many stories about the future, but I've had difficulty finding any that were compelling. That's because the future is unpredictable. It's difficult to tell a convincing story about it. Even if a story about the future is momentarily convincing as it is told, the future inevitably changes in some unexpected direction, and so the story becomes unbelievable.

A related approach is to offer an enticing word-picture of the future, as was done in the famous examples of Winston Churchill's "We shall fight on the beaches" speech in 1940, or Martin Luther King Jr.'s "I have a dream" speech in 1963.

These speeches are sometimes said to contain compelling future stories. In fact, the relevant passages don't have the central characteristics of a story, namely, a set of events held together by causal connection. They are brilliant word-pictures of a future state. They clearly required a high degree of linguistic skill—they might even be called prose poems. For Winston Churchill or Martin Luther King, who possessed those skills, crafting a dazzling prose poem was a feasible option. But most of us don't happen to have such linguistic skills. And without the incandescent poetry, word pictures of the future risk being unconvincing and are liable to be satirized.

Generally Ineffective Methods

And here are some ways of stimulating desire for the future that rarely perform as intended:

- Present arguments and reasons.
- Tell "burning platform" stories.
- Create dissatisfaction to sell your point.
- Pose an unexpected question.
- Depict an actual image of the future.
- Employ satire and irony.
- Tell fictional stories.

Present Arguments and Reasons

If a leader presents arguments to people who are skeptical, cynical, or hostile to their change idea, the audience will be listening to the arguments through the lens of their negative attitude, silently answering every argument with a rejoinder. As a result of the confirmation bias, the audience will be mentally fencing with the speaker. Bob Nardelli may say, "I've got great financial results." But the listener will be thinking, "What about customer service in the stores?" When Nardelli offers a new argument, say, "Look at the potential of the wholesale building supply sector!" the listener will be thinking, "Yes, but the margins there are very low, whereas your pay package is astronomically high." Nardelli might retort that his pay package was negotiated long ago and was scaled to persuade him to leave his lucrative position at GE. And on it goes. There is never any winner in such an argument. The more strenuously Nardelli argues his point of view, the deeper the listeners dig in to defend their own entrenched opinions, and prepare to fight again another day. So a direct approach of giving arguments and reasons doesn't elicit desire for a different future. It typically ends in a continuation of the adversarial relationship, with the audience more opposed than before the speaker said anything.

Tell "Burning Platform" Stories

Writers on leadership often suggest the need for "a burning platform" story to create a sense of urgency for change. The term derives from a situation when North Sea oil platform *Piper Alpha* caught fire and a worker was trapped by the fire on the edge of the platform. Rather than face certain death by fire, he chose probable death by jumping into the freezing sea below.[18] It's now used as a metaphor to describe a situation where people are forced to act by dint of the alternative's appearing far worse. Doing nothing will result in disaster, so that ceases to be a viable option.

In a burning platform story, the disaster scenario is described in such shocking detail that by comparison even disruptive change looks safe. This is typically how wars of choice are sold: in the effort to paint a sufficiently horrific picture, the dangers are exaggerated. Once the exaggeration is discovered, however, the motivation may evaporate so that any forward action stalls.

Burning platform stories are excellent for getting attention. For instance in 1993, when IBM was going through a near-death experience, the dire situation made it easier for the new CEO, Lou Gerstner, to get people to listen to the case for change.

The limitation of burning platform stories is that they create fear and stimulate the listeners' reptilian brain. Without more, they are likely to provoke grudging compliance with change directives rather than the enduring enthusiasm that transformational change requires. So burning platform stories can be used to get people's attention, but they need to be followed with a positive message to ignite desire to do something different.

Create Dissatisfaction to Sell Your Point

Leading and selling have some features in common. They both involve getting people to do things without hierarchical power: the leader can't compel people to change, any more than the seller can compel people to buy the product or service on offer. Both work by persuasion.[19]

The approach known as "spin selling" puts emphasis on making the customers dissatisfied with their current lot and thus ready to seek something new. It involves asking a series of carefully crafted questions that are meant to "push the customer down the ladder of satisfaction," so that people who are initially content or feeling only minor irritation with the current situation end up realizing that the issues are so serious that they become ready to buy the seller's product.[20]

However, large and complex sales typically involve significant innovation. Merely being dissatisfied with the current situation won't be enough to push an organization to incur the expense and run the risk of making the change. In any major innovation, unseen decision makers will have to review the offering and assess how it helps to further their strategic agenda.[21] For this to happen they will need to see positive value in making the change. Unless the buyers develop a strongly positive view of the future, they are likely to muddle along in their current situation, putting up with its attendant problems and dissatisfactions, all the while hoping that the problems will go away if they just work a little harder or faster. They won't take the risk of making the leap to do things differently until they believe in a different kind of future.

The fact is that making customers dissatisfied with the current situation doesn't elicit desire for a different future. To be successful in making sales entailing disruptive change, sellers must make a positive appeal. In effect, after generating dissatisfaction to get attention, sellers must inspire buyers to believe that they can make the current situation demonstrably better. How? Positive stories will usually be the route.[22]

Pose an Unexpected Question

In *Building the Bridge as You Walk on It,* Robert Quinn gives the example of the company executive who was involved in a large project that was hopelessly behind schedule. He wandered around the firm asking everyone, "What would it take for us to deliver this project one week ahead of schedule?" Quinn suggests that the project was eventually completed ahead of schedule because of the persistent questioning.[23]

In this instance, the question appears to have been enough to focus attention on meeting the instrumental goal of completing that particular project, and thus accelerate the schedule. But would it have worked for a second project and a third project?

A further problem with such questions is that they have a hidden premise: "There is something we can do to accelerate the schedule, if only we knew what it was." If people accept the premise, the question may work. But if they don't, the question risks turning into an argument.

Moreover, it's tough to formulate a question that will elicit enthusiasm for an activity on a sustained basis. Questions are good for getting attention, but less effective for stimulating positive desire for sustained change, unless they point to a positive story.

Depict an Actual Image of the Future

If the change idea is a very simple one (buy this handbag or this hamburger), it may be possible to find an image that can make the emotional connection directly. But when it comes to the more complex challenges of leadership, of getting people to embrace complex new ideas with enduring enthusiasm, it isn't easy to find single images that can encapsulate the idea. Where is the image that communicates the idea of knowledge management? I was never able to find one.

So images may be effective in simple communication challenges, but it's hard to make them work for the task of getting people to dream a wholly new future.

With these more complex ideas, an image may become associated with a story, in the way that photos of 9/11 became associated with the stories of that terrorist attack. These photos became emblematic of 9/11 through the story of 9/11: it's the story that's doing most of the work here, not the image.

Employ Satire and Irony

In rhetorical theory, derisive, ironical abuse of a person is known as *insultatio*.[24] For example, Hamlet says to his mother (when he is trying to get her to abandon her marriage with his uncle):

> Look on this picture, and on this,
> The counterfeit presentment of two brothers.
> See what a grace was seated on this brow:
> Hyperion's curls, the front of Jove himself. . . .
> This was your husband. Look you now what follows.
> Here is your husband, like a mildew'd ear,
> Blasting the wholesome brother. Have you eyes?
> Could you on this fair mountain leave to feed,
> And batten on this moor? Ha! Have you eyes?[25]

The problem here is that satire may win the argument, but as with all arguments, it doesn't lead to action. Hamlet's mother may be persuaded, but in the end she does nothing.

Tell Fictional Stories

The right fictional story can get us to dream. As a result, companies sometimes use fiction in an effort to give authenticity to their stories and get people to see them differently. Thus McDonald's Corporation uses the story of Ronald McDonald to help prompt a new story in the mind of the listener about what sort of company it is. If Ronald McDonald can get interested in healthier food, maybe customers will follow suit. Paradoxically, a fictional character like Ronald McDonald may have more credibility than the McDonald's Corporation to communicate the message.[26] However, fictional stories run the risk of being easily satirized. This is not to say that such stories aren't useful: as discussed in the next chapter, they tend to play their most useful role in personifying the reasons for change. But they're not reliable tools for stimulating desire in difficult audiences.

The Productivity of Communication

This chapter has reviewed the tools that are—or are not—effective in eliciting a desire in a new and different future. Table 9.1 summarizes these tools. The irony is that the less effective techniques tend to be the standard communication practices of the modern corporation. A shift toward more productive communication tools would lead to a significant improvement in the productivity of organizational communications.

Thus, imagine a leader speaking to a group of fifty people and trying to persuade them to implement a change by traditional means. Each of those fifty people is in a different situation. If the leader adopts the conventional approach to communications, it might take months, just trying to understand those fifty different situations. It might take more months to craft action plans for each of those fifty different situations. And it might take still more months to get those fifty people to implement those fifty action plans. So it might take a year or more to implement the change just for those fifty people.

When narrative is working at its best, as the fifty people listen to the speaker, they are mentally crafting action plans, plans perfectly adapted to each of these fifty different situations. And what's more, because the action plans are their own action plans, they believe in them. They own them. They are already figuring out how to implement them. The speaker has achieved in minutes what might otherwise take many months—a huge gain in the productivity of communications.

Of course eliciting desire isn't enough by itself to make persuasion sustainable. The listener may have second thoughts and wonder whether it was just a dream. So leaders need to follow up with rational reasons why the seed of the new idea that has been sown does indeed make sense. In the next chapter, I discuss ways to do this—not with grinding abstract arguments but with compelling narratives.

TABLE 9.1 Utility of the Various Communication Devices for Getting Attention

	Communication Device	Example	Value in Eliciting Desire*	Comments
Tools That Generally Work	Actual live experience	J. Allard demonstrates the Web at Microsoft.	High	Experiential evidence is the most compelling.
	A springboard story	"Let me tell you about an example where this is already happening."	High	The happy ending must be credible and positive for the audience.
	Externalization accompanied by a new story	Abraham Lincoln proposes a "new Union" committed to liberty for all.	High	Effectiveness depends on listeners seeing themselves as living a new story.
	A metaphor	"If you want to enjoy the fruits of the tree, you must keep the tree healthy."	High	Make sure that the metaphor points to a story.
	The story of who we are	Henry V's "band of brothers"	High	The audience needs to identify with the community.
	A common memory story	"You all remember when we . . ."	High	The story should be positive and related to the change.
	A positive challenge	"Who can help solve this problem?"	High	It's hard to craft challenges that elicit enduring enthusiasm.
Tools That Require Special Talents	Music	"La Marseillaise"	High	Requires extraordinary musical talent.
	A memorable aphorism	Lincoln: "government of the people, by the people, for the people"	High	Requires extraordinary linguistic talent.
	An enticing word picture of the future	Winston Churchill's "We shall fight them on the beaches" in 1940, or Martin Luther King Jr.'s "I have a dream speech" in 1963.	High	Requires extraordinary linguistic talent.

TABLE 9.1 Utility of the Various Communication Devices for Getting Attention, Cont'd.

	Communication Device	Example	Value in Eliciting Desire*	Comments
Generally Ineffective Methods	Arguments and reasons	The XYZ Corporation has 41,000 employees and sales of over $1 billion.	Low	It may win the argument, but it doesn't lead to action.
	Burning platform story	The firm will go bankrupt unless we implement this change.	Low	It is good at getting attention, but not for stimulating desire for action.
	Creating dissatisfaction	Your problems here are bigger than you realize.	Low	It needs to be accompanied by something more positive.
	A surprising question	"What would it take for us to deliver this project one week ahead of schedule?"	Low	It depends on the answer's being positive and surprising.
	An image	A picture of the change idea under discussion	Low	It can work if the image is genuinely enticing or interesting and it points to the change idea.
	Satire and irony	People who don't use an Apple computer are lifeless nerds.	Low	It may win an argument, but rarely leads to action.
	Fictional stories	Using Ronald McDonald to create a different view of the McDonald's Corporation	Risky	Fictional stories are easy to satirize.

*The ratings reflect experiential judgments that warrant further quantitative research.

10

REINFORCING
WITH REASONS

" We recognize the truth, not only with
the reason, but also by the heart. "

—**Blaise Pascal**[1]

Some years ago, when I was program director for knowledge management at the World Bank, I attended a meeting organized by George Mason University for large organizations in the Washington, D.C., area. It was a kind of show-and-tell session where each organization shared its experience with assembling the metrics of knowledge management programs. It had the usual Washington organizations from the public and private sector, such as the Mitre Corporation and the Marriott group. We listened to presentations that showed how each organization had gone about measuring the status and progress of its programs. Some of them were truly impressive in their scope and sophistication.

Then, toward the end of the session, somebody asked the fateful question: In any organization, had these sophisticated metrics ever been effective in winning a battle over budgets in a time of crisis? The universal answer from all participants was no. In a time of crisis, the metrics were there as a kind of background music to the discussion. But decisions were never based directly on them. In a time of crisis, the question was, Which of a number of programs were going to get new funding and which were going to be cut and by how much? In the end, decisions were based not on analyzing the numbers but rather on a gut feeling of what was important for the organization at that time. The amount of passion that different executives felt for different programs was the key determinant of the decisions that were made.

One reason for this was that every competing program was able to come up with statistics that purported to show that it was performing well and why it was valuable to the organization. So the statistics by themselves didn't provide guidance as to what to do. The decision always came down to gut questions: What makes sense? What do the statistics mean? Into which story do the statistics fit?

The illusion that statistics and analytics alone can resolve difficult questions of choice and goals is stubbornly persistent and has even survived formal proof by Kurt Gödel of the incompleteness of arithmetic. The misguided faith in pure statistical reasoning overlooks the fact that statistical systems by themselves don't generate meaning. There are always questions outside the statistics: Why are these particular numbers being gathered and analyzed in the first place? And what actions are to be taken based on the outcomes of the statistical analyses? What other considerations beyond the numbers bear on the decision?

The comfort that is provided by apparently hard numbers is thus to some extent illusory: it rests on a swamp of soft assumptions. The surface appearance of objectivity depends on agreed relationships and practices of the people who are generating and interpreting the statistics. Those relationships and practices determine which statistics are gathered, what the field of operation of the statistics will be, with what rigor they will be analyzed, what attention will be paid to them, and what actions will be taken on the basis of the answers that emerge. Statistics work well when the practices and the relationships in which they are embedded are accepted by all involved.[2] The trouble begins when either the practices or the relationships—or both—are in question. And, of course, that is normally the situation in the case of transformational change. When basic change is being proposed, the underlying practices and assumptions are precisely the elements that are controversial.

So statistics and analyses don't necessarily win battles on their own, but they can provide a kind of entry card to serious discussion and they can reinforce the desire for change that has been kindled by other methods. What form does the entry card take? It depends on the particular organization. Each organization has its own preferences and fetishes and, once established, these preferences and fetishes are hard to change. In any kind of discussion, the organization will expect certain kinds of analytic material to be presented in certain ways. And if the organization doesn't get them, it may go into a spasm.

In some organizations, it will be a knee-jerk call for the rate of return on investment—the notorious ROI. In other firms, it will be insistence on a detailed implementation schedule, with costs for every step spelled out in microscopic detail. In other organizations, the discussion cannot proceed in the absence of a detailed PERT chart. In other firms, the requirement will be the calculation of net present value, based on multiple interest rate predictions.

There is usually little point in questioning whether these expectations reflect a realistic ability to predict and quantify the future. Rather than argue about the requirement of the particular organization, it's generally better to meet the expectation. Give the organization its ROI, its PERT chart, its NPV, whatever. Give the beast what the beast feels it needs!

But there's no point wasting precious presentation time dwelling on such metrics, or giving lengthy PowerPoint presentations explaining them. Instead, make sure that the required metrics are available, for instance in handouts, and let the audience know that they are available. And get on with presenting reasons that will really resonate with your audience, reasons that will show them what makes sense, particularly how it works and why it works—that is to say, give people reasons in the form of stories.

Instead of relying on pure reason, on mere facts and figures and arguments, you can give your reasons an emotional punch. Stories appeal to the heart as well as the mind, so as to cement the reasons in place and make the reasons memorable.

Characteristics of the Stories
That Reinforce with Reasons

These features characterize stories that reinforce the reasons for change:

- The stories are typically set in the *present or immediate future*, and hence, like all future stories, are generally fictitious in nature.

- Although the stories are fictitious, it is vital that they give a *plausible* account of how the future is likely to unfold.

- They tend to be *minimalist* in form, that is, told without a great deal of context or detail.

- They tend to be *neutral in tone. Negative* stories about the implications of not implementing the change idea may also be useful. However, the emphasis is less on the emotional impact of the story than on clarifying the underlying rationale for the change idea.

- They often depict one or more *archetypical characters* through whose eyes the audience can understand the main elements of a complex idea. The stories depict characters the audience can easily understand, though they aren't necessarily characters the audience needs to identify with.

- The effectiveness of these stories is usually *dependent on prior stories* that have stimulated desire for change. Without this prior stimulation of desire, the confirmation bias is likely to kick in and the reasons will risk being rejected by the audience, or worse, interpreted to mean the opposite of what the speaker intends.

Tell the Story of "What the Change Is"

Leaders can explain what the change idea is by a simple story showing how a typical user might actually implement the idea when it is developed. For instance, this is how, back in 1996 at the World Bank, I communicated what the idea of knowledge sharing might look like. I told a story about what a typical desktop might look like and how typical World Bank staff might go about using it in the course of their work. (This story is set

out in full in Appendix 1.) In this way, a complex set of ideas was communicated in a simple, memorable story.

Or suppose you were introducing a complex set of changes to a
health insurance scheme. You might explain it by a set of stories of typical
users: what the insurance data means for Sally, the hip young single, or
for Fred, the young father, and for Jack, who is two years from retirement.
The stories highlight what the change idea is and what it means for the
people involved.

Tell the Story of "How It Will Work"

A business model is a story that explains how an organization will operate. It explains the theory of the business. It's a story set in the present or
near future. The narrative is linked to the relevant numbers of the business. It addresses questions like these: Who is the customer? What does
the customer value? How is the company going to make money in this
business? What is the underlying economic logic that reveals how it can
deliver value to its customers at a suitable cost? The validity of the business model depends both on its narrative logic—does the story ring
true?—and its analytic dimension—do the numbers add up?[3]

The story of "how it will work" is a future story—a story telling how
the future will unfold. As with all future stories, the issue is credibility.
The effectiveness of this kind of story depends on listeners who want to
understand how the change idea will play out. It appeals to the mind by
linking the elements of the change idea together with credible causal connections and suggesting that the broad order of magnitude of the numbers is plausible. It lends the voice of reason to desire that has already
been ignited in a prior step.

Tell the Story of "How to Get from Here to There"

A complex change being introduced into an organization can often seem
overwhelming to beleaguered staff. How could such a complex change possibly be implemented? Confusion can morph into discouragement unless
people have a sense of the way forward. And although implementation
may involve hundreds or even thousands of steps, it is usually possible to

synthesize the trajectory of getting from here to there into a simple story of the main steps: "We are here. If we do A, and then B, X will happen. Then we will do C, and then D, and bingo, we will be there." In this way, a massively complicated implementation plan can become broadly intelligible.

For example, in the 1996 presentation shown in Appendix 1, I laid out five simple "road maps" as to how one might go about turning the lending organization known as the World Bank into a knowledge sharing organization. As it turned out, actual implementation over the following four years didn't follow these road maps exactly, but in 1996, the five road maps provided a mental guide for listeners and gave them reassurance that the immensely complex change program was indeed manageable.

Tell the Story of "Why It Will Work"

As you'd expect, the story of "why it will work" is related to the story "how it will work." The difference between them is that the story of "how it will work" tends to be a story set in actual time and space in the future, whereas the story of "why it works" tends to be a story set in imaginary time and space, some kind of timeless Platonic world where the basic causal mechanisms of reality are (seemingly) revealed. Rather than dwelling on the specific conditions that will make the change idea viable, it focuses on the broader causal elements that make the change idea inevitable.

Here's an example from one of my own presentations about why the springboard story needs to be positive in tone:

> And so you see, Hollywood is right: a story aimed at sparking action has to have a happy ending. I've had no success in telling a story: "Let me tell you about an organization that didn't implement knowledge management and it went bankrupt." No success at all with this kind of story.
>
> And there is actually some neurological evidence suggesting why this is so. Over the last four hundred years or so, most of the attention on the brain has been focused on the cortex, that is to say, the human brain. But in the past couple of decades, a lot of the attention has been on other parts of the brain that hadn't been accessible in the past. In particular, we have been looking at the mammal brain and the limbic system, which sits just under the human brain, and the reptilian

brain, that we all have and which sits just under the mammal brain. These mammal and reptilian brains are not very smart, but they are very quick and they make a lot of noise.

And so if I tell you a story with an unhappy ending, about that company that went bankrupt because it didn't implement knowledge management, what seems to be happening is that these ancient parts of the brain, the reptilian brain kicks into action and sends a message to the cortex: "Fight! Flight! Get out of here! Trouble! Something bad is happening!" and so on. Now the human brain, the cortex, can intervene and override the reptilian brain and say something like, "Now calm down, reptilian brain, let's analyze this, and we may be able to learn something from this experience." And the cortex will generally win that debate. But by the time the commotion is over, the opportunity to invent a new future is past. Learning may take place, but no rapid action ensues. There is no springboard effect.

But by contrast, if I tell you a story with a happy ending, what seems to be happening is that the limbic system kicks in with something called an "endogenous opiate reward" for the human brain, the cortex. Basically, it puts the human brain on drugs. It pumps a substance called dopamine into the cortex, which leads to a warm and floaty feeling—the kind of feeling you have after you have just seen a wonderful movie. This is the perfect frame of mind to be thinking about a new future, a new identity for yourself or your organization.

In this jokey re-creation of what's going on inside the human brain, audience identification with the protagonist isn't important. The protagonist of the first story is the reptilian brain, which urges a fight-or-flight response upon encountering a negative story. In the second story, it's the limbic system which is the protagonist. The emphasis is on understanding the underlying neurological mechanism. My aim is to show to listeners that it's not just my personal preference for positive stories at work here: there's an underlying scientific reason why it's ineffective to use negative stories for the purpose of sparking action.

Such explanatory stories aspire to describe a stable and universal pattern of the underlying causal factors that drive the operation of the brain. The story explains the operation of not just one person's brain, but rather the brain of every human being.

Turn Arguments into "Common Memory" Stories

Common memory stories are stories that draw on common experiences and remind people of things that they already know. For instance, on December 29, 1940, Franklin Roosevelt gave a radio address from the White House, appealing for aid to the democracies fighting Nazi aggression. He opened his speech by recalling the common memory of successfully dealing with the banking crisis of 1933:

> Tonight in the presence of a world crisis, my mind goes back eight years to a night in the midst of a domestic crisis. It was a time when the wheels of American industry were grinding to a full stop, when the whole banking system of our country had ceased to function.
>
> I well remember that while I sat in my study in the White House, preparing to talk with the people of the United States, I had before my eyes the picture of all those Americans with whom I was talking. I saw the workmen in the mills, the mines, the factories; the girl behind the counter; the small shopkeeper; the farmer doing his Spring plowing; the widows and the old men wondering about their life's savings.
>
> I tried to convey to the great mass of American people what the banking crisis meant to them in their daily lives.
>
> Tonight I want to do the same thing, with the same people, in this new crisis which faces America.
>
> We met the issue of 1933 with courage and realism. We face this new crisis—this new threat to the security of our nation—with the same courage and realism.[4]

The common memory story draws on the audience's memory of some experience that all or most of the audience will have encountered. It invites the audience to recall that experience and imagine its implications. It depends on the presenter's being aware of an experience that will appear immediately plausible to all or most members of the audience. Ideally, the audience experiences a shock of recognition: "Yes, that's so true!" The common memory story makes the reason memorable.

Communicate the Reason Through Someone's Eyes

Suppose you are trying to explain to an audience what a complex change program will mean. Instead of presenting the arguments as arguments and describing the details of the multiple components of the program as abstractions, you can tell the story of how a typical participant will be affected by the program.

Suppose you are talking about a new business model in which a single channel of communication is replaced by multiple channels. Instead of describing the channels of the model separately in abstract terms, you tell the story of how a single individual—let's call her Ann Haines, a mother of two, who lives in Boise—would encounter the various channels of the program.

"First, Ann reads the magazines and sees. . . . Then she goes online and notices that. . . . Then she watches television and observes that. . . . Finally she is intrigued sufficiently to go and visit the model home that has been constructed at. . . ."

Instead of experiencing the changes as inert abstractions of magazines, Web site, television programs, and shopping centers, we experience those components through the eyes of Ann Haines and what they mean to her as another human being. Even if she is an imaginary creature, we start to see the world through her eyes, and begin to feel what it would be like, and what it means.

Support the Story with Images

A picture can be worth a thousand words. So where you have a relevant, powerful image, use it. For instance, when I gave my presentation at the World Bank in May 1996, I showed a slide with an image of the desktop of a World Bank professional and another with an image showing the change in relationship that would occur if the World Bank pursued a knowledge-sharing strategy. Both were helpful in reinforcing the logic of the change idea with reasons.

But at the same time, recognize the limits of images. Some ideas can't easily be depicted in images. For instance, why do we need words to explain that images are powerful? And images tend to simplify complex ideas. In creating a simplified visual map of an immensely complex phenomenon, images may isolate several variables out of perhaps ten or twenty that are actually active. In doing so, they may give the audience a misleading picture of the whole phenomenon. That's because two-dimensional charts are usually partial truths. They reflect only a fraction of a multidimensional reality. If more dimensions are added to a chart in an effort to capture more of the reality, the chart soon collapses into incomprehensibility at about the fourth dimension.[5] Multidimensional phenomena are generally more easily communicated in narratives than in images.

Closing the Presentation

So you've captured the audience's attention. You've stimulated desire for a different future. You've reinforced the audience's desire for change with powerful reasons in the form of stories. Now what? How do you close the presentation?

It's a truism that all good presentations end strongly. The presentation's closing ties the elements of the presentation together. It brings out the point of the presentation. It ends with a bang, not a whimper.

And here lies a pitfall. When speakers know that they have to end strongly, they risk sliding back into a preaching, lecturing, instructional, hierarchical mode of closure. Just when they are about to triumph, they snatch defeat from the jaws of victory by arguing with the audience, thus undermining any narrative momentum they have been able to develop.

If speakers are using their narrative intelligence, they stay in a narrative mode. They appeal to both the emotions and the mind by inviting the audience to daydream and imagine a different future. They don't tell. They entice.

Normally, closure isn't a separate phase of the presentation: it's a seamless continuation of reinforcing the desire for change with reasons. It simply adds a final reason why what is being proposed makes sense and must—inexorably—be implemented. It may be a striking, unexpected reason. It may be your most powerful reason. It may be your most eloquently articulated reason, but it isn't qualitatively different. It appeals to the emotions as well as the imagination. But in the end, it's another reason.

The ending reinforces where the leader wants the audience to be at the end of the presentation: ideally, the audience is in a state of enthusiastic reverie, fleshing out in their minds what the new future could be like. The ending should reinforce this state and of course do nothing to detract from it.

One easy option is to end with a moving story that exemplifies the change idea under discussion.

Another option, used by many of the greatest speeches in history, is to end on this note: "Let us go forward into the future together and—" This approach epitomizes the spirit of joint action and collaboration that is the hallmark of transformational leadership.

Thus, Pericles' great funeral oration in 431 B.C., given as a memorial to the first Athenian soldiers who fell in the Peloponnesian war, ends: "Now let everyone respectively indulge in becoming grief for his departed friends, and then retire."

And Winston Churchill ended one his most eloquent speeches with another "let us" phrase: "Let us therefore brace ourselves to our duties and so bear ourselves that, if the British Empire and its Commonwealth last for a thousand years, men will still say, 'This was their finest hour.'" Of course, at the time, the British nation hadn't yet done much to warrant the conclusion that this was to be the finest hour in the entire history of the nation. Here Churchill nudges the listeners to join him in imagining what kind of conduct might justify such a conclusion. Since it is the audience who imagines what those actions might be, those imaginings can easily become self-fulfilling prophecies.

A moving line of poetry, or a pithy quotation, might also be able to bring out the point of what you've been saying in powerful, unforgettable language.

Still another elegant option, one that ties everything together, is to refer back to the story with which you began the presentation, and continue and reinforce it. The story then serves as a pair of bookends to the presentation, giving it a sense of symmetry and closure.

When leaders have got their audience's attention, stimulated their desire for change, and reinforced that desire with reasons, they have begun the leadership conversation. But it is only a beginning. As the change idea gets conceptualized and implemented by the audience, it will evolve. New insights will emerge. Problems will be encountered. Questions will be raised. Resistance will surface. If forward momentum is to be maintained, the conversation between leaders and their followers must continue. It is to this issue that I turn in Chapter Eleven.

11

CONTINUING THE CONVERSATION

" When minds meet, they don't just exchange facts:
they transform them, reshape them, draw different
implications from them, engage in new trains of thought. "

—Theodore Zeldin[1]

If the initial task of the language of leadership is to spark energy and initiate forward motion, its never-ending task is to ensure that the change idea continues to be pursued with sustained élan, spirit, and passion. The first steps aim at creating the spark; once that's happened, the flames need to be fanned and turned into an unstoppable conflagration. Thus it's one thing to get people excited about a worthwhile idea: it's another to keep that energy flowing.

Three Challenges

The challenges here are threefold.

From within, there's a tendency toward *entropy*. As problems arise, blockages are encountered, and the inevitable resistance to change surfaces. Joint activity is what keeps energy flowing so that enthusiasm builds on enthusiasm and energy becomes infectious. If leaders or followers are pursuing the change idea alone, the potential energy of the collectivity may never coalesce. Leaders and their followers are most likely to overcome resistance if they can confront challenges together, reminding each other why the change idea is worthwhile, energizing each other, spurring each other on, collectively raising their sights and their game to maintain forward progress. People need to be building the kind of trust that can help them to remain resolute in the face of difficulty. In concerted activity, information, insights, knowledge, and wisdom can be shared. Mobilizing many minds in a joint dialogue can both enhance understanding of the problems and increase the likelihood of finding solutions.

A second danger is *loss of focus*. As energy is unleashed, as opportunities open up and new avenues become apparent, there is a vast new scope for Machiavellian scheming, individualism, and careerism to reemerge. In a scramble for new positions, new turf, and new careers, clan warfare may break out, and the goal may be lost from sight. In the first instance, it may be an issue of conducting a conversation to see whether a focus on common goals can be reestablished. If that doesn't work and dissidents continue to pursue counterproductive action, then it may be necessary to separate them from the committed change agents. Of course, what is productive adaptation and what is counterproductive disruption will be matters of judgment. Not everyone may agree. Dialogue offers the best possibility of reaching a consensual solution.

Leadership also faces *dangers from outside*. When energy has been generated and implementation is under way, all this bustling, enthusiastic activity risks being seen by those in authority as chaos. The top management may become alarmed. Or outside investors may see the change as unproductive turbulence rather than progress toward a goal. The danger is most acute when implementation has started and costs are being incurred, while benefits are still ahead. With all this flowing, bubbling, kinetic energy, the authoritarian mind-set lurking in reptilian brains may reassert itself and seek to reestablish order in the name of common sense and efficiency, and so kill exuberance and energy. Those in authority—managers, politicians, teachers, parents, outsiders—may begin taking steps to reestablish order in ways that deenergize and stop momentum. Authority may begin to speak in a contrived, institutional language that impresses, intimidates, blusters, browbeats, and subdues, while all the time unwittingly signaling just how inhuman that institutional authority is.

Overcoming the Challenges

If these three dangers are to be averted, a balance needs to be achieved between making forward progress and discussing issues that have to be resolved. All forward progress and no discussion can be just as disastrous as all discussion and no forward progress. If the energy is to keep flowing and growing, ideally leaders elicit a process of interaction. Articulating a change idea and sparking action toward its accomplishment is thus only the beginning of leadership. To continue forward momentum, leaders need to make it easy and comfortable for people to contribute their insights. They need to give people the chance to converse, person-to-person. The process is a conversation.

Leadership Conversation

There's nothing special or technical or mysterious about a leadership conversation. It's a conversation in the way the word is used in everyday speech.

We all know what a good conversation is, even if we enjoy it all too rarely. Think of an interesting dinner party where participants have fresh points of view but don't try to thrust their opinions upon others; where the discussion is inclusive and participants create openings for each other, drawing everyone into the discussion and drawing each other out; where the talk is lively but participants speak respectfully even when they disagree; where they share relevant stories rather than make abstract pronouncements; where participants are willing to speak on a variety of subjects but are not afraid to admit ignorance or mistakes; where the language is intelligible and free from jargon; where the flow of serious thought is lightened by periodic laughter; where people feel it is easy to make their contribution; where they listen to each other with genuine curiosity and learn.

Such interchanges are atypical in the communications of managers with their staff, of teachers with pupils, of parents with teenagers, or of politicians with their electors. The communications of authority figures traditionally follow a different path, starting from what the authority figure "knows," what the system or program "requires," what the institution "wants." It's talking *at* people rather than *with* people. All too often, it involves lecturing and preaching rather than participating in a conversation that makes everyone want to continue the dialogue.

What Is a Conversation?

A conversation is an exploration in which the parties agree for the duration of the interchange to try to develop a larger understanding of the issues. Conversations allow people with different views of a topic to learn from each other.

A conversation isn't a *negotiation*. A negotiation is a process of resolving disputes and conflicts through talks and discussions. The parties bargain for individual or collective advantage or try to craft outcomes that will serve their common interests. In a negotiation, typically the parties come with the relatively fixed positions and goals and seek to promote those positions and goals, accommodating those of the other parties to the extent necessary. By contrast, the object of a conversation is collective learning.

Nor is a conversation an *argument*. An argument is inherently adversarial, in which each party tries to win by persuading the other party to accept their point of view. By contrast, a genuine conversation is inherently collaborative, in which the object is shared exploration and discovery rather than to secure the victory of any preconceived viewpoint.

Conversation is *person-to-person*—not role-to-role. Conversation is conducted on the same level, one human being to another, not people acting out roles, saying what they've been told to say or what's expected of them, representing their organization or functions or jobs, or watching over their shoulders to see what the boss wants them to say. Nor is it a bunch of exhibitionists shouting, "Listen to me! Aren't I just something!" where no one is really listening to what anyone else is saying.

Those in authority have a special responsibility for making a conversation person-to-person, because in a hierarchical setting subordinates will assume initially that the interchange is role-to-role, where they're expected for the most part to listen and obey. Leaders can do several things to launch a genuine conversation:

- Ask questions.
- Level with people.
- Show vulnerability.
- Build on the inputs of others.
- Share stories.
- Encourage others to share their stories.
- Have participants tell one another's stories.

Ask Questions   One way to stimulate real discussion is for leaders to ask questions. Instead of making assertions, they explore what others think, particularly with open-ended questions—such as "what if?"—questions that minimize the limiting assumptions built into them. But be careful: it's possible to overdo the questions. If managers do nothing but ask questions, distrust and frustration can break out as participants begin to suspect manipulation. The ancient Greek philosopher Socrates taught the world a great deal, but he would have been an annoying conversation partner when he refused to answer questions and carried on—at least as recorded in some of Plato's dialogues—with the pretence of knowing nothing.

Level with People   Hidden agendas kill conversations. Even the suspicion of their existence can prevent frank discussion. Be willing to say where you stand and say what you think, at least provisionally, while showing yourself open to entertaining alternative viewpoints.

Show Vulnerability   As Mark McCormack suggests in *What They Don't Teach You at Harvard Business School,* learning to utter three hard-to-say phrases—"I don't know," "I need help," and "I was wrong"—can help hierarchical leaders promote conversations.[2] By setting aside the pretences of invulnerability and omniscience, the manager invites subordinates to trust.

Build on the Inputs of Others   Hierarchical leaders have a special responsibility to listen carefully to what others are saying, searching for scintillas of good sense and exploring the implications. The discussion proceeds in a "yes and" mode, rather than "yes but."

Share Stories   An important route for getting into a person-to-person interchange is for leaders to share stories. When a story is shared, listeners don't need to accept or reject the story: it's something that they can live together. It's a mutually shared experience, something in which they all participate. The normal response is neither acceptance nor rejection but rather to tell another story. It might be a story in the same vein. Or it might be, "I have a different experience of that!" followed by a story that reflects another point of view. Either way, one story leads to another. A story is neither right nor wrong. It simply *is*. In this way, storytelling is naturally collaborative. Story is the natural language of conversation.[3]

Encourage Others to Share Their Stories   Obviously, leaders don't just tell their own stories. They share their stories so as to make it easy for others to share *their* stories. In the process, everyone learns about what progress has been made, what setbacks have been encountered, what needs exist, how issues are being tackled, who is grappling with them, and what new steps need to be taken. Through the exchange of stories, everyone gains insight on what is going on and what is possible.

Have Participants Tell One Another's Stories   Where people have conflicting viewpoints, they are living in different constructions of reality. If a conversation is organized among such antagonistic parties, the risk is that the confirmation bias will kick in and participants will simply interpret other viewpoints as a confirmation and reinforcement of their own version of reality. They may fail to explore the possibility of a new story that might be a more compelling version of their ongoing life narrative. If participants can be encouraged to understand and tell the story of the other party as coherently and convincingly as they can, then the mere process of learning about others and their viewpoints may be enough to catalyze change.[4] (See the exercise in Appendix 2.)

How Stories Promote Conversation

When we hear a powerful story, we have the feeling that it is somehow unique, somehow without precedent. We perceive a sense of the "new-bornness" of the entire world, as if there has been nothing like this, ever, anywhere. It is the same feeling that we get when we perceive a beautiful object that "fills the mind and . . . gives the 'never before in the history of the world' feeling."[5]

Story stimulates creativity. It causes us to gape and suspend analytic thought, to set aside the inclination to slice and dice experience into abstract categories. Instead, the mind is prompted to search backward to earlier examples and parallels. And simultaneously we are prompted to new acts of creation, to imagine other analogous examples in the future. One story leads to more stories.

A story thus moves us to bring new things into the world. It hurtles us forward and backward, requiring us to break new ground but obliging us also to refer back to territory we thought we had left behind. In this way, stories, like all beautiful objects, carry greetings from other worlds.[6]

Just as the moment of hearing a powerful story makes the listener more lively, so the fact of listening to the story turns it into a living thing. The seeming aliveness of the story makes listeners want to pass it on.[7]

The experience of following a story thus has two parts. Our attention is involuntarily given to the story, and then this quality of heightened attention is—almost involuntarily—extended to other persons or things. We now have a pivot point from which to survey the universe. Suddenly the world coheres. A story provides the kind of plausibility and reasonableness that enables people to make sense of complex ideas.

A powerful story causes us to undergo a "radical decentering."[8] We give up our imaginary position as the center of our perceptual universe. A transformation takes place in our perspective on the world. We cease to be locked in our own story. We become interested in others.

Conversation is about bringing such stories together, so that the stories flirt with each other, learning to dance and embrace.

Conversations Are About Learning

Conversations are crucial to leadership because leadership entails the co-creation of innovation. Leaders depend on their followers to help complete the change idea in action. Since no complex new idea survives contact with reality intact, adaptation is inevitable. And adaptation will require the inputs of those involved in implementation. As the contexts in which the idea is being implemented will differ, so the knowledge of those differences will be important. And the contributions of those who have such knowledge will be critical.

Conversation facilitates learning. It allows people with different views and experiences to understand each other. A good conversation has "trapdoors, secret gardens and hidden staircases."[9] It is full of surprises and unexpected discoveries. Conversations allow participants to explore these different pathways, construct their own meaning from what's being said, and learn how to adapt a change idea to their specific contexts.

In conversations, there is the laughter of recognition: it's a stretching exercise for the brain and the heart. Conversations are seriously playful. When participants engage openly, there is no telling in advance how things will turn out. "To be playful is not to be trivial or frivolous or to act as though nothing of consequence will happen. . . . When we are playful with each other. . . the relationship is open to surprise; *everything* that happens is of consequence."[10] By contrast, "seriousness is a dread of the unpredictable outcome of open possibility."[11] To be serious is to press for a predetermined conclusion. To be playful is to allow for unanticipated possibility.

Conversation is the intersection of multiple stories. As conversationalists, participants live on the threshold of different worlds. They come ready to explore other stories, other ways of seeing things, other universes. As Theodore Zeldin says in his delightful little book *Conversations:* "Conversation doesn't just reshuffle the cards: it creates new cards."[12]

Conversations Need a Container

Stimulating conversation entails creating an empty space where the interchange can take place. In stressing the need to create conversations to enhance energy and reinforce forward progress, I don't mean to imply that all traditional meetings of managers, politicians, teachers, or parents should be discarded. But many of them could benefit from being restructured from one-way pronouncements to interactive conversations.

Indeed, managers, when they act as managers, will go on making their slideshows. Sellers will go on doing sales presentations. Teachers will go on giving the lessons that the syllabus prescribes. Politicians will go on running their campaigns.

Nonetheless, when managers, teachers, politicians, or parents force their staff, their pupils, their electors, their teenagers to sit through prepackaged presentations, they are creating dynamics inimical to enduring enthusiasm. One-way presentations push audiences into passive listening roles, as well as making presenters appear pompous know-it-alls, more concerned about having their view prevail than about helping resolve the issues of the people they are talking to.

In the workplace, managers can't connect with staff unless they know what problems they're having difficulty with. In the marketplace, sellers can't really write a proposal until they find out which version of success a client wants with this project. In the schoolroom, teachers can't really help students unless they know where students are stuck. In the family, parents can't really engage teenagers to become adults unless they can get inside their world and see where they are coming from.

By contrast, when these people act as leaders, they launch conversations to solve problems, share experiences and generate new options. Once they've developed a minimal amount of consensus on where a joint activity is heading, leaders need to sit down at eye level with the people—with staff, with clients, with pupils, with teenagers, with electors—and say: "Let's talk!"

Virtual Conversations

Healthy groups get better over time, in part because their members get to know one another's' stories. They learn what the other group members are thinking, what their strengths and tendencies are likely to be, and so they can anticipate what their fellows will deliver and adjust their performance accordingly. This process happens easily and naturally when people meet face-to-face.

Virtual teams and communities are, however, pervasive in forward-looking organizations, especially for knowledge work and for work that involves people on the road much of the time. In such arrangements, members of teams or communities interact electronically by e-mail, the Web, telephone, and videoconference.

Virtual teams and communities have a number of advantages over groups that only meet physically. They can be larger, more diverse, and collectively more knowledgeable than those that depend on face-to-face communications: members can be scattered around the world and still stay in touch. As a result, widely dispersed expertise can be brought to bear on complex issues quickly and efficiently.

However, periodic face-to-face meetings are generally necessary for the group to become and remain a dynamic living entity. If members of a community have never met, the group tends to remain somewhat blurred, with participants rarely feeling altogether comfortable as to who is in the group, and willingness to pitch in for group activities is difficult to elicit. Of course, it depends on the complexity of the task at hand as to what is the most suitable mode of interaction: simple updates on project status or requests for information can be conveniently done by virtual means. But when it comes to solving complex problems, figuring out what the group should be doing, or creating new designs and concepts, it may be more efficient to meet.

One reason why people need to meet face-to-face is that asking for advice is an implicit admission of ignorance. In low-trust organizations, public admissions of ignorance may lead to career setbacks or worse. Hence before people will be willing to show ignorance and ask for advice, they need to have a sense of whom they are exposing their ignorance to. Once people have met and exchanged stories so that they have established a minimum level of trust, then they can disperse around the world and exchange views openly.

What can be done to boost trust levels in conversations online? One key can be found in the first two lines of Shakespeare's *Hamlet:*

Bernardo: *Who's there?*

Francisco: *Nay, answer me: stand, and unfold yourself.*

The uncertainty as to "who's there" is usually the biggest constraint to open conversation online. One way to address this is to make explicit who's there so that participants know (or can find out) who's listening or reading. A second step is to find ways to have those people "unfold" themselves.

How do you unfold yourself? Revealing how you have dealt with adversity can be one of the most effective ways. It can bring into focus what sort of person you are. People might not agree with you, but they learn quite a bit about you. All going well, they may start to think of you as a human being, not simply as a manager or expert or bureaucrat—a mere voice on the end of the line.

The success of the "facebook" technology among young people suggests that it is possible to have people unfold themselves online. When so many people are doing it, it starts to feel normal. Older generations are generally more reticent to reveal themselves in a facebook world. They don't seem to be comfortable being too open, perhaps considering possible repercussions.

In webinars, it's also possible to organize audience polls before or during the webinar. Carefully designed polls can quickly reveal what the audience as a whole is thinking about the issues under discussion as it occurs. The audience polls can enable the audience to unfold itself in a fashion and so embolden people to speak up, in the process helping the discussion focus on issues that people are really interested in.

In using audience polls like this in a webinar, the speaker and the audience sometimes have more information about what people are thinking than they would have in a live, face-to-face discussion.

The other aspect to keep in mind with online discussions is to allow enough time for the group to get comfortable with itself. In my experience, a webinar is usually just getting going after about ninety minutes, which is often when the webinar is scheduled to end. Planning a series of sessions can help the group have enough time to unfold itself so that conversation can blossom.

Leadership and Innovation

A leadership presentation that generates enthusiasm is a remarkable thing. But at its best, at its most convincing, in its most superlative deployment of the language of leadership, it's simply a beginning. The way for leaders to continue and accelerate enthusiastic implementation and deepen the relationship is by having regular, ongoing conversations with the people they are leading, about the things going on in their context and how they can address emerging threats or opportunities. Leadership is thus a continuing set of experiments, not all of which will succeed as planned. Seeing leadership as experimentation can help prevent setbacks from producing discouragement.

Real leadership shows us that people have more than the two choices of being either cynical or naive.[13] Somewhere between blindly accepting whatever we are told and second-guessing everyone's motives, leadership creates a space where joint commitments can be made to do what is worthwhile.

Leadership conversations involve a balance between having a ferocious determination to achieve the goal and having the openness and curiosity and willingness to listen to other ideas about how to get there, even including whether it's the right goal to be pursuing at this time. The leaders' conception of what needs to be done is simply the "best version of that idea so far": it remains perpetually provisional and contingent. Leaders remain continually on the lookout for an improvement, an evolution, a maturer version that will lead to better results.

In the process of discovery both leaders and followers will be touched. Something changes between them. Their relationship opens forward dramatically. The strength of conversation is to invite all parties into the drama.

12

EPILOGUE

> ❝ Less is more. ❞
> **—Ludwig Mies van der Rohe**

For too long, we imagined that leadership and change were the work of a few exceptional people. We were mistaken. In fact, leadership and change are driven by ordinary people who speak and act in a different way. Once we learn the language of leadership, then we can all drive change, if we want to.

The language of leadership is a language with simple principles and patterns and sequences that can make any worthwhile change idea resonate and sing. Learning these principles and patterns and sequences implies making relatively small changes to the way and the order in which we say things. But introducing those small changes can make a massive difference in how an audience reacts. As Malcolm Gladwell has noted, the difference between generating resistance and enthusiasm is narrower than we imagine.[1] Through the language of leadership, ordinary people can have extraordinary impact.

In a way, the language of leadership is no more than common sense. Stress the negative and people pay attention. Tell people about examples where a change has already happened and they begin to imagine how it could occur in their lives. Get people interested in the change and suddenly they're willing to listen to reasons. Put reasons in the form of stories and people remember them. Commit to a clear, worthwhile goal and you find this helps generate sustained enthusiasm. Understand the stories that your listeners are living and you discover they're not as intransigent as you imagine. Use body language that reflects an intention to communicate and people can see that you mean it. Implementing these simple principles and patterns and sequences in our discourse has a dramatic effect on whether people listen to and act on what we say—or not.

And the impact of the language of leadership happens in a hurry. This is not about applying grinding arguments, each piled on top of the other, until the audience concedes defeat, begs for mercy, and signifies willingness to sign a surrender agreement. The language of leadership is nimble, light-footed, entertaining as well as educational. It's accompanied by laughter and infectious energy. When discourse is conducted in the language of leadership, the world sounds very different from much of the world we live in now. It makes the exchange fresh, stimulating, and inviting.

And the application of the language of leadership has a wide range. It applies to people with immense power who will lose it if they can't inspire enthusiasm for what they are doing. It applies to people with no power, who can move mountains when they learn how to generate excitement for their cause. It applies to huge global organizations as well as intimate situations in schools and families. For the most part, the principles play out the same way regardless of the context. The language of leadership can empower anyone—managers, professionals, politicians, teachers, parents, anyone who wants to change the world for the better—to do so.

Why Does It Work?

The language of leadership communicates quickly and simply and meaningfully. It involves using narrative intelligence to say a whole lot less while conveying a whole lot more. The greater richness of communication doesn't come from transmitting more information. It comes from the additional content that listeners themselves generate. The leader says less: the listeners understand more. This paradox happens because the leader communicates in a way that fits the way human beings think. It mirrors the peculiarities of the human mind and heart. As a result, people are able to see possibilities that were hitherto invisible to them. As these new possibilities open up, the listeners find themselves willing to assist with the task of reimagining and re-creating the future.

Communication between human beings doesn't function in the way we've been taught to expect, with people systematically processing information and carefully listening to reason and analysis. To become effective leaders, we have to adjust some of our most fundamental assumptions. The truth is that we've been living for several millennia with some counterproductive myths. They push us to go on acting ineffectively, often achieving the opposite of what we want.

We have spent so much time celebrating the power of science and reason and analysis that we have a hard time accepting that bland, simple narratives could be apter to get action than sophisticated analysis. Surely this can't be true. But in reality it is no more than an obvious consequence of what we know about how human beings think and make decisions. If people think in narrative and make decisions in narrative, then talking to people in abstractions is akin to hammering the square pegs of analytical thought into the round holes in their brains. The pain and wasted time of those efforts have been enormous. When we see how easily round-edged stories can slide into people's minds, why shouldn't we apply this finding? Should it really be any surprise that once we talk to people in a way that matches how their brains are made, they listen to and connect with our message?

Instead of arguing with our listeners in an adversarial fashion, so that energy is consumed unproductively in conflict, we can elicit their active participation in a judo-like manner, causing collective energy and intelligence to flow into productive channels.

Narrative Is More Important Than We Thought

Story is important. This much is straightforward. But narrative intelligence is more than that. Narrative intelligence is about knowing the different patterns of story, knowing which pattern works in which context, intuiting which stories one's listeners are living, and having the capacity to judge how they will respond to new stories.

Narrative intelligence means understanding the role of protagonists and whether the audience is likely to empathize with them. It means being able to assess the tonality of the narrative and judge whether it will be positive, negative, or neutral for any particular listener. It's knowing when a story should be minimalist or maximalist to achieve its particular purpose. It's knowing how to weave together a sequence of narratives so that the listener is led inexorably from distrust and cynicism to understanding and enthusiasm. It's understanding the difference a single word or a single emphasis or a single gesture can make in an entire presentation. It's recognizing that we're not just sensitive to the meaning of narratives: we're acutely sensitive to them.

The language of leadership has its own grammar. Just as in the English language an adjective comes before its noun, and the subject generally comes before the verb, the language of leadership requires that getting attention comes before anything else, and that stimulating desire for change comes before providing reasons for change. Why is this so? It's a function of the way human beings are structured. Underlying psychological mechanisms make these patterns and sequences more resonant than others.

In the same way that once we have grasped the grammar of the English language we can put together an infinite number of effective sentences, so when we have mastered the language of leadership we can communicate an infinite array of change ideas and spark people into action—whether in organizations, in the marketplace, in politics, in communities, in schools, in families, wherever.

Before we understand its grammar, the accomplishment of leadership can look like spooky black magic. After we figure out what's going on, we can see that the feat is nothing special. It's something anyone can do. It's a matter of knowing what to look for, how to recognize it when you find it, how to develop it so that it's ready for prime time, and how to deliver it with maximum impact.

The Language of Leadership Can Be Learned

Some talents—like Olympic sprinting—are innate. But for the most part, mastery of the language of leadership isn't something we're born with. Apart from a few esoteric areas, such as Abraham Lincoln's way with aphorisms or Martin Luther King's ability to paint brilliant word pictures of the future, the abilities involved in applying the principles of the language of leadership aren't extraordinary.

Learning the language means doing a limited number of things right and doing them in the right order. The principles can be grasped rather rapidly and modest competence can often be accomplished even within a day. But mastery of any language takes a lifetime of learning and practice. Using the language of leadership effectively means seeing the world differently and understanding its dynamic in narrative terms. It means continuing to sharpen our narrative intelligence.

One reason why rapid initial progress is possible is that we already practice many elements of narrative intelligence in our social lives. In our organizational lives we have gotten into some very bad habits, talking to each other in tangles of abstractions and boring bullet points. This abstract way of speaking is more difficult to deliver and harder to listen to or understand. It takes more time and it communicates less.

When we transpose the narrative intelligence we practice in social life to more purposeful settings, we find that only minor adjustments are required. These minor adjustments make an immense difference to the impact of what we are trying to communicate.

This is not to imply that leadership is just a matter of words. Obviously over time our actions as leaders must be consistent with what we say. And saying the right things in the right way will have more effect if the enabling conditions of the language of leadership are in place. It will help if the leader is fully committed to a clear, worthwhile change idea. It will help if the leader can intuit the stories the listeners are living. It will help if the leader is authentically truthful. It will help if the leader's body language is consistent with the words that are used. These enabling conditions are important. But by themselves they are not sufficient for leadership. The most immediate impact will come from what leaders say and how they say it.

The Ethics of Leadership

If the language of leadership is so powerful in getting people to change their minds and do things they initially had no intention of doing, is there something unethical about it? Is it manipulative to appeal to people's feelings? I don't think so. Provided leaders live by a commitment to be authentically truthful, I don't see that it is evil or Machiavellian to communicate with people so as to fit the way their brains are made and make it easy for them to understand or remember what we are saying. Does anyone really think that we should communicate with people in ways that make it hard for them to understand or remember what we're saying? As it happens, we've been doing that unknowingly for an embarrassingly long time. To go on doing it knowingly would be unhelpful as well as self-destructive.

In making the case for narrative, I am in no way trying to undermine science or drag the world back to the dark ages of myth and superstition. On the contrary, I am committed to science and its self-correcting methodology. We need to apply double-blind controls in experiments, where neither the subjects nor the experimenters know the experiment's objectives during data collection. We need to vet our results at professional conferences and in peer-reviewed journals. We should insist that research be replicated by others unaffiliated with the original researcher. In our reports, we need to include any evidence to the contrary, as well as alternative interpretations of the data. We need to encourage colleagues to be skeptical and to raise objections. If extraordinary claims are being made, we must put forward extraordinary evidence. Those methods need to be applied to the language of leadership as well as to everything else.

But when we've done all that, and it's vital that we do it, how do we communicate the results of what we have discovered, particularly if our findings are highly disruptive to people's lives? If we try to communicate those findings by the same methods through which the findings were derived, what usually happens? Pushback. Resistance. Cynicism. Hostility. If we use narrative intelligence and employ the language of leadership, the results can be very different.

It's a matter of using science and analysis for what they are good at, and using the language of leadership to communicate science's findings and get them implemented. Just think for a moment. Would it be scientific to go on using the language of analysis for an activity for which it isn't suited, while refusing to use a different language that does work? To adopt such an approach would be the height of unscientific behavior.

The Age of Leadership

We are entering an era with a rapidly growing need for leadership. This is caused by the convergence of irresistible socioeconomic forces. Accelerating economic and social change in the global economy, the consequent imperative for ever faster innovation, the emergence of global networks of partners, the rapidly growing role of intangibles, which can't be controlled like physical goods, the increasing ownership of the means of production by knowledge workers, the escalating power of customers in the marketplace, and the burgeoning diversity in both the workplace and marketplace—all these forces imply a vastly more important role for transformational leadership in the future. The ability to get results in the face of these challenges will depend at least as much on leadership as on management. It will depend on a capacity to inspire enduring enthusiasm in people over whom we have no hierarchical control.

These irresistible forces will drive organizations to develop genuine leadership capability as a necessary competence. Leadership—the ability to connect people to meaningful goals without hierarchical power to compel compliance—will become a requirement for organizational survival.

Management won't disappear. We'll continue to have much to thank management for. It has helped us achieve the wonders of the modern global economy—its stunning scientific accomplishments and the massive improvements in the physical standard of living of most people, at least in the developed countries—and it will go on doing so.

But the challenges now facing the human race won't be solved by better management alone. Management will still be needed, but it will be less pivotal. In fact, it will be mostly taken for granted. Our capacity to manage will give us the technical means to solve our most intractable problems. What is needed now is the will to solve them. So goals, ends, purposes—what we are trying to accomplish—move to center stage.

In the world of management, the goals are largely given. Management is about finding the quickest, cheapest, and best way to reach those goals. The language of management is naturally abstract. Human goals are naturally absent from its discourse.

Once the emphasis shifts toward goals, ends, and purposes, then it is natural for the language to shift from abstractions to narratives, which have goals built into them.

The goals of human beings are embedded in their stories. The clarification and focusing of our goals will necessitate a sharper narrative intelligence. It will entail understanding our own story and its connection with other stories. We will need to understand the web of stories in which we found ourselves when we were born, and which will continue after we die. It is only within these continuing, communal narratives that we will be able to make sense of our lives and our goals.

Initially our goals are derived from the stories of those who have gone before us, but gradually they become ours as we embark on our own quests. These quests are narrative in nature. They address the question: Where is our story heading? The question itself is both purposeful and also part of its own answer. This is not a journey toward a specified destination but rather a quest whose goals will unfold themselves in the course of the journey. [2]

As we change others, we ourselves will change. In our roles as leaders—as managers, change agents, politicians, professionals, teachers, parents—we will see the narrative character of our own lives through the stories of our listeners. The stories that we hear and tell will touch us and initiate new thinking. The end of each leader's story will thus be a beginning. It will generate new narratives for the leader as well as for the listeners.

In pursuing our quest, narrative intelligence will be key. As the focus shifts increasingly to goals, and the discourse becomes increasingly more concrete and less abstract, it is natural and indeed inevitable that narrative intelligence—an ability to listen to and decode the meaning of stories, to understand how and when to use stories, and to anticipate the effect of stories—will come to the fore. It will rest on a recognition of how exquisitely sensitive human beings are to even the smallest details of the stories we hear. That's why leadership is so tricky and difficult.

But in its trickiness and difficulty, there's also a measure of hope. Understanding the stories of the people we are talking to can have a decisive effect on our ability to say something that will resonate and engage. Sharing our story in a different way can dramatically change the impact of what is said. Understanding the grammar of narrative can help us navigate through this turbulent, quicksilver context of interacting narratives. The language of leadership can help all those who would like to be able to operate more effectively in this context and change the world for the better. That ability isn't a privilege that is restricted to those who were born with a silver tongue or the gift of gab. Once the principles of the language of leadership are mastered, any determined person can accomplish the feat.

Ultimately the implication of the language of leadership is this: there is a pattern of simple narratives that, under the right enabling conditions, will make any worthwhile change idea difficult to resist. The task of leadership is to find it.

PRESENTATION TO THE CHANGE MANAGEMENT COMMITTEE OF THE WORLD BANK: APRIL 1996

In April 1996, I was asked to explain my ideas on information and knowledge management to the Change Management Committee of the World Bank. This committee comprised the managing directors as well as a few vice presidents and some influential senior advisers to the president of the bank. They were charged with "orchestrating change" in the World Bank.

Initially, I had been allotted half an hour to speak. Then I was told that someone else was being added to the agenda, so that I would only have fifteen minutes. Then I heard that yet another presenter was being inserted into the time slot, so that I would only have ten minutes. At the time, I was upset: how could I possibly convince a difficult, change-resistant audience of a new strategic thrust in ten minutes?

As it turned out, it was probably fortunate that I was allowed only ten minutes, as this induced me to concentrate on the elements that would really make an impact. This also led me to focus on narrative components of my presentation, since those were most succinct. At the time, I wasn't "thinking in narrative terms" at all. I was simply being pragmatic.

The New Triad

The time constraint also pushed me into abandoning the traditional triad of

Problem >> Analysis >> Solution

Instead, the presentation reflected the pattern that I have outlined in this book for any communication aimed at getting change:

Get Attention >> Stimulate Desire >> Reinforce with Reason

I begin with a story with several surprise elements—a good way to get attention.[1]

Getting Attention

I say that the World Bank already had experience in building knowledge infrastructure. This in itself would have been news to many of the members of the World Bank Change Management Committee, who had paid scant attention to such matters in the past and were uninformed about the innovations taking place in the Africa Region.

In my presentation, I explain how, in March 1995, the Africa Region had decided to implement a best practice system. Four months later, after checking on the experience in private sector organizations such as McKinsey and Company, in July 1995, we issued an instruction to the technical staff to start compiling their best practices.

Two months after that, in September 1995, the best practice system opened for business by Internet, phone, and e-mail. By December 1995, use of the system was widespread in two areas of expertise: gender and participation. Here I lull the audience into thinking that this is going to be a success story, even possibly a self-serving commercial for the Africa Region, where I had been the director.

I then outline the unexpected obstacles that the effort had encountered.

First, skepticism was pervasive, with people saying, "It won't work in the World Bank." That was plausible, as this response tended to greet every management initiative. However, the next elements were surprising: the news that the top experts in the Africa Region weren't sure what best practice was, or that the central vice presidencies, who were supposed to be the guardians of institutional best practice, didn't agree on best practice either. In fact, it was shocking that only one central vice presidency had any best practice managers.

When an instruction was given to compile best practice, our technical experts said that wasn't their job, and compliance with the instruction was minimal. Even in the two areas that did gain compliance, the volume of material expanded so rapidly that the user-friendliness of the system made it problematic. Now the audience is worried: ladies and gentlemen, we have a problem!

I have now begun to get the audience's attention with a couple of worrying stories.

Then I pique their interest by making a positive assertion—the World Bank is a treasure house of information and knowledge—and I ask three questions:

- What would be involved in exploiting the treasure house?
- How would we get from here to there?
- What does "there" look like?

Stimulating Desire

Now that I have the audience's attention, the conventional communication approach would be either to begin an analysis of the problems that need to be resolved, or to launch into a description of what the future knowledge and information sharing environment might look like. The former tack would probably lose the audience in a morass of difficulties. The latter would run the risk that the description would appear futuristic and the stuff of science fiction, unfeasible anywhere, let alone at the World Bank. Moreover it would be technically impossible for the clients of the World Bank—developing countries who lacked physical infrastructure and human skills for any high-tech endeavor.

Instead, I dive into the recent past, with a springboard story about an organization that is very similar to the World Bank—the Centers for Disease Control and Prevention—where such a system is already in place and is already solving real-world problems, not for people of a developed country like the United States, but in one of the poorest countries in the world: Zambia.

> In June of last year, a health worker in a tiny town in Zambia went to the Web site of the Centers for Disease Control and got the answer to a question about the treatment of malaria.

I emphasize that this isn't science fiction, posting the giant title, "FACT." No one can seriously argue that this is incredible. It has already happened!

And I reinforce the unusual aspects of the story:

- It's not about something happening in June 2015—it already happened in June 1995—nine months ago.
- It's not even something that happened in the capital of the country, but rather in a small village six hundred kilometers away from the capital—that is, exactly the kind of environment that the World Bank deals with.
- And remember, this isn't a developed country—this is Zambia, one of the poorest countries in the world.

The implicit argument I'm making is simple: If this could happen here, why not anywhere?

Then I link the story to the change idea:

- I say that the most important part of the picture is that the World Bank isn't in the picture. The World Bank doesn't have its knowledge organized to share with all the millions of people who make decisions about poverty.
- But—and here is where I invite the audience to dream—what if? What if the World Bank was organized to share its knowledge with the world? Just imagine what an organization it could become?

At the time, I didn't attach much importance to this particular slide. The story was only twenty-nine words long and it was one slide out of nineteen. If asked at the time, I would have said that what made the presentation effective was the substance in the following fourteen slides.

In one sense, this is true: the substance of the next fourteen slides *was* important. But I also discovered over the coming months and years that when I included a story like the Zambia story, the presentation worked like a charm. Listeners seemed to "get it." But when I didn't include a story like the Zambia story, everything ended in turmoil and confusion: the substance seemed to the audience like science fiction.

As a result, I eventually came to see that the inclusion of a story like the Zambia story—a springboard story—was a sine qua non for the audience to relate to the substance in an attentive, sympathetic way. Without a springboard story, the substance sounded futuristic and unbelievable. With the story, the listeners themselves began to imagine the future, and so it became credible. So although the Zambia story was only a tiny part of the whole presentation, it was actually the linchpin, the element that made the whole presentation work.

Reinforcing with Reasons

I know from the subsequent reactions of the audience that many of them began to dream. "That's right! We do have knowledge! We could reach many more people with our knowledge than we currently are. Suppose we were to do this? What would it look like?"

At this point I offer five linked "road maps," or stories, showing how we would get from "here" to "there."

Story #1

The first road map flows from the fact that the World Bank is a paper-based organization where everything happens at an incredibly slow pace. This is not just a problem inside the organization: disbursements to clients take weeks to be processed, creating significant client dissatisfaction. The obvious solution is to switch to digital systems, so that all information is available instantly, and so that disbursements, for instance, could be handled in hours, not weeks.

Story #2

In 1996, if you wanted to find out the current situation of the balance of payments of a country, you would have to go on a paper chase and calculate it yourself, or try to find the country economist and get the current assessment. It was obvious if we could organize systematic data banks of all commonly needed data, we could make that kind of data available both to staff and clients, saving both large amounts of time and effort for both.

Story #3

Once we had these rudimentary information systems in place, then we could go on to the more challenging task of assembling and sharing knowledge through the establishment of best practice systems, including incentives to encourage people to contribute. And if we could do this for staff, why not directly for clients? Not only would this help World Bank staff "get it right" again and again, it would also exponentially speed up client access to World Bank best practice.

Story #4

Our experience in the Africa Region had shown that merely establishing databases was only part of the challenge. It was also essential to create conversations among professionals across organizational boundaries so that we could actually generate common understanding of good and bad practice in specific knowledge domains. (These arrangements, which were then called "colleges," later came to be called "thematic groups" in the World Bank, and are known as "communities of practice" in many other organizations.)

Story #5

Once these arrangements were in place, we could then create electronic task-specific desktops for task teams.

And what would these electronic desktops look like?

- *Best practice:* Our teams would not want every best practice under the sun, but just the lessons of experience relevant to the particular work they are doing.

- *Bibliography:* Our teams would not want the whole Library of Congress, just the references and citations relevant to the particular project.

- *Policies and guidelines:* Our teams didn't need the whole massive operational manual and all the other policy guidelines that have accumulated over decades—just the sections relevant to the job under way.

- *Country information:* Our teams didn't want everything we knew about the countries, just the people and correspondence that led up to the work now ongoing—in effect, the story so far.

- *Reports:* Our teams didn't want all the old reports—just the reports that had been done in the same field as the task at hand.

- *Identifying experts:* Our team wanted to know, not who are the gurus generally, but rather who can answer questions on key issues relevant to the particular area of work.

- *Analytical tools:* Our team wanted spreadsheets showing economic, financial, and technical analyses of earlier work in the same area, not everything that has been done.

If we could do this for our staff, why stop there? Why not provide the same material directly for our clients, who needed exactly the same information and know-how for their own purposes. In this way, the clients could undertake more of the preparation effort and we could thus confine ourselves to guidance, as and when needed.

What Impact Would These Changes Have?

First, the impact in terms of efficiency would be huge. We could accelerate Bank response times exponentially—make them ten to twenty times faster, not just 10–20 percent faster.

Second, the improvement to the organization's effectiveness could be equally huge once we provided electronic access to information and knowledge to a massively expanded clientele.

Providing direct client access to real best practice would secure the World Bank's real comparative advantage as a development organization.

How much would it cost? Detailed estimates weren't available at the time, but it was fairly obvious that the significant investment costs (most of which had to be made anyway) would be offset by substantial savings in big data systems (by having fully integrated systems instead of multiple incompatible systems) and in terms of traditional operating costs.

The World Bank and its clients would no longer have to face each other across tall boundary walls. Instead, the World Bank and its clients would be fully integrated so that the sharing of information and knowledge would create major gains in efficiency and effectiveness. It would create the genuine partnership that was often talked about, but had proven so elusive to create in practice.

The vision is that of a *new kind of organization* that would be acknowledged as a world leader in leveraging information and knowledge. It amounts to a comprehensive new strategy for the organization with cost savings in information and operational benefits from knowledge.

Postscript: What Actually Happened?

That was the presentation that I made in April 1996. What happened? In due course, the bank's top management espoused most elements of the game plan, although information and knowledge followed two very different routes. Information was handled by conventional management practices, while knowledge was dependent on leadership.

Over the next several years, substantial investments were made to upgrade the World Bank's information systems. Accounting systems were standardized and integrated. A single e-mail system was introduced. An intranet and an external Web site were built.

On the knowledge side, the "stretch goal," approved by the Board of Directors in March 1997, was to become "a world leader in knowledge management by the year 2000." As outlined in the Preface, tremendous obstacles to implementation emerged in the years that ensued, including lack of authority, funding, and consistent top management support. But by 2000, most of the knowledge program had been successfully implemented. Leadership—in the form of a clear and inspiring vision, compellingly communicated—had overcome the obstacles. The World Bank was indeed being benchmarked as a world leader in sharing knowledge.

APPENDIX 2

TEMPLATES
AND EXERCISES

The use of narrative by leaders is a performance art and one learns it by practice. This appendix provides a brief discussion of what exactly a story is, as well as some templates that I use in workshops to accelerate the learning process.

What Is a Story?

In this book, *narrative* and *story* are used as synonyms, in the broad sense of an account of a set of events that are causally related. One could fill a whole library with the academic discussion swirling around such a simple commonsense notion. Here, I will allude to only a few of the issues.

Various practitioners have suggested different definitions. For some, *story* should be defined in the narrower sense of a well-told story, with a protagonist, a plot, and a turning point leading to a resolution. For them, *narrative* might be used in the broader sense that I employ in this book. In this view, locutions that lack the traditional elements of a well-told story are not so much stories as ideas for possible stories yet to be told, or fragments of stories.[1]

Others have suggested that *story* should be used in the broader sense I am suggesting, while *narrative* should be used in the narrower sense of "a story as told by a narrator." On this view, "narrative = story + theme": the theme is a layer added to the story to instruct, to provide an emotional connection, or to impart a deeper meaning.[2]

In practice, the actual everyday usage of both *story* and *narrative* is very broad. Polkinghorne and others have suggested that we accept this broad meaning and treat *story* and *narrative* as synonyms.[3] Within the broad field of story, we can then distinguish classically structured stories, well-made stories, minimalist stories, anti-stories, fragmentary stories, stories with no ending, stories with multiple endings, stories with multiple beginnings, stories with endings that circle back to the beginning, comedies, tragedies, detective stories, romances, folk tales, novels, theater, movies, television mini-series, and so on, without the need to get into quasi-theological discussions as to what is truly a story.[4]

In common usage, *story* is a large tent, with many variations within the tent. Some variations are more useful for some purposes than others. There are probably many variations that haven't yet been identified. If we start out with predetermined ideas of what a "real story" is, we may end up missing useful forms of narrative.

Exercise #1: The Story of the Change

This exercise aims at clarifying the goal, as discussed in Chapter Two.

Tell the five elements of the story of the change:

- What is the domain of the change?
- What is the problem?
- What will the future state look like once the change has been implemented?
- How will we get from here to there?
- Will the change:
  - Be seen as worthwhile for its own sake?
  - Enable the participants to grow and develop?
  - Generate benefits for everyone involved in the change?
  - Be devoid of instrumental harm to others?

Exercise #2: The Leader's Own Story

This exercise addresses committing to the change, as discussed in Chapter Three.

Tell your story:

- Are you clearly committed to making the change happen, come what may? Have you thought through what's at stake for yourself, your spouse, your children?

- Are you willing to make the necessary changes in your own life to make this happen? Are you willing to give whatever it takes, in terms of time, energy, effort, patience? Are you ready to sacrifice yourself and your ego and ambition and pride in order to make the change happen? Are you willing to commit to making the change happen, even if it involves personal loss, humiliation, and lack of recognition?

- Imagine that the change has gone very well: Are you ready for success and its ramifications? What are likely to be the repercussions for you and your family? On your relationships with friends and colleagues?

- Imagine that the change has gone badly: Are you ready for failure and its ramifications? Are you ready for the impact on you and your family? On your relationships with friends and colleagues? Can you live with all that?

Exercise #3: The Story of the Person Who Must Change

This set of exercises helps build an understanding of the audience's story, as discussed in Chapters Four and Eleven. The point of the exercises is to

- Give practice in telling stories.
- Give practice in listening to stories.
- Help you understand the world, the values, the mind-set of the person who needs to change.

Try to tell the stories as coherently and persuasively as you can.

1. Pick one (or more) of the people who need to change, someone who finds the change difficult, perhaps the person who is most likely to be opposed to the change.

2. Tell the story of that person. Tell the story of why they feel the way they do, how they have come to feel that way. It will include what their values are, as well as their hopes, their dreams, and their fears. The story will end, "That's why the person doesn't want to change." Tell the story of that person as coherently and persuasively as possible, making sense of the world of that person.

3. Put yourself in the world of that person, and tell his or her story in the first person. The story will end: "And that's why I don't want to change."

4. Tell the story in the second person. The story will end: "And that's why you don't want to change."

Exercise #4: Crafting the Springboard Story

This exercise addresses stimulating the desire for change, as discussed in Chapter Nine.

1. What is the *specific change* in the organization or community or group that you hope to spark with the story?

2. Think of an *incident* (either inside or outside your organization, community, or group) where the change was in whole or in part successfully implemented? Describe it briefly.

3. Who is the *single protagonist* in the story?

4. Is the single protagonist *typical* of your specific audience? If not, can the story be told from the point of view of such a protagonist?

5. What are the *date* when and *place* where the *single protagonist* began the story? For example, "In July 2003, in London, Tony Smith . . ."

6. Does the story *fully embody the change idea?* If not, can it be extrapolated so that it does fully embody the change idea?

7. Does the story make clear *what would have happened without the change idea?*

8. Has the story been *stripped of any unnecessary detail?*

9. Does the story have an *authentically happy ending?* Can it be told so that it does have such an ending?

10. Does the story *link to the purpose* to be achieved in telling it? "What if . . . ?" or "Just imagine . . ." or "Just think . . ."

WHAT'S YOUR NARRATIVE INTELLIGENCE?

Narrative intelligence is the capacity to understand the world in narrative terms. It means being familiar with the various components and dimensions of narratives and knowing the different patterns of stories that exist, as well as which narrative patterns are most likely to have what effect in which situation. It involves knowing how to overcome the fundamental attribution error and understand the audience's story. It entails the capacity to navigate the quicksilver world of interacting narratives, anticipating the dynamic factors that determine how the audience will react to a new story and whether a new story is likely to be generated in the mind of any particular audience by any particular communication tool.

Narrative intelligence can be seen as having several dimensions:

- *Explicit understanding of the theory of how narratives work:* The things for which you can explain the underlying principles.

- *Tacit understanding of how narratives work:* The things you know but can't explain. (This is analogous to knowledge about how you ride a bicycle: you can do it, even if you can't explain the underlying principles of physics that make it possible.)

- *Narrative performance skills:* The ability to operate in real-life situations in listening to stories, performing stories, and intuiting what stories other people are living.

The following is a simple quiz through which you can explore the current state of first dimension—your explicit understanding of how narratives work. *Note:* The quiz sheds no light on your tacit understanding of narrative or your narrative performance skills.

Narrative Intelligence Quiz

Indicate whether you consider the following statements to be true (T) or false (F), or whether you are uncertain (U). The correct answers are given at the end, along with the reasons why they are the correct answers.

The Practice of Business Narrative

1. Storytelling is a feature of every country and human culture.   T   F   U

2. Human beings find stories easier to remember than abstractions.   T   F   U

3. Storytelling is a rare skill in which relatively few human beings excel.   T   F   U

4. Storytelling is a relatively rare phenomenon in business.   T   F   U

5. The effective use of storytelling in organizations involves the crafting and performing of "well-made stories," with a hero or heroine, a plot, a turning point and a resolution.   T   F   U

Nature of Persuasion

6. The most powerful way to convince someone of something is through a story.   T   F   U

7. Big persuasive impacts require big narratives.   T   F   U

8. The best way to persuade a skeptical, cynical, or hostile audience to change their minds is to give them compelling, rational reasons why their views are not well founded.   T   F   U

9. Communications are always more effective if they begin with a clear statement of what the speaker intends to say.   T   F   U

10. Providing abstract reasons to change people's minds
has little or no effect on an audience that is skeptical,
cynical, or hostile.   T   F   U

11. The opponents of constructive change ideas in
organizations usually act the way they do because
they are obstinate and closed-minded.   T   F   U

12. Once people understand the nature of cognitive biases
such as the fundamental attribution error or the
confirmation bias, they find it easy to overcome them.   T   F   U

Nature of Leadership

13. The tools of management—the right to exact
obedience, to impose incentives and disincentives,
to hire and fire—make it easier to inspire enthusiasm.   T   F   U

14. You can't become a leader unless you already have
charisma.   T   F   U

15. A principal function of a leader is to tell compelling
stories about the future.   T   F   U

16. No one can lead who does not first acquire power.   T   F   U

17. There is now solid evidence that those organizations
that are good at storytelling have better business
results than those that don't.   T   F   U

18. Once you discover the leader deep within yourself,
people automatically recognize you as a leader.   T   F   U

Using Different Types of Stories

19. "Burning platform" stories will by themselves
motivate people to buy in to transformational change
in organizations.   T   F   U

20. Since the rumor mill has existed in organizations
since time immemorial, there's nothing you can do to
stop an untrue rumor.   T   F   U

21. Beyond establishing the enabling conditions for teamwork, such as right membership, clear goals, adequate resources, and so on, there's nothing a manager can do to generate high-performance teams: it's up to the team itself.   T   F   U

22. Negative stories have no place in a presentation aimed at generating enthusiasm for a new course of action.   T   F   U

23. A story to transmit values has to be uplifting in tone.   T   F   U

Navigating the World of Interacting Narratives

24. The most effective thing public relations can do is to persuade the public that your organization did the right thing.   T   F   U

25. The easiest way to brand an organization is for the organization to tell its own story.   T   F   U

Ethics of Narrative

26. In telling a story that purports to be true, the leader's responsibility is fulfilled by making sure that all the facts in the story are true.   T   F   U

27. It's necessarily manipulative to try to change people's minds by appealing to their feelings.   T   F   U

Answers to the Quiz

Except for the first two statements, all the statements are false.

Score 1 for every correct answer, and 0 for any "wrong" or "uncertain" answer.

High explicit understanding of narrative: 18+
Medium explicit understanding of narrative: 9–17
Embryonic explicit understanding of narrative: 0–8

Here are the answers—and why.

1. "Storytelling is a feature of every country and human culture." TRUE: Multiple anthropological studies show that every culture is permeated by storytelling.

2. "Human beings find stories easier to remember than abstractions." TRUE: Psychological studies show that stories are more memorable than abstract statements.

3. "Storytelling is a rare skill in which relatively few human beings excel." FALSE: Human beings master the basics of storytelling when they are young children and retain this capability throughout their lives. Just watch what goes on in an informal social setting—a restaurant, a coffee break, a party—and you will see that all human beings know how to tell stories. Storytelling is an activity that is practiced incessantly by everyone. It is so pervasive that it has almost become invisible to us. We are like fish swimming in a sea of narratives.

4. "Storytelling is a relatively rare phenomenon in business." FALSE: Persuasion is 28 percent of GDP.[1] If storytelling is—conservatively—at least half of persuasion, then storytelling amounts to 14 percent of GNP, or more than a trillion dollars. See Chapter One of *The Leader's Guide to Storytelling*.

5. "The effective use of storytelling in organizations involves crafting and performing a 'well-made story,' with a hero or heroine, a plot, a turning point and a resolution." FALSE: Aristotle suggested that all stories have a plot, a turning point with a resolution, and are told with a lot of

context. This overlooks the minimalist storytelling tradition. The statement can only be "made correct" by adopting an artificial definition of story as "a well-told story" that requires the inclusion of those elements. This would have the result of excluding many of the locutions that are usually regarded in organizations as stories.

6. "The most powerful way to convince someone of something is through a story." FALSE: Direct experience is usually more powerful than a story. See Chapter Five of *The Secret Language of Leadership*.

7. "Big persuasive impacts depend on big narratives." FALSE: Some of the biggest impacts of narrative come from modest, unpretentious narratives, such as the Biblical parables, or springboard stories in organizations. Narrative is a nonlinear phenomenon. See Chapter Five of *The Secret Language of Leadership*.

8. "The best way to persuade a skeptical, cynical, or hostile audience to change their minds is to give them compelling, rational reasons why their views are not well founded." FALSE: Many psychological studies show that, as a result of the *confirmation bias*, difficult audiences are likely to be more entrenched in their viewpoint by encountering evidence showing that their beliefs are unfounded: see Chapter One of *The Secret Language of Leadership*.

9. "Communications are always more effective if they begin with a clear statement of what the speaker intends to say." FALSE: This is generally true for a supportive audience. But for a difficult, cynical, or skeptical audience, announcing what you're going to say can cause the confirmation bias to kick in, so that the listeners interpret everything you say as evidence for the contrary position: see Chapter One of *The Secret Language of Leadership*.

10. "Providing abstract reasons to change people's minds has little or no effect on an audience that is skeptical, cynical or hostile." FALSE: Many psychological studies show that, as a result of the confirmation bias, difficult audiences are likely to be more entrenched in their viewpoint by encountering evidence showing that their beliefs are unfounded: see Chapter One of *The Secret Language of Leadership*.

11. "The opponents of constructive change ideas in organizations act the way they do because they are obstinate and closed-minded." FALSE: This is an illustration of the cognitive bias known as the *fundamental attribution error*. This is the tendency that we have as human beings to assign the cause for actions of other people to dispositions or personality-based explanations of behavior, whereas we tend to assign the causes of our own actions to the situation we are in. See Chapter One of *The Secret Language of Leadership.*

12. "Once people understand the nature of cognitive biases such as the fundamental attribution error or the confirmation bias, they find it easy to overcome them." FALSE: Cognitive biases are typically not removed by intellectual understanding of them: the fact that people can talk more eloquently about cognitive biases does not mean that they become less subject to them. Overcoming our cognitive biases usually requires repeated experience and feedback from making the same error.[2]

13. "The tools of management—the right to exact obedience, to impose incentives and disincentives, to hire and fire—make it easier to be a leader." FALSE: The tools of management make it easier to be a manager and compel compliance. They tend to get in the way of inspiring enduring enthusiasm for change. See Chapter Three of *The Secret Language of Leadership.*

14. "You can't be a leader unless you already have charisma." FALSE: Charisma is generally the result of successful leadership, not the cause of it: see Chapter Seven of *The Secret Language of Leadership.*

15. "A principal function of a leader is to tell compelling stories about the future." FALSE: It's very difficult to tell compelling stories about the future: since listeners know that the future is unpredictable, future stories typically lack credibility. It's true that effective leaders often tell compelling stories, but generally they're not about the future. See Chapter Ten of *The Leader's Guide to Storytelling.*

16. "No one can lead who does not first acquire power." FALSE: Many famous leaders, including Martin Luther King Jr., Nelson Mandela, and Gandhi, became leaders without having political power. See Chapter Three of *The Secret Language of Leadership.*[3]

17. "There is now solid evidence that those organizations that are good at storytelling have better business results than those that don't." FALSE: There is anecdotal evidence of many individual instances of storytelling having significant impact. However, there are not yet any systematic studies showing that organizations that are good at storytelling have better business results overall than those that don't. See Chapter One of *The Leader's Guide to Storytelling*.

18. "Once you discover the leader deep within yourself, people automatically recognize you as a leader." FALSE: If leaders' inner commitment to change is to have any effect, they have to communicate it compellingly to the people they aspire to lead. True, the leaders' actions will eventually speak louder than words, but in the short run, it's what leaders say—or don't say—that has the impact.

19. "Burning platform" stories will by themselves motivate people to buy in to transformational change in organizations." FALSE: Burning platform stories are effective at getting people's attention, but not for motivating people to change: see Chapter Nine of *The Secret Language of Leadership*.

20. "Since the rumor mill has existed in organizations since time immemorial, there's nothing you can do to stop an untrue rumor." FALSE: Where the rumors are false or unreasonable, it may be possible to satirize the rumor out of existence. See Chapter Nine of *The Leader's Guide to Storytelling*.

21. "Beyond establishing the enabling conditions for teamwork, such as right membership, clear goals, adequate resources, and so on, there's nothing a manager can do to generate high-performance teams: it's up to the team itself." FALSE: Narrative can inspire teams to lift their game and reach a higher level of performance. See Chapter Seven of *The Leader's Guide to Storytelling*.

22. "Negative stories have no place in a presentation aimed at generating enthusiasm for a new course of action." FALSE: Although negative stories are unlikely to stimulate desire for change, they are good at getting people's attention, particularly if the subject is a matter of personal concern to the audience: see Chapter Eight of *The Secret Language of Leadership*.

23. "A story to transmit values has to be uplifting in tone": FALSE: For instance, many of the biblical parables are negative in tone. See Chapter Six of *The Leader's Guide to Storytelling*.

24. "The most effective thing public relations can do is to persuade the public that your organization did the right thing." FALSE: The most effective thing that public relations can do is to tell the public the truth. Getting the truth out fully and quickly is generally the most effective way to quell controversy: see Chapter Six of *The Secret Language of Leadership*.

25. "The easiest way to brand a firm is for the firm to tell its own story." FALSE: The level of cynicism and mistrust in today's marketplace make it very difficult for a firm to tell its own story credibly. It's generally easier and more effective to induce the firm's customers to tell its story. See Chapter Five of *The Leader's Guide to Storytelling*.

26. "In telling a story that purports to be true, the leader's responsibility is fulfilled by making sure that all the facts in the story are true." FALSE: It's equally important for the speaker to make sure that relevant facts are not omitted. Half-truths are a larger problem in organizations than pure falsehoods: see Chapter Six of *The Secret Language of Leadership*.

27. "It's necessarily manipulative to try to change people's minds by appealing to their feelings." FALSE: The idea that it is possible to appeal to reason apart from the emotions is an illusion. Neurological studies show that feelings are tightly interwoven with reasoning in all human discourse.[4] Manipulation is the use of deception or dissembling to cause people to change their minds.

$\begin{bmatrix}\ \end{bmatrix}$ NOTES

PREFACE

1. The advice and encouragement that Professor Paul Strebel offered at IMD was invaluable to me.

2. The curious thing is that I have some evidence of what I anticipated. I spent some time in the summer of 1996 at a management course at IMD in Switzerland. As part of the course, we were asked to write ourselves a letter expressing our boldest hopes about the change that we were considering in our organization. The letter was to be posted back to us in three months' time, to remind us what we had envisaged. When I received my letter in November 1996, the boldest hope that I had been able to envisage in the summer of 1996 was that the idea of knowledge sharing would be accepted for implementation in one vice presidency. In fact, by November 1996, the idea had been announced by the bank's president at the annual meeting of the organization as a new strategy for implementation across the entire organization.

3. See S. Mallaby, *The World's Banker* (New York: Penguin Press, 2004), p. 159.

4. People sometimes ask me whether it is really plausible that the managing directors didn't support knowledge management and continued to undermine it. The fact that they didn't support knowledge management, however, is not in question. The managing directors were interviewed by Sebastian Mallaby for his book, *The World's Banker.* In response to a direct question from Mallaby, Gautam Kaji said: "Steve will say that we didn't support him and he's right!" (*The World's Banker,* p. 415, note 19). According to Kaji, the managing directors were looking at the world from the perspective of personnel management. They saw my push for knowledge management as "more linked to [my] need for a new job than to the virtues of knowledge management" (*The World's Banker,* p. 415, note 19). On this account, the managing directors weren't listening to or thinking about the substance of the arguments I was making. It was merely another unsurprising example of the confirmation bias at work.

5. Teleos benchmarked the World Bank as one of the world's Most Admired Knowledge Enterprises for a number of years from 1999 onward. APQC repeatedly selected the World Bank as a best practice organization for knowledge management from 1999 onward.

6. See, for example, "What the World Bank Knows," *Economist,* January 13, 2007, p. 67.

INTRODUCTION

1. Annual message to Congress, Dec. 1, 1862; Abraham Lincoln Online: Speeches and Writings. Available online: http://showcase.netins.net/web/creative/lincoln/speeches/congress.htm. Access date: April 14, 2007.

2. *An Inconvenient Truth* is the third-highest-grossing documentary ever, with a worldwide box office of $45 million: W. Booth, "Oscar Hopeful May Be America's Coolest Ex-Vice President Ever," *Washington Post*, February 25, 2007. Available online: www.washingtonpost.com/wp-dyn/content/article/2007/02/24/AR2007022401586_pf.html. Access date: April 14, 2007.

3. M. Henneberger, "Gore Sells Out Idaho's 10,000 Seat Taco Bell Arena 'Faster Than Elton John,'" *Huffington Post*, January 23, 2007. Available online: www.huffington post.com/2007/01/23/huffpos-melinda-henneber_n_39362.html?p=5. Access date: April 14, 2007.

4. C. Heath and D. Heath, *Made to Stick: Why Some Ideas Stick and Others Die* (New York: Random House, 2007).

5. D. Maraniss and C. Connolly, "A Nominee Still in Search of Definition," *Washington Post*, August 17, 2000, p. A-1.

6. D. Morris, *Power Plays: Win or Lose—How History's Great Leaders Play the Game* (New York: Regan Books, 2002), p. 86.

7. Maraniss and Connolly, "A Nominee Still in Search of Definition."

8. H. Kurz, "Ephemeral Analysis," *Washington Post*, October 5, 2000, p. C-1.

9. M. Kelly, "Conan the VP," *Washington Post*, October 5, 2000, p. A-35.

10. R. E. Denton Jr., ed., *The 2000 Presidential Campaign: A Communication Perspective* (Westport, Conn.: Praeger, 2002), p. 105.

11. Political Jokes: Bush/Gore Presidential Debate Transcript. Available online: http://politicalhumor.about.com/library/bldebateparody.htm. Access date: April 14, 2007.

12. Gore never claimed to have invented the Internet. What he actually said (in a CNN interview with Wolf Blitzer) was, "During my service in the United States Congress, I took the initiative in creating the Internet. I took the initiative in moving forward a whole range of initiatives that have proven to be important to our country's economic growth and environmental protection, improvements in our educational system." Seth Finkelstein has assembled some fascinating resources on how the words were twisted over time. Available online: http://sethf.com/gore/. Access date: April 14, 2007. The political reality was that Gore was never able to set the record straight in people's minds, and perception became more important than what he had actually said.

13. M. Halperin and J. F. Harris, *The Way to Win* (New York: Random House, 2006), p. 129.

14. W. Safire, "Bush Wins by Not Losing," *New York Times*, October 5, 2000.

15. K. Sack, "Gore Admits Being Mistaken But Denies He Exaggerates," *New York Times*, October 8, 2000.

16. F. Ahrens, "It Happened Under Me—Blame Him," *Washington Post*, October 5, 2000, p. C-8.

17. C. A. Smith and N. Mansharamani, "Challenger and Incumbent Reversal," in Denton Jr., *The 2000 Presidential Campaign,* pp. 117–134.

18. N. Lemann, "The Word Lab," *New Yorker,* October 16, 2000, pp. 100–117.

19. For example, on October 27, 2006, Senators Jay Rockefeller and Olympia Snowe sent a letter to ExxonMobil CEO Rex Tillerson requesting him to stop Exxon's campaign of disinformation about global warming. Available online: http://opinionjournal.com/extra/?id=110009337. Access date: April 14, 2007. In 2007, Al Gore's movie won the Oscar for Best Documentary, and he was nominated in 2007 for the Nobel Peace Prize.

CHAPTER ONE

1. M. Gladwell, *The Tipping Point: How Little Things Can Make a Big Difference* (New York: Little, Brown, 2000), p. 258.

2. R. Quinn, *Deep Change: Discovering the Leader Within* (San Francisco: Jossey-Bass, 1996).

3. J. C. Maxwell, *The 21 Indispensable Qualities of a Leader: Becoming the Person Others Will Want to Follow* (Nashville, Tenn.: Nelson Business, 1999).

4. M. Buckingham, *Now, Discover Your Strengths* (New York: Free Press, 2001).

5. D. Goleman, A. McKee, and R. E. Boyatzis, *Primal Leadership: Realizing the Power of Emotional Intelligence* (Boston, Harvard Business School Press, 2002).

6. B. J. Avolio, "Authentic Leadership Development: Getting to the Root of Positive Forms of Leadership," *Leadership Quarterly,* 2005, *16,* 315–338.

7. R. Byrne, *The Secret* (Hillsboro, Ore.: Beyond Words, 2006).

8. C. Lord, L. Ross, and M. R. Lepper, "Biased Assimilation and Attitude Polarization: The Effects of Prior Theories on Subsequently Considered Evidence," *Journal of Personality and Social Psychology,* 1979, *37,* 2098–2109.

9. F. Bacon, *Novum Organum,* XLVI.

10. D. Westen, P. S. Blagov, K. Barenski, D. Kilts, and S. Hamann, "Neural Bases of Motivated Reasoning: An fMRI Study of Emotional Constraints on Partisan Political Judgment in the 2004 U.S. Presidential Election," *Journal of Cognitive Neuroscience,* 2006, *18*(11), 1947–1958.

11. The most active parts of the brain were the orbital frontal cortex, which is involved in the processing of emotions; the anterior cingulate, which is associated with conflict resolution; the posterior cingulate, which is concerned with making judgments about moral accountability, and—once subjects had arrived at a conclusion that made them emotionally comfortable—the ventral striatum, which is related to reward and pleasure. See M. Shermer, "The Political Brain," *Scientific American,* July 2006.

12. Shermer, "The Political Brain."

13. Gladwell, *The Tipping Point,* pp. 216–252.

14. Interview with Craig Dunn, December 2005.

15. B. Gates, *Business @ the Speed of Thought: Using a Digital Nervous System* (New York: Warner Books, 1999).

16. The following paragraphs draw on Gates, *Business @ the Speed of Thought*, pp. 160–174.

17. Gates, *Business @ the Speed of Thought*, p. 169.

18. T. Davenport and J. Beck, "Getting the Attention You Need," *Harvard Business Review* (September-October 2000): 118–126.

19. M. Gladwell, *Blink: The Power of Thinking Without Thinking* (New York: Little, Brown, 2005). In his classic work on the subject, *Sources of Power*, Gary Klein tells how he discovered the way in which people actually dealt with tough choices. It was a study that set out to improve the way people used reason to wrestle with the pros and cons of difficult issues. What he found was that people generally didn't wrestle with tough choices or make reasoned decisions at all. Experts looked at complex situations and made their decisions in an instant. They didn't seem to examine alternatives. They didn't pause and reflect. They seemed to "know" the right course of action right away. "Their experience," says Klein, "let them identify a reasonable reaction as the first one they considered, so they did not bother thinking of others. They were not being perverse. They were being skillful." *Sources of Power* (Cambridge, Mass.: MIT Press, 1999), p. 17.

20. The process of generating a new story is akin to the practice of narrative therapy. See K. Gergen and M. Gergen, "Narrative in Action," *Narrative Inquiry*, 2006, *1*, 112–121.

21. R. Goffee and G. Jones, "Leading Clever People," *Harvard Business Review*, March 2007.

22. R. Levine, C. Locke, D. Searles, and D. Weinberger, *The Cluetrain Manifesto: The End of Business As Usual* (Cambridge, Mass.: Perseus Books, 2000), p. xxvi.

23. J. P. Carse, *Finite and Infinite Games* (New York: Random House, 1987), p. 31.

24. J. Welch and S. Welch, *Winning* (New York: HarperCollins, 2005). Is winning the only thing? "The quotation which is so often attributed to Coach Lombardi is, 'Winning is not everything, it's the only thing!' (although the actual quote is 'Winning isn't everything—but wanting to win is.') The hard work, discipline, and dedication of Lombardi's Green Bay Packers resulted in five NFL championships and two Super Bowls, and many Americans began to believe that winning and coming in first was the only acceptable position. Our society became obsessed with winning. We first noticed this attitude in the sports world, but soon we found it in the business world, in the legal profession, and in every corner of our society." M. F. Wright Jr., "Is Winning Really The Only Thing?" North Carolina Court System, *State Bar Journal*, Fall 2001. Available online: www.nccourts.org/ Courts/CRS/Councils/Professionalism/Winning.asp. Access date: January 2005.

25. M. Csikszentmihalyi, *Flow: The Psychology of Optimal Experience* (New York: HarperCollins, 1990), p. 65. When an activity is pursued for its own sake, Csikszentmihalyi notes, a person "invests all her psychic energy into an interaction—whether it is with another person, a boat, a mountain, or a piece of music—she in effect becomes part of a system of action greater than what the individual self had been before. The system takes its form from the rules of the activity; its energy comes from the person's attention. But it is a real system—subjectively as real as being part of a family, a corporation, or a team—and the self that is part of it expands its boundaries and becomes more complex than what it had been before." Participation in fundamentalist relationships, mass movements, and political parties also generates a welcome extension of the boundaries of the self, but in these cases, the true believers are not really interacting with the belief system: they merely let their psychic energy be absorbed by it. As Csikszentmihalyi notes, "From this submission, nothing new can come; consciousness may attain a welcome order, but it will be an order imposed rather than achieved."

26. Available at http://www.wisdomquotes.com/cat_reason.html. Access date: May 15, 2007.

27. F. Heider, *The Psychology of Interpersonal Relations* (New York: Wiley, 1958). See also L. Ross, "The Intuitive Psychologist and His Shortcomings: Distortions in the Attribution Process," in L. Berkowitz (ed.), *Advances in Experimental Social Psychology*, Vol. 10 (Orlando, Fla.: Academic Press, 1977), pp. 173–240; E. E. Jones and R. E. Nisbett, "The Actor and the Observer: Divergent Perceptions of the Causes of the Behavior," in E. E. Jones, D. E. Kanouse, H. H. Kelley, R. E. Nisbett, S. Valins, and B. Weiner (eds.), *Attribution: Perceiving the Causes of Behavior* (Morristown, N.J.: General Learning Press, 1972), pp. 79–94; E. E. Jones and V. A. Harris, "The Attribution of Attitudes," *Journal of Experimental Social Psychology*, 1967, *3*, 1–24.

28. D. McAdams and J. L. Pals, "A New Big Five: Fundamental Principles for an Integrative Science of Personality," *American Psychologist*, 2006, *61*, 204–217.

29. P. Goldie, *The Emotions: A Philosophical Explanation* (New York: Oxford University Press, 2000).

30. A. MacIntyre, *After Virtue* (Notre Dame, Ind.: University of Notre Dame Press, 1981), p. 216.

31. D. P. McAdams, "The Psychology of Life Stories," *Review of General Psychology*, 2001, *5*(2), 100–122.

32. To my knowledge, the term *narrative intelligence* was first used at MIT in the 1990s, by a multi-disciplinary discussion group focused on resolving problems in artificial intelligence. See M. Davis and M. Travers, "A Brief Overview of the Narrative Intelligence Reading Group," 1999. Available online: www.cs.cmu.edu/afs/cs/user/michaelm/www/nidocs/DavisTravers.pdf. Access date: April 14, 2007. The

term is being used in a different sense in this book. Carol Pearson, in *The Hero Within: Awakening the Heroes Within* (San Francisco: HarperSanFrancisco, 1991), emphasizes the need to develop narrative intelligence to understand the nature of archetypal stories and what they inspire in oneself, others, and whole social systems. Narrative intelligence is especially important in leadership storytelling, so that the desired end is realized without creating unforeseen and negative side effects. To aid in this process, she (with Hugh Marr) has developed a self-assessment instrument, the Pearson-Marr Archetype Indicator, and an organizational culture assessment instrument, the Team and Organizational Culture Indicator.

33. Levine, Locke, Searles, and Weinberger, *The Cluetrain Manifesto*, p. 89.

CHAPTER TWO

1. G. B. Shaw, *Man and Superman*, "Epistle Dedicatory to Arthur Bingham Walkey," cited in A. Quiller-Couch (ed.), *Oxford Book of English Prose* (New York: Oxford University Press, 1925), p. 952.

2. C. M. Christensen, M. Marx, and H. H. Stevenson, "The Tools of Cooperation and Change," *Harvard Business Review*, 2006, *84*(10).

3. Christensen, Marx, and Stevenson, "The Tools of Cooperation and Change."

4. J. Heilemann, "The Perceptionist: How Steve Jobs Took Back Apple," *New Yorker*, September 8, 1997.

5. K. R. Jamison, *Exuberance: The Passion for Life* (New York: Knopf, 2004), p. 5.

6. Jamison, *Exuberance*, p. 5.

7. For more on this topic, see my Web site, www.stevedenning.com/knowledge_management.htm. Access date: April 14, 2007.

8. M. Csikszentmihalyi, *Flow: The Psychology of Optimal Experience* (New York: HarperCollins, 1990), 39–40. Csikszentmihalyi tells the story of Rico Medellin, who had to perform the same task on an assembly line six hundred times a working day. Most people would grow tired of the work, but Rico, according to Csikszentmihalyi, still enjoyed it because he approached it the way an Olympic athlete approaches his event: how can I beat my record? Rico trained himself to upgrade his performance every day and so was still finding challenge in his work. But even for Rico, there are limits: though still enjoying his job, he was studying electronics at night, and when he had his diploma, he would leave to find a more complex job.

9. Csikszentmihalyi, *Flow*, p. 91; A. Solzhenitsyn, *The Gulag Archipelago: 1918–1956* (New York: Harper Perennial, 2001); V. E. Frankl, *Man's Search for Meaning* (New York: Pocket Books, 1997; originally published in 1946).

10. Csikszentmihalyi, *Flow*, pp. 39–40, 67, 91–92.

11. Csikszentmihalyi, *Flow*, p. 41.

12. A. MacIntyre, "Social Structures and Their Threats to Moral Agency," *Philosophy*, 1999, *74*, 311–329. The nastiest fanaticisms and cults in history—from the Inquisition to Nazism, the Ku Klux Klan, and Islamic terrorism—were perceived by the participants as good in themselves. Among the aspects that participants failed to pay sufficient attention to were the negative instrumental effects on those who were killed, wounded, tortured, or otherwise damaged by those fanaticisms and cults.

13. When we view the activity in this way, we could be seen as having some affinities to what Alasdair MacIntyre has called a "practice," or what James Carse called "an infinite game," or what Mihalyi Csikszentmihalyi has called a "state of flow." There are, however, differences. For instance, MacIntyre at times appears to regard a practice as being inherent in the nature of certain activities: For example, he wrote in 1981: "Bricklaying is not a practice; architecture is. Planting turnips is not a practice; farming is." See A. MacIntyre, *After Virtue* (Notre Dame, Ind.: University of Notre Dame Press, 1981), p. 187. The view adopted in this book is that bricklaying or planting turnips might conceivably become practices, just as architecture and farming in the modern economy are often not practices as defined by MacIntyre. It is a matter of fact in any instance whether a particular activity is being pursued as a practice, or otherwise.

14. MacIntyre, *After Virtue*, p. 196.

15. Gertner, J. "From 0 to 60 to World Domination," *New York Times* Magazine, February 18, 2007.

16. J. Collins and J. I. Porras, *Built to Last: Successful Habits of Visionary Companies* (New York: HarperBusiness, 1994), pp. 58–61.

17. A. Barry, "Everybody's Store," *Barrons*, February 12, 2007. Available online by subscription: http://online.barrons.com/article/SB117106867214804322.html. Access date: April 14, 2007.

18. B. Burlingham: *Small Giants: Companies That Choose to Be Great Instead of Big* (New York: Portfolio, 2007).

19. The question concerning the goals of companies like GE and Costco is: Will the stated goal of the corporation survive the term of the current chief executives and come to pervade those corporations?

20. As Alasdair MacIntyre noted in 1964: "The production of consumption is as much a mark of our society as the consumption of what is produced. Hence each becomes a means to the other and we find once more a chain of activity in which everything is done for the sake of something else and nothing is done for its own sake." A. MacIntyre, "Against Utilitarianism," in S. Wiseman (ed.), *Aims in Education* (Manchester, UK: University of Manchester Press, 1964), pp. 1–23. The result can be the obliteration of ends, a condition that typifies many modern organizations and the men and women who work there. When ends disappear, the difference between manipulative and manipulative behavior can vanish.

21. W. Shakespeare, *Hamlet*, Act 3, Scene 1.

CHAPTER THREE

1. E. Young, "Conjectures on Original Composition," cited in R. H. Fiske, *101 Elegant Paragraphs* (Rockport Mass.: Vocabula Books, 2005), pp. 6–7.

2. R. C. White Jr., *The Eloquent President: A Portrait of Lincoln Through His Words* (New York: Random House, 2005), p. 189.

3. White, *The Eloquent President*, p. 251.

4. White, *The Eloquent President*, p. 256.

5. White, *The Eloquent President*, p. 257.

6. N. Machiavelli, *The Prince* (New York: Bantam, 1966), p. 99. (Originally published 1513)

7. Machiavelli, *The Prince*, p. 99. In the United States it is of particular importance that a politician have an appearance of religiosity, even though the practice of hardball politics is hard to reconcile with the moral precepts of any major religion. The modern politician is thus typically an intermittent practitioner of religion. The values of religion are typically put to one side when politicians turn to the specific actions needed to be successful in politics.

8. Machiavelli, *The Prince*, p. 31.

9. M. Bai, "The Way We Live Now: The Last 20th-Century Election?" *New York Times* Magazine, November 19, 2006.

10. Bai, "The Way We Live Now."

11. J. M. Burns, *Leadership* (New York: HarperCollins, 1978), p. 1.

12. To *preside* has two main senses, neither of which is explicitly concerned with leadership. One sense is "to occupy the place of authority or control." This is nothing active. It is to be a caretaker, a symbolic role–to chair, head up, officiate, or oversee. The other sense is "to exercise management or control." It is an active role, but it's managerial, not a leadership role. A president is someone who administers, conducts, controls, directs, governs, handles, operates, runs, and supervises an ongoing enterprise. There is nothing here explicitly about change, or inspiring change.

13. A. Klapmeier, "Passion," *Harvard Business Review*, 2007, *85*(1), 22–23.

14. M. E. Porter and M. R. Kramer, "The Competitive Advantage of Corporate Philanthropy," *Harvard Business Review*, 2002, *80*(12).

15. M. E. Porter, J. W. Lorsch, and N. Nohria, "Seven Surprises for New CEOs," *Harvard Business Review*, 2004, *82*(10).

16. G. A. Williams and R.B.L. Miller, "Change the Way You Persuade," *Harvard Business Review*, 2002, *80*(5). See also G. A. Williams and R.B.L. Miller, *The Five Paths to Persuasion: The Art of Selling Your Message* (New York: Warner Business Books, 2004).

17. See S. L. Katz, *Lion Taming: Working Successfully with Leaders, Bosses and Other Tough Customers* (Naperville, Ill.: Sourcebooks, 2004), p. 32. I find the analogy of lion taming an intriguing one for dealing with CEOs.

18. D. Keltner, D. H. Gruenfeld, and C. Anderson, "Power, Approach, and Inhibition," *Psychological Review,* 2003, *110*(2), 265–284.

19. D. Whyte, *Crossing the Unknown Sea* (New York: Riverhead Books, 2001), p. 8.

20. S. Scott, *Fierce Conversations: Achieving Success at Work and in Life One Conversation at a Time* (New York: Viking Penguin, 2004), p. 74.

21. C. Vogler, The *Writer's Journey: Mythic Structure for Writers* (Studio City, Calif.: Michael Wiese Productions, 1998), p. 99.

22. J. Milton, *Areopagitica* (Chicago: Henry Regnery Company, 1949), pp. 55–56.

CHAPTER FOUR

1. Quoted online at ThinkExist.com: http://thinkexist.com/quotes/robert_mccloskey/. Access date: April 16, 2007.

2. K. Auletta, "The Howell Doctrine," *New Yorker,* June 10, 2002.

3. H. Raines, "My Times," *Atlantic Monthly,* May 2004.

4. Raines, "My Times."

5. Raines, "My Times."

6. Raines, "My Times." Also see A. H. Eagly, "Achieving Relationship Authenticity: Does Gender Matter?" *Leadership Quarterly,* 2005, *16,* 459–474.

7. Aristotle, *The Art of Rhetoric* (New York: Penguin Books, 1991), p. 249.

8. M. Buber, *I and Thou* (New York: Scribner, 1970), p. 58. (Originally published 1923)

9. D. P. McAdams, "The Psychology of Life Stories," *Review of General Psychology, 5,* June 2001, 100–122.

10. L. Prusak and T. Davenport, *What's the Big Idea? Creating and Capitalizing on the Best New Management Thinking* (Boston: Harvard Business School Press, 2003).

11. R. T. Pascale and J. Sternin, "Your Company's Secret Change Agents," *Harvard Business Review,* 2005, *83*(5).

12. Raines, "My Times."

CHAPTER FIVE

1. J. Austen, *Persuasion* (New York: Barnes & Noble Classics, 2005), p. 15. Originally published 1817)

2. S. Zhang, F. Bock, A. Si, J. Tautz, and M. V. Srinivasan, "Visual Working Memory in Decision Making by Honey Bees," *Proceedings of the National Academy of Sciences of the United States of America,* April 5, 2005, pp. 5250–5255.

3. For example, see E. P. Phelps, "Emotion and Cognition," *Annual Review of Psychology,* 2006, *47,* 27–53.

4. While the majority of researchers believe that bee dances give enough information to locate pollen, proponents of the odor plume theory, such as Adrian Wenner, argue that the dance alone is insufficient to give other bees guidance to the nectar source. They argue that bees instead are primarily recruited by odor. The purpose of the dance is to attract attention to the returning worker bee so she can share the odor of the nectar with other workers who will then follow the odor trail to the source. Further discussion available online: http://en.wikipedia.org/wiki/Bee_learning_and_communication. Access date: April 17, 2007.

5. E. A. Phelps, "Emotion and Cognition: Insights from Studies of the Human Amygdala," *Annual Review of Psychology,* 2006, *47,* 27–53. See also A. Damasio, *Descartes' Error: Emotion, Reason, and the Human Brain* (New York: Avon Books, 1994), chap. 7.

6. Phelps, "Emotion and Cognition." There are subtle differences between experiential, observed, and symbolic learning: see pp. 29–33.

7. W. James, *The Principles of Psychology* (New York: Henry Holt, 1890), p. 670.

8. D. Dorner, *The Logic of Failure* (New York: Basic Books, 1997).

9. T. Kelley and J. Littman, *The Ten Faces of Innovation: IDEO's Strategies for Defeating the Devil's Advocate and Driving Creativity Throughout Your Organization* (New York: Doubleday Currency, 2005).

10. Phelps, "Emotion and Cognition." In this review, passive learning alone through messages had no effect at all.

11. Damasio, *Descartes' Error,* p. 171.

12. Damasio, *Descartes' Error,* p. 171.

13. K. E. Weick and L. D. Browning, "Argument and Narration in Organizational Communication," *Journal of Management,* 1986, *12,* 243–259; see pp. 245–246. It ties in with the widely believed mythology that organizations conduct their affairs in a fully rational fashion.

14. D. Albarracin, J. C. Gillette, A. N. Earl, L. R. Glasman, M. R. Durantini, and M.-H. Ho, "A Test of Major Assumptions About Behavior Change: A Comprehensive Look at the Effects of Passive and Active HIV-Prevention Interventions Since the Beginning of the Epidemic," *Psychological Bulletin,* 2005, *131,* 856–897.

15. See, for example, R. B. Cialdini, *Influence: the Psychology of Persuasion,* rev. ed. (New York: Morrow, 1993).

16. M. C. Green and T. C. Brock, "The Role of Transportation in the Persuasiveness of Public Narratives," *Journal of Personality and Social Psychology,* 2000, no. 79, 701–721.

17. R. G. Hurley, The Decision to Trust, *Harvard Business Review,* 2006, *84*(9). In a survey of 350 executives in thirty companies, roughly half didn't trust their leaders.

18. L. M. Lodish, M. Abraham, S. Kalmenson, J. Livelsberger, B. Lubetkin, B. Richardson, and M. E. Stevens, "How T.V. Advertising Works: A Meta-Analysis of 389 Real World Split Cable T.V. Advertising Experiments," *Journal of Marketing Research*, 1995, *32*, 125–139.

19. L. A. LaClair and R. P. Rao, "Helping Employees Embrace Change," *McKinsey Quarterly*, 2002, no. 4.

20. J. Bruner, *Actual Minds, Possible Worlds* (Cambridge, Mass.: Harvard University Press, 1986), p. 11. For a number of decades, cognitive psychology did its best to turn the human mind into an information processor and reduce narrative to argument. Meanwhile Walter Fisher was doing his best to reduce argument to narrative: W. R. Fisher, "Narration as Human Communication Paradigm: The Case of Public Moral Argument," *Communication Monographs*, 1984, *51*, 1–22. Neither project succeeded. I believe that Bruner is right: you can't reduce one to the other.

21. A. MacIntyre, *After Virtue* (Notre Dame, Ind.: University of Notre Dame Press, 1981), p. 216.

22. N. Tichy, *The Leadership Engine* (New York: HarperCollins, 1997), pp. 173–175.

23. For example, *Narrative Inquiry*, 2006, *6*(1), tries to answer three questions: What was it that made the original turn to narrative so successful? What has been accomplished over the last forty years of narrative inquiry? What are the future directions for narrative inquiry?

24. See, for example, "Storytelling That Moves People: A Conversation with Screenwriter Coach, Robert McKee," *Harvard Business Review*, June 2003, *18*(6), 51–57, and S. Denning, "Telling Tales," *Harvard Business Review*, May 2004, *82*(5), 122–130.

25. Much less research in experimental psychology has been done on the use of narrative in persuasion than on abstract thinking. In psychology, the role of story in persuasion has been slow to get recognition, in part because "story was not considered to be the proper focus of the social sciences." See I. I. Mitroff and R. H. Kilmann, "On Organizational Stories: An Approach to the Design and Analysis of Organization Through Myths and Stories," in R. H. Kilmann, L. R. Pondy, and D. P. Slevin, eds., *The Management of Organizational Design*, vol. 1 (New York: North-Holland, 1976), pp. 189–207; see p. 191. Even though other fields such as child psychology, therapy, literature, theology, law communication, history, economics, and advertising have embraced the importance of narrative, in experimental psychology only a few studies have been done, compared to the thousands of studies that have been done on persuasion by argument or intuition.

26. J. M. Kouzes and B. Z. Posner, *Credibility: How Leaders Gain and Lose It, Why People Demand It* (San Francisco: Jossey-Bass, 2003).

27. Green and Brock, "The Role of Transportation in the Persuasiveness of Public Narratives."

28. H. Gardner, *Leading Minds: An Anatomy of Leadership* (New York: HarperCollins, 1995), p. 49.

29. In public relations, the practice of issuing talking points has been perfected, so that a chorus of different people tell the same story at the same time in many different media, thereby creating an illusion of verisimilitude and consensus, even when the story is totally fictitious. This is called the *echo chamber effect.*

30. These principles apply to persuasion aimed at getting basic changes in behavior, with implementation marked by enthusiasm and gusto. Where the object of persuasion is a simple, one-time change in behavior of trivial significance, then appeals to intuition may be more appropriate.

31. A. Stark, "The Great Storyteller: Ronald Reagan and the Political Uses of Anecdote," *Times Literary Supplement,* November 12, 1999.

32. Stark, "The Great Storyteller."

33. M. Marquardt, *Leading with Questions: How Leaders Find the Right Solutions by Knowing What to Ask* (San Francisco, Jossey-Bass, 2005).

34. A. Miller, *Metaphorically Selling* (New York: Chiron, 2004).

35. E. Tufte, E. *The Visual Display of Quantitative Information* (Cheshire, Conn.: Graphics Press, 2001).

36. Scott, *Fierce Conversations.*

37. M. Joyner, *The Irresistible Offer: How to Sell Your Product or Service in 3 Seconds or Less* (Hoboken, N.J.: Wiley, 2005).

38. A. Simmons, *The Story Factor* (Cambridge Mass.: Perseus Books, 2006).

39. Howard Gardner in *Frames of Mind: The Theory of Multiple Intelligences* (New York: Basic Books, 1983).

40. W. L. Payne, "A Study of Emotion: Developing Emotional Intelligence; Self-Integration; Relating to Fear, Pain and Desire (Theory, Structure of Reality, Problem-Solving, Contraction/Expansion, Tuning in/Comingout/Letting Go)" (doctoral dissertation, Union for Experimenting Colleges and Universities, Cincinnati, Ohio, 1985). See also Goleman, *Emotional Intelligence* (New York: Bantam Books, 1995).

41. Gardner uses eight criteria to judge whether a candidate ability can be counted as an intelligence: (1) Potential of isolation by brain damage; (2) existence of savants, prodigies, and other exceptional individuals; (3) an identifiable core operation or set of operations; (4) support from experimental psychological tasks; (5) support from psychometric findings; (6) a distinctive developmental history with a definable set of expert "end-state" performances; (7) evolutionary plausibility; (8) susceptibility to encoding in a symbol system. See S. Veenema, L. Hetland, and K. Chalfen, "Multiple Intelligences: The Research Perspective," Project Zero, Harvard Graduate School of Education, 1997. Available online: www.learner.org/channel/workshops/socialstudies/pdf/session3/3.MultipleIntelligences.pdf. Access date: April 17, 2007. Although further research is obviously needed, prima facie

all but the first of these criteria can be met by narrative intelligence. Further studies should be undertaken to see how closely narrative intelligence correlates with other intelligences such as emotional, interpersonal, and intrapersonal intelligences.

42. D. P. McAdams and J. L. Pals, "A New Big Five: Fundamental Principles for an Integrative Science of Personality," *American Psychologist*, 2006, *61*(3), 204–217. Stories are even more powerful when they are mythic universal stories—that is, stories that are find in all cultures and resonate deeply with human motivations and that convey a complex of meanings. Carol S. Pearson's work on such stories emphasizes the way that people actually live stories and in the process gain certain human abilities and virtues (*The Hero Within, Awakening the Heroes Within*). Pearson emphasizes the need to develop narrative intelligence to understand the nature of archetypal stories and what they inspire in oneself, others, and whole social systems.

43. LaClair and Rao, "Helping Employees Embrace Change"; J. Martin and M. E. Power, "Organizational Stories: More Vivid and Persuasive Than Quantitative Data," in B. M. Staw, *Psychological Foundations of Organizational Behavior* (Glenview, Ill.: Scott, Foresman, 1982). See also N. Pennington and R. Hastie, "Explaining the Evidence: Tests of the Story Model for Juror Decision Making," *Journal of Personality and Social Psychology*, 1992, no. 62, 189–206.

44. E. Borgida and R. E. Nisbett, "The Differential Impact of Abstract vs. Concrete Information on Decisions," *Journal of Applied Technology*, 1977, *7*(3), 258–271; R. Zemke, "Storytelling: Back to Basics," *Training*, March 1990, 44–50. A. L. Wilkens, "Organizational Stories as Symbols Which Control the Organization," in L. R. Pondy, J. Frost, G. Morgan, and T. C. Dandridge, *Organizational Symbolism* (Greenwich, Conn.: JAI Press, 1983); J. A. Conger, "Inspiring Others: The Language of Leadership," *Executive*, 1991, *5*(1), 31–45.

45. Green and Brock, "The Role of Transportation in the Persuasiveness of Public Narratives."

CHAPTER SIX

1. F. W. Nietzsche, *Beyond Good and Evil, Prelude to the Philosophy of the Future* (New York: Vintage Books, 1989), p. 9. (Originally published 1886)

2. L. S. Paine, *Value Shift: Why Companies Must Merge Social and Financial Imperatives to Achieve Superior Performance* (New York: McGraw-Hill, 2003).

3. J. Campbell, *The Liar's Tale: A History of Falsehood* (New York: Norton, 2001).

4. S. Godin, *All Marketers Are Liars: The Power of Telling Authentic Stories in a Low Trust World* (New York: Portfolio, 2005).

5. Godin, *All Marketers Are Liars*, pp. 2, 6.

6. Godin, *All Marketers Are Liars*, p. 104.

7. Ed Keller, CEO of Keller Fay Group, a market-research firm based in New Brunswick, N.J., quoted in G. G. "How to Get Attention In a New-Media World." *Wall*

Street Journal, September 25, 2006, p. R1. Available online by subscription: http://online.wsj.com/article/SB115885283520170125.html. Access date: April 18, 2007.

8. D. Holt, *How Brands Become Icons: The Principles of Cultural Branding* (Boston: Harvard Business School Press, 2004), pp. 65–93.

9. Under U.S. Law, "misbranding" is a crime involving mislabeling a drug, fraudulently promoting it or marketing it for an unapproved use. The consequences of infringement can be significant. On May 20, 2007, Purdue Pharma, the company that markets the painkiller OxyContin, agreed to pay some $600 million in fines and other payments to resolve criminal and civil charges related to the drug's misbranding. B. Meier. "In Guilty Plea, OxyContin Maker to Pay $600 Million," *New York Times,* May 11, 2007, p. 1.

10. P. Street, "Iraq Is Not Vietnam: Part 1: Imperial Continuities," ZNet Iraq, April 22, 2006. Available online: www.zmag.org/content/print_article.cfm?itemID=10138&sectionID=15. Access date: April 18, 2007.

11. Bush administration officials don't see the parallels between Vietnam and Iraq. "This is a different set of circumstances, with different stakes for the United States," Stephen J. Hadley, the president's national security adviser, said in November 2006 about Vietnam. Vietnam historian Stanley Karnow notes both similarities and differences. "We got lied into both wars," he says, but adds: "The easy summation is that Vietnam began as a guerrilla war and escalated into an orthodox war—by the end we were fighting in big units. Iraq starts as a conventional war, and has degenerated into a guerrilla war. It has gone in an opposite direction. And it's much more difficult to deal with." D. E. Sanger, "On to Vietnam, Bush Hears Echoes of 1968 in Iraq 2006," *New York Times,* November 17, 2006.

12. A British insider at the time concluded that the Bush administration was intent on removing Hussein through military action, justified by the conjunction of terrorism and weapons of mass destruction: in effect, the intelligence and facts were being fixed around the policy, rather than the policy being developed out of the facts. See "The Downing Street Memo(s): Seeking the Truth Since May 13, 2005." Available online: www.downingstreetmemo.com. Access date: April 18, 2007.

CHAPTER SEVEN

1. P. Brook, *Threads of Time: A Memoir* (New York: Random House, 1998), p. 85.

2. B. L. Halpern and K. Lubar, *Leadership Presence: Dramatic Techniques to Reach Out, Motivate and Inspire* (New York: Gotham Books, 2003), p. 3.

3. Mehrabian's study of 1971 is often quoted to show that only 7 percent of the meaning of a communication is in the content of the words that are spoken, while 93 percent of meaning comes from nonverbal communication: A. Mehrabian, *Silent Messages* (Belmont, Calif.: Wadsworth, 1971). This study was, however, based on artificial laboratory studies, involving the use of single, mostly

ambiguous words, and Mehrabian didn't claim that his findings were applicable beyond the resolution of simple, inconsistent messages.

4. V. Hearne, *Adam's Task* (New York: Vintage Books, 1987), pp. 229–230.

5. Malcolm Gladwell has written about this in the *New Yorker*. M. Gladwell, "What the Dog Saw," *New Yorker,* May 22, 2006. Available online: www.gladwell.com/ 2006/2006_05_22_a_dog.html. Access date: April 19, 2007. See also his blog for May 22, 2006. Available online: http://gladwell.typepad.com/gladwellcom/2006/ 05/the_dog_whisper.html. Access date: April 19, 2007. Video excerpts from *The Dog Whisperer* are available at http://channel.nationalgeographic.com/channel/ dogwhisperer/videoPreview.html. In the United States, the program airs on the National Geographic Channel.

6. Halpern and Lubar, *Leadership Presence;* A. Pease and B. Pease, *The Definitive Book of Body Language: How to Read Others' Thoughts by Their Gestures* (New York: Bantam, 2006); P. Collett, *The Book of Tells: From the Bedroom to the Boardroom: How to Read Other People* (New York: HarperCollins, 2003).

7. M. Gladwell, *The Tipping Point: How Little Things Can Make a Big Difference* (New York: Little, Brown, 2000), p. 131.

8. Brook, *Threads of Time,* p. 85.

9. G. Yukl, *Leadership in Organizations* (Upper Saddle River, N.J.: Pearson, 2002), p. 243.

10. It's also the case that some leaders deliberately set out to stage-manage their performances so as to attract attention—using props such as the pearl-handled pistols carried by General George Patton or the strangely formed hats and long pipe of General Douglas MacArthur.

11. V. Mehta, "Mahatma Gandhi and His Apostles," Part 1, *New Yorker,* May 10, 1976, p. 44.

12. V. Mehta, "Mahatma Gandhi and His Apostles," Part 2, *New Yorker,* May 17, 1976, p. 47.

13. N. C. Roberts, "Transforming Leadership: A Process of Collective Action." *Human Relations,* 1985, *38,* 1023–1046. And see Yukl, *Leadership in Organizations,* pp. 258–259.

14. W. Bennis and B. Nanus, *The Strategies for Taking Charge* (New York: Harper-Collins, 1985). See also Yukl, *Leadership in Organizations,* p. 258.

15. D. A. Kaiser, "Interest in Films as Measured by Subjective & Behavioral Ratings and Topographic EEG," doctoral dissertation, University of California, Los Angeles, 1994. Available online: www.skiltopo.com/papers/applied/articles/ dakdiss1.htm#toc. Access date: April 19, 2007. See especially Chap. 4, "QEEG Correlates of Film Presentations: Experiment 2: Gender Effects in Topographic EEG, which summarizes the evidence discussed here.

16. Basic Principles of PowerPoint Hygiene: http://www.stevedenning.com/Power-Point.htm.

CHAPTER EIGHT

1. J. S. Brown, S. Denning, K. Groh, and L. Prusak, *Storytelling in Organizations* (Boston: Butterworth-Heinemann, 2005).

2. T. Davenport and J. C. Beck, *The Attention Economy* (Boston: Harvard Business School Press, 2001), p. 58.

3. C. Perelman and L. Olbrechts-Tyteca, *The New Rhetoric* (Notre Dame, Ind.: University of Notre Dame Press, 1970), p. 147.

4. Perelman and Olbrechts-Tyteca, *The New Rhetoric,* p. 147. As Joseph Stalin once said, "A single death is a tragedy. A million deaths is a statistic." See Paul Slovic: "If I Look at the Mass I Will Never Act: Psychic Numbing and Genocide," *Judgment and Decision Making,* 2007, *2*(2), 79–95

5. Davenport and Beck, *The Attention Economy,* pp. 68–69.

6. D. Kahneman and A. Tversky, "Choices, Values, and Frames," *American Psychologist,* 1984, *39,* 341–350; F. Pratto and O. P. John, "Automatic Vigilance: The Attention-Grabbing Power of Negative Social Information," *Journal of Personality and Social Psychology,* 1991, *61,* 380–391.

7. Pratto and John, "Automatic Vigilance."

8. Pratto and John, "Automatic Vigilance."

9. Quoted by Tom Asacker on his Web site, "A Clear Eye," October 15, 2006. Available online: www.sandboxwisdom.com/sandbox_wisdom/2006/10/jose_ortega_y_g.html. Access date: April 20, 2007.

10. R. Wolf, "A 'Fiscal Hurricane' on the Horizon," *USA Today,* November 14, 2005. Available online: http://www.usatoday.com/news/washington/2005-11-14-fiscal-hurricane-cover_x.htm. Access date: April 20, 2007.

11. S. Sengupta, "The 2000 Campaign: The Viewers—Georgia: 'Skewering' The Politicians," *New York Times,* October 4, 2000.

12. J. Bauer and M. Levy, *How to Persuade People Who Don't Want to Be Persuaded* (Hoboken, N.J.: Wiley, 2005).

13. W. Safire, "Obamarama," *New York Times Magazine,* February 4, 2007.

14. S. Vedantam, "In Politics, Aim for the Heart, Not the Head," *Washington Post,* September 18, 2006, p. A02. Available online: www.washingtonpost.com/wp-dyn/content/article/2006/09/17/AR2006091700401_pf.html. Access date: April 20, 2007.

15. H. M. Boettinger, *Moving Mountains: Or the Art of Letting Others See Things Your Way* (New York: Macmillan, 1969), p. 94.

16. Perelman and Olbrechts-Tyteca, *The New Rhetoric,* p. 17.

CHAPTER NINE

1. E. Kolbert, "Mr. Green," *New Yorker,* January 22, 2007, p. 34.

2. B. Grow, D. Brady, and M. Arndt, "Renovating Home Depot," *Business Week,* March 6, 2006. Since 2001, 98 percent of Home Depot's 170 top executives are

new to their positions and, at headquarters in Atlanta, 56 percent of job changes involved bringing new managers in from outside the company.

3. Grow, Brady, and Arndt, "Renovating Home Depot."

4. A. Murray, "Executive's Fatal Flaw: Failing to Understand New Demands on CEOs," *Wall Street Journal,* January 4, 2007, p. A1.

5. G. Klein, *Sources of Power: How People Make Decisions* (Cambridge, Mass.: MIT Press, 1999); D. Kahneman, "Maps of Bounded Rationality: A Perspective on Intuitive Judgment and Choice," Prize Lecture, Princeton University, December 8, 2002; M. Gladwell, *Blink: The Power of Thinking Without Thinking,* (New York: Little, Brown, 2005).

6. S. Denning, *The Springboard: How Storytelling Ignites Action in Knowledge-Era Organizations* (Boston: Butterworth-Heinemann, 2000).

7. NPR interview with William Gibson, November 30, 1999. Available online: www. npr.org/templates/story/story.php?storyId=1067220. Access date: April 20, 2007.

8. K. Gergen and M. Gergen, "Narrative in Action," *Narrative Inquiry,* 2006, *1,* 112–121.

9. An excellent source of metaphors is A. Miller, *Metaphorically Selling: How to Use the Magic of Metaphors to Sell, Persuade and Explain Anything to Anyone* (New York: Chiron Associates, 2004). See also D. Weiss and E. Sommers, *Metaphors Dictionary* (Detroit, Mich.: Visible Ink Press, 2001).

10. For these and other metaphors, see "What Does *All Hat No Cattle* Mean?" n.d. Available online: www.allhatnocattle.net/what_does_it_mean.htm. Access date: April 20, 2007.

11. C. W. Dugger, "Dead Zones: Fighting Back in India.; Calcutta's Prostitutes Lead the Fight on AIDS," *New York Times,* January 4, 1999.

12. N. Tichy, *The Leadership Engine* (New York: HarperCollins, 1997), pp. 173–179.

13. D. Tapscott and A. D. Williams, *Wikinomics: How Mass Collaboration Changes Everything* (New York: Portfolio, 2006), pp. 7–9.

14. *Encyclopedia Britannica* (1972), 24:955.

15. The scene emulated a similar one in Jean Renoir's 1937 film *Grand Illusion,* five years earlier.

16. R. Lanham, *Handlist of Rhetorical Terms* (Berkeley: University of California Press, 1991), p. 33.

17. N. Tichy, *The Leadership Engine* (New York: HarperCollins, 1997), pp. 173–179.

18. J. P. Kotter, *The Heart of Change: Real-Life Stories of How People Change Their Organizations* (Boston: Harvard Business School Press, 2002), pp. 27–28.

19. *Selling* has acquired a pejorative sense that has not yet attached to *leadership,* and so leaders and writers on leadership are often at pains to distinguish themselves from mere sellers.

20. M. T. Miller and J. M. Sinkovitz, *Selling Is Dead* (Hoboken, N.J.: Wiley, 2005).

21. Miller and Sinkovitz, *Selling Is Dead,* p. 174.

22. Miller and Sinkovitz, *Selling Is Dead*, p. 173.

23. R. E. Quinn, *Building the Bridge as You Walk on It* (San Francisco: Jossey-Bass, 2004).

24. Lanham, *Handlist of Rhetorical Terms*, p. 91.

25. W. Shakespeare, *Hamlet*, Act 3, Scene 4.

26. D. M. Boje and C. Rhodes, "The Leadership of Ronald McDonald: Double Narration and Stylistic Lines of Narration," *Leadership Quarterly*, 2006, *17*, 94–103.

CHAPTER TEN

1. B. Pascal, *Pensées* (London: Penguin Books, 1961), p. 64.

2. C. Tilly, *Why?* (Princeton, N.J.: Princeton University Press, 2006).

3. J. Magretta, "Why Business Models Matter," *Harvard Business Review*, May 2002, pp. 87–92.

4. "President's Call for Full Response on Defense; Sees New Crisis for America," *New York Times*, December 30, 1940, p. 6.

5. Knowledge management might be seen as comprising multiple dimensions, including knowledge strategy, communities of practice, help desks, knowledge bases, knowledge capture, knowledge storage, knowledge dissemination, knowledge taxonomies, quality assurance, authentication procedures, budget, incentives, and knowledge measures. It's difficult to devise an image that can accurately and clearly communicate these multiple dimensions.

CHAPTER ELEVEN

1. T. Zeldin, *Conversation* (London, UK: Hidden Spring, 1998), p. 14.

2. M. McCormack, *What They Don't Teach You at Harvard Business School* (New York: Bantam, 1984).

3. For other books that have some affinity with the concept of leadership as conversation, see M. Buber, *I and Thou* (translated by Walter Kaufmann) (New York: Scribner, 1970), and D. Abram, *The Spell of the Sensuous: Perception and Language in a More-Than-Human World* (New York: Vintage, 1997).

4. See, for example, the Public Conversation Project: (www.publicconversations.org), access date: April 23, 2007, as well as K. Gergen and M. Gergen, "Narrative in Action," *Narrative Inquiry*, 2006, *1*, 112–121.

5. E. Scarry, *On Beauty and Being Just* (Princeton, N.J.: Princeton University Press, 1999), p. 22.

6. Scarry, *On Beauty and Being Just*, pp. 30–46.

7. Scarry, *On Beauty and Being Just*, pp. 69–70.

8. Scarry, *On Beauty and Being Just*, pp. 111–113.

9. Peter Elbow, in *Writing with Power* (New York: Oxford University Press, 1981), used the phrase to describe readerly writing, that is, writing that creates the opportunity and space for readers to construct their own meaning with the text.

10. J. P. Carse, *Finite and Infinite Games: A Vision of Life as Play and Possibility* (New York: Ballantine, 1986), p. 19.
11. Carse, *Finite and Infinite Games*, p. 19.
12. Zeldin, *Conversation*, p. 14.
13. Compare this to Zeldin, *Conversation*, p. 78.

CHAPTER TWELVE

1. M. Gladwell, *The Tipping Point: How Little Things Can Make a Big Difference* (New York: Little, Brown, 2000), p. 132.
2. A. MacIntyre, *After Virtue* (Notre Dame, Ind.: University of Notre Dame Press, 1981), pp. 217–219.

APPENDIX 1

1. The slides used at this presentation can be viewed at: http://www.stevedenning .com/slides/PresentationApr26-1996.pdf.

APPENDIX 2

1. Y. Gabriel, *Storytelling in Organizations: Facts, Fictions and Fantasies* (New York: Oxford University Press, 2000).
2. L. Vincent, *Legendary Brands: Unleashing the Power of Storytelling to Create a Winning Market Strategy* (Chicago: Dearborn Trade, 2002).
3. D. E. Polkinghorne, *Narrative Knowing and the Human Sciences* (Albany: State University of New York Press, 1988).
4. Polkinghorne defines both *narrative* and *story* as "the fundamental scheme for linking individual human actions and events into interrelated aspects of an understandable composite." Polkinghorne, *Narrative Knowing and the Human Sciences*, p. 13.

APPENDIX 3

1. D. D. McCloskey and A. Klamer, "One Quarter of GDP Is Persuasion (in Rhetoric and Economic Behavior)," *American Economic Review*, 1995, *85*, 195.
2. D. Dorner, *The Logic of Failure* (New York: Basic Books, 1997).
3. The assertion that power is essential is made in "Lessons in Power: Lyndon Johnson Revealed: A Conversation with Historian Robert A. Caro," *Harvard Business Review*, April 2006.
4. E. A. Phelps, "Emotion and Cognition: Insights from Studies of the Human Amygdala," *Annual Review of Psychology*, 2006, *57*, 27–53.

ACKNOWLEDGMENTS

It is hard to thank all of the many people who have contributed to the creation of this book. Obviously I am drawing on both the rich tradition of storytelling that dates back many thousands of years and the huge literature on management and leadership. I have done my best throughout the book to note the sources of my thinking so that readers can immerse themselves more deeply in these vast streams of thought.

I am grateful for the many helpful suggestions from readers of my newsletter and from people who have volunteered ideas at the workshops I have held. I particularly thank members of the Golden Fleece Group in Washington, D.C., who made many worthwhile suggestions.

At the risk of slighting some people by mentioning others, I especially thank Pam Barry, Julia Beardwood, Barbara Bickford, Madelyn Blair, Maja Grolimund Daepp, Johan Dhaeseleer, Cindy Dieck, Lyn Dowling, Lynne Feingold, Mary Fowler, Bryan Frew, Don Gallagher, Karen Gilliam, Eustoquio García, Brian Guest, Scott Hiegel, Jessica Hill, Seth Kahan, Gus Krauss, Laurie Lock Lee, Denise Lee, Stewart Marshall, Michael Margolis, Marla McIntosh, Bill Moffett, Carol Mon, Kate Muir, Pamela Occhino, Larry Prusak, Tony Quinlan, Ashraf Ramzy, Dan Rasmus, Ellen Rintell, Sandy Robinson, Lisa Rose, Shelley Rosen, Sam Sandarni, Jim Schultz, Virginia Steffen, Dave Snowden, Kathe Sweeney, John Thompson, Martha Vahl, Dirk Van Den Steen, Harsh Verma, Tony Walker, Susan Williams, Andy Wolvin, and Peter Young.

ABOUT THE AUTHOR

Steve Denning is a senior fellow at the James MacGregor Burns Academy of Leadership at the University of Maryland. He is the former program director of knowledge management at the World Bank.

Denning, who was born in Sydney, Australia, studied law and psychology at Sydney University and worked as a lawyer in Sydney for several years. He then did a postgraduate degree in law at Oxford University. In 1969, he joined the World Bank, where he held various management positions, including director of the Southern Africa Department from 1990 to 1994 and director of the Africa Region from 1994 to 1996. From 1996 to 2000, as program director of knowledge management, he led the knowledge-sharing program there. Since 2000, he has been working with organizations in the United States, Europe, Asia, and Australia on leadership, innovation, and business narrative, including several of the companies mentioned in this book.

Denning is the author of *The Springboard: How Storytelling Ignites Action in Knowledge-Era Organizations* (2000), *Squirrel Inc.: A Fable of Leadership Through Storytelling* (2004), and *The Leader's Guide to Storytelling: Mastering the Art and Discipline of Business Narrative* (2005). He has published a novel and a volume of poetry.

In November 2000, Denning was selected as one of the world's ten most admired knowledge leaders by Teleos. In April 2003, he was ranked as one of the world's top two hundred business gurus in Tom Davenport and Larry Prusak's book, *What's the Big Idea?* (Boston: Harvard Business School Press, 2003). In November 2005, the Innovation Network named *The Leader's Guide to Storytelling* as one of the twelve most important books on innovation in the past couple of years. Denning is also a fellow of the Royal Society of Arts.

Denning's Web site (http://www.stevedenning.com) has a collection of materials on organizational storytelling and knowledge management.

[INDEX]

269

Index

Blair, Jayson, 82, 84
Body language, 132–139
    animal trainers' insights on, 133–135
    basic elements of, 135–136
    as enabling condition, 47–48
    importance of, 133, 258n3
    incongruent, as leadership mistake, 7–9
    practicing, 137–139
    resources on, 136–137
Boeing, 56
Boettinger, Henry, 162
Book of Tells (Collett), 137
Boyd, Gerald, 81, 82
Brain activity, when listening, 25, 247n11
Branding
    communication of, 121–124
    and truthfulness, 120–121
Bristol-Myers Squibb, 90
Brook, Peter, 132, 149
Bruner, Jerome, 105, 255n20
Budweiser, 123–124
Building the Bridge as You Walk on It
    (Quinn), 182
Built to Last (Collins and Porras), 56
Burke, James, 117
Burlingham, Bo, 60, 73
"Burning platform" stories, 180–181,
    186
Bush, George H. W., 16, 133
Bush, George W., 8, 13
Business @ the Speed of Thought (Gates),
    29

C

The Call to Adventure (Vogler), 79
Campbell, Jeremy, 118
Canadian Imperial Bank of Commerce,
    90
Capital punishment, and confirmation
    bias, 23–24
Carse, James, 251n13
Celebrity pressure, 103
CEOs
    encouraging leaders of change, 90
    failing to stimulate desire for change,
        166–167

as leaders, 71–73
    speaking to, 74–76, 253n17
Challenges
    to get attention, 156, 164
    to stimulate desire for change,
        176–177, 185
Change
    challenges when implementing,
        199–200
    disruptiveness of, 86–87
    leaders' commitment to making,
        77–78
    middle managers as leaders of, 90
    politician' commitment to, 70–71,
        252n12
    situations where desiring, 21–22
    See also Stimulating desire for change
Changing others' minds. *See* Persuasion
Changing your mind
    Author's personal experience of, 92–96
    conditions resulting in, 96–99
    See also Learning
Charisma, 139–142, 259n10
Chiasmus, 178
Churchill, Winston, 178–179, 197
Clever people, leading, 35
Clifford, Clark, 63
Clinton, Bill, 4–5, 5, 81
Closing presentations, 196–197
Cohen, Roger, 81
Collaboration, and truthfulness, 118, 119
Collett, Peter, 137
Collins, Jim, 56, 84
Commitment to goal, 65–79
    by CEOs, 71–73
    as enabling condition, 41–42
    exercise on, 232
    lack of, as leadership mistake, 6–7, 41
    by leaders, 76–79, 232
    by Lincoln, 65–68
    by politicians, 68–71
    and speaking to CEO, 74–76, 253n17
"Common memory" stories, 176, 185, 194
Communication
    of brands, 121–124
    to CEOs, 74–76, 253n17

270